Roots of English

What is the explanation for the nature, character and evolution of the many different varieties of English in the world today? Which changes in the English language are the legacy of its origins, and which are the product of novel influences in the places to which it was transported? *Roots of English* is a groundbreaking investigation into four dialects from parts of northern Britain, out of which came the founding populations of many regions in the other parts of the world. Sali Tagliamonte comprehensively describes and analyses the key features of the dialects and their implications for subsequent developments of English. Her examination of dialect features contributes substantive evidence for assessing and understanding bigger issues in sociolinguistic theory. Based on exciting new findings, the book will appeal to those interested in dialects, from the Anglophile to the syntactician.

SALI A. TAGLIAMONTE is a professor of linguistics at the University of Toronto, Canada. She has been a university-level teacher since 1995 and her research focuses on variation and change in the evolution of English. Her previous publications include *Analysing Sociolinguistic Variation* (Cambridge University Press) and *Variationist Sociolinguistics: Change, Observation, Interpretation.*

Roots of English

Exploring the History of Dialects

Sali A. Tagliamonte

CAMBRIDGE
UNIVERSITY PRESS

CAMBRIDGE UNIVERSITY PRESS
Cambridge, New York, Melbourne, Madrid, Cape Town,
Singapore, São Paulo, Delhi, Mexico City

Cambridge University Press
The Edinburgh Building, Cambridge CB2 8RU, UK

Published in the United States of America by Cambridge University Press, New York

www.cambridge.org
Information on this title: www.cambridge.org/9780521681896

First published 2013

Printed and Bound in Great Britain by the MPG Books Group

A catalogue record for this publication is available from the British Library

Library of Congress Cataloguing in Publication data
Tagliamonte, Sali.
  Roots of English : exploring the history of dialects / Sali A. Tagliamonte.
    p. cm.
  Includes bibliographical references and index.
  ISBN 978-0-521-86321-6 (hardback) – ISBN 978-0-521-68189-6 (pbk)
  1. English language–Dialects–Great Britain. 2. English language–
  Dialects–Great Britain–Colonies. 3. English language–Variation. I. Title.
  PE1711.T34 2012
  427–dc23   2012019847

ISBN 978-0-521-86321-6 Hardback
ISBN 978-0-521-68189-6 Paperback

For:
Honorah H. Williamson, piano teacher, mentor, friend
David Robinson, blood brother
Una Coghlan, sister in spirit
Bev and Gerry Boyce, parents-in-law
My roots by love
With appreciation, Sali

Contents

Figures

Tables

Preface

> But you see in England and all those places, each place had a sort of their own
> dialect. They knew by the sound of the voice and the words they used where
> they came from. (Margaret Aldaine, 80, Swords, Canada, 1982)

My native language is English – Canadian English. It was the mother tongue
of my mother and my father, both of whom were born in Canada. But it is
my mother's language that was my linguistic model because, like many of
my generation, my mother was a homemaker and the one who raised me. My
mother's parents were also born in Canada. Yet if I go back just one generation
more, to my mother's grandparents, one was born in Ireland and the other was
born in England, and both my grandfathers were Scots. Each one of my great-
grandparents was a pioneer in a new frontier, the rich farmlands of southern
Ontario. They all migrated during the 1800s when thousands of Scots, Irish
and English settlers went to North America, the new world of opportunity. To
trace my roots back to the ancestors of my great-grandparents in the British
Isles is murky. The links are long lost. Or are they?

Have you ever wondered how your ancestry affects the way you speak? For
me, it is certain that the dialects of my fore-parents are not directly reproduced
in my variety of English. Yet in the bigger picture, Canadian English is a product of development from these founding populations of Scots and Irish and
English migrants who first settled in what was then known as Upper Canada.
As Canadian English evolved over the late nineteenth and early twentieth centuries it developed into the variety I speak, a variety pretty much indistinguishable from other Canadians like me.

Then I moved to Yorkshire, England in 1995. To my surprise, I shared many
linguistic features with my colleagues from Scotland and Ireland, many more
than I did with my colleagues from England. I certainly do not *sound* Scots or
Irish, and yet features at all levels of grammar from phonetics to discourse-
pragmatics are the same. I have the *cot/caught* merger, the form *gotten* for the
past participle of 'got'; I am *r*-full, I say *wee* for 'small' and *it's a good job* for
'it's a good thing'. I wouldn't use verbal *–s* outside 3rd person singular but I
know what it means and where it is 'normal', i.e. in constructions such as *The*

cows eats and *I says*. I can recall that my mother said things like this occasionally and my great aunts and uncles certainly did. The same is true of regularized preterits *come*, *give* and *run*, zero adverbs such as *go quick* and *speak slow*, sentence-final *like* and many other linguistic phenomena.

If there are correspondences between my variety of English and those of my northern colleagues, the interesting questions are how and why do similarities and differences like these between dialects long separated by time and distance endure? How do the roots of communities and regions and countries play out in the way their dialects are used by contemporary speakers several hundred years later? These are the questions I asked myself, and they are the questions that spurred me to embark upon the 'Back to the Roots' project and to write this book. May it help you explain some strange turn of a word or an unusual name or a unique expression that you or someone else you know uses. May it offer you a fresh perspective on your own roots.

Acknowledgements

The formative part of my academic career was spent in Yorkshire at the University of York in the Department of Language and Linguistic Science. I interviewed for the post in March of 1995 and was overjoyed to accept a position as Lecturer A in the department, which was to start five months later. A portent of things to come came in a light blue airmail envelope from Lowfield House in Heslington (near York) in June of 1995. It was a letter welcoming me to the department, 'You will enhance it' the letter said, and it was signed 'Bob Le Page'. To me, it was as if the queen herself had greeted me with open arms.

I arrived in York in early August 1995 with three children in nappies and a huge amount of enthusiasm. I left in early August 2001 to take up a position at the Department of Linguistics at the University of Toronto in Canada. The children were not in nappies anymore, my intellectual life had totally changed and Bob had become a confidante and a friend. My sojourn in the UK left a defining imprint on me both personally and professionally. I count among my dear friends many of the people I met between 1995 and 2001 especially Joan Beal, Jenny Cheshire, Karen Corrigan, Paul Foulkes, Paul Kerswill, Jane Stuart-Smith, Jen Smith, Ros Temple, Peter Trudgill and Anthony Warner. Living and working among the British sociolinguistic scene was a mind-blowing experience. My myopic North American-centric perspective changed gear. Many of the non-standard features reported as innovations in Canadian and US circles were alive and well among the people I met on the street and encountered in the pubs and hiked with in the peaks and dales. My own perfectly respectable middle-class Canadian accent had – to my mortification – transmuted into an ill-regarded American drawl. My children started sounding incrementally more and more foreign. The idea that shepherds in Yorkshire counted their sheep in an ancient Celtic tongue was a source of amazement. In sum, I had embarked on the experience of a lifetime. There I was, a neophyte sociolinguist specializing in language variation and change in English, living on the very ley lines where it all began.

As it happens, I am an early riser, so I would go to work early in the morning. It was dark and damp, but the cheery cleaning ladies were my cherished companions. They taught me how to pronounce British words properly, such as 'Scarborough' and 'Barbican' and railed me with stories about their lives and children. Listening to these raconteurs, I first conceived of the idea to create a data repository from the York speech community, which became the York English Corpus collected in 1997. By 1998 I had met Jennifer Smith who collected the Buckie English Corpus. Other students followed, each one did fieldwork in her home town: Elizabeth Godfrey collected the Tiverton data, Megan Jones the Wincanton data, Elyse Ashcroft the Henfield data, and Danielle Martin the Wheatley Hill data. By 1999 I had secured funding to create a corpus of the dialect data from my students' projects. By 2000, I dreamed of finding the roots of English in the counties that had contributed settlers to North America. I was awarded a large research grant for 'Back to the roots: The legacy of British dialects', which enabled me to collect the Roots Archive, the data this book is largely based upon. My academic daughters Jennifer Smith and Helen Lawrence were research assistants and collaborators on this research project. Both of them were in the field (Jennifer in Maryport and Cumnock, and Helen in Portavogie), as well as in the lab and in the office and now appear as co-authors on many of the papers arising from the fieldwork. Before the last draft of the book went to press, I benefited greatly from the input of an anonymous Cambridge University Press reviewer as well as the suggestions of my supervisee Shannon Mooney, who read through the entire manuscript from a student's point of view.

I am indebted to The Economic and Social Research Council of the United Kingdom (ESRC) for funding these projects in research grants spanning 1997–2001. I am also indebted to the Arts Humanities Research Board of the United Kingdom (AHRB) for providing a research grant to fund 'Vernacular roots: A database of British dialects'. The latter grant enabled me to compile and transcribe the piles of cassette tapes from the student projects and turn them into a functioning archive of English dialects.

Of course the true heroes and heroines of this book are the women and men from the far north shore of Scotland to the rural countryside of south-west England, who shared their life histories, stories and experiences. Their words infuse this book with colour, nuance and wise humanity. May their stories live long and prosper wherever the offshoots of their roots now bloom.

Counting

She used to get me to count in you know, yan, tan, thethera. You know, t'old yan, tan three. (Andrew Meyers, 63, MPT)[1]

Abbreviations

BCK	Buckie
CLB	Cullybackey
CMK	Cumnock
DVN	Devon
MPT	Maryport
NI	Northern Ireland
PVG	Portavogie
SAM	Samaná
TIV	Tiverton
TOR	Toronto
WIN	Wincanton
WHL	Wheatley Hill
YRK	York

1   Introduction

You just can nae but help but speak your mother tongue.

(Joan Dewar, 67, CMK)[1]

This book is about the roots of language and how they are reflected in the way the language is spoken from one place to the next and from one generation to the next. The particular language I focus on is English. As English becomes the dominant global language, its development and the changes it is undergoing are dramatic. Which changes are the legacy of its origins and which are the product of novel influences in the places to which it was transported? This book provides a unique perspective on these questions by going back to where the roots still show – dialects spoken in remote areas of Northern Ireland, Lowland Scotland and north-west England as represented by lengthy conversations with elderly people in selected communities in these areas. Each community is situated within the counties that were heavily implicated in migrations to other locations in the world during the early colonization period. The interesting and uncommon features of English found in these locales may contribute to a greater understanding of the English language, how it has changed over time and why. Indeed, I argue that these dialects provide a window on the past – hence the *Roots of English*.

In order to give readers a profound sense of the dialects that are the subject of this book, I have sprinkled the chapters with quips, stories and interchanges from the conversations upon which the linguistic analyses are based. In many cases, readers may notice a relationship between the excerpt and the topic of discussion – sometimes they will contain an illustrative example of the linguistic feature. In other cases, I have simply chosen a poignant quote that illustrates a particular dialect word or expression that arose spontaneously in the conversations, e.g. *weans* and *it's a good job* in the quip below. Every one of these excerpts comprises innumerable linguistic features typical of the community. I have made note of some of them in the notes to each excerpt. Many of the features are ubiquitous, well known across English vernaculars, including regularized pasts, e.g. *knowed*, *come*, past tense *seen* and *done*, among others (Trudgill, 2004: 14–15; Wagner, 2004: 169–70). Others, such as 2nd person plural *youse*, *till* for 'so that', punctual *whenever*, sentence-final *but*, *for* as a conjunction and plurals such as *sheafs* are reported to be typical of Ireland or Scotland (see Trudgill and Hannah, 1985). Many features can be found in compendia of varieties of English (e.g. Britain, 2007; Kortmann, Burridge, Mesthrie and Schneider, 2004; Milroy and Milroy, 1993; Trudgill, 1984, 1990). A few have only rarely been reported and offer readers fresh new possibilities for investigation. Some of the features in the quotes are examined in depth in this book; others are still in the long queue of features awaiting study in my research lab.

Weans

Aye, they just come on the phone– 'Morag could you come out the night there's some-body, ken. Such and such a body can nae manage yin'. 'Aye, Aye, I'll just come out aye'. She's just leaving the dogs. Says I, it's a good job it's no weans you've got for you would nae– could nae go! (Elizabeth Stevenson, 78, CMK)[2]

This book comprises a series of linguistic studies that draw on the theory and practice of several sub-fields of linguistics: sociolinguistics, dialectology and historical linguistics. Some of the terminology and technical terms may not be familiar to every reader. Therefore, I have also included, at relevant points in the discussion, definitions of the technical terms and notes explaining con-cepts. To further bolster the argumentation, I have on occasion added a claim or observation from an expert in the field, labelled 'words from the wise'.

The chapters are organized as follows. Chapter 1 introduces the topic and situates the analyses that follow. Chapter 2 discusses the justification for studying dialects as a window on the past. Chapter 3 describes the distinctive archive of dialect materials used as a reference database and resource for the present book – The Roots Archive and The British Dialects Archive. Chapter 4 explains the methodology employed to explore the linguistic features of the dialects. While descriptive reports of words, features and phonological differ-ences are common in traditional studies of dialect, the approach I take in this book is to uncover the underlying patterns in the grammar. This requires a quantitative approach and the set of methodological practices that have come to be known as 'comparative sociolinguistics' (Poplack and Tagliamonte, 2001; Tagliamonte, 2002a). Chapters 5–8 present case studies of key linguis-tic variables from morphology to discourse-pragmatics. Each chapter intro-duces the variable(s), considers where the variation may have originated (a historical perspective) and where the variation is reported in the present day (a synchronic perspective). Then, I problematize what hypotheses can be put forward to examine the feature in the archive of data and the most appropriate method for studying the feature. Each analysis proceeds first by assessing the distribution of the linguistic feature by community and, where possible, the patterns underlying the use of the linguistic feature across communities. Each section ends by providing an answer to the question 'What does this feature tell us about dialects and history?' Chapter 9 synthesizes the results from all the features and offers an interpretation based on comparative sociolinguistic principles. Chapter 10 offers some overarching interpretations that explain and evaluate the legacy of British and Northern Irish dialects.

Thee and thou

But see villages such as them, Dearham, where our Robert comes frae, they do– they're 'thee/thou'. Well the older, you divn't hear it now as much, eh. But they use lots of 'thee' and 'thou' and 'eh'. (Janice Mortimer, 60, MPT, 012)[3]

Legacies of English

It is fascinating to consider why the many varieties of English around the world are so different. Part of the answer to this question is their varying local circumstances, the other languages that they have come into contact with and the unique cultures and ecologies in which they subsequently evolved. However, another is the historically embedded explanation that comes from tracing their roots back to their origins in the British Isles. Indeed, leading scholars have argued that the study of British dialects is critical to disentangling the history and development of varieties of English everywhere in the world (Hickey, 2004; Montgomery, 2001; Trudgill, 1997: 749; 2004). Thus, another goal of this book is to contribute new evidence to the debates about why and how world Englishes differ (Mufwene, 2001).

Research exploring the transatlantic relationship between British and American dialects is now nearly a century old. Tracking the origins of North American English, in particular, has emerged as an important focus of research in language variation and change (Clarke, 1997a, b; Hickey, 2004; Jones and Tagliamonte, 2004; Montgomery, 2001; Poplack, 2000). Critical evidence for this enterprise comes from the original input varieties, many of which were from Ireland, Scotland and England:

Understanding the character and evolution of American English, as well as its regional differences and much else of interest to linguistics, cultural historians, and others, rests, among other things, on *an adequate account of its antecedents from the British Isles.* [Italics mine] (Montgomery, 2001: 87–8)

There are several problems with this prescription. First, there is a longitudinal lack of awareness of northern English dialects, both in the British Isles themselves (Wales, 2006), but most acutely in North America. Second, in considering the relationship between British and transplanted dialects, many previous investigations have relied on secondary source materials (dialect grammars and literary works) for comparison (see, e.g., Hickey, 2004; Kurath, 1964), with only rare exceptions (see Kurath, 1964, who based his research on Lowman's fieldwork in England). The problem is that dialectological reports are often selective and tend not to provide reliable structural analyses. Even in the case where investigations have targeted more informal sources (personal letters and court records), there is always the question of whether or not these materials approximate the spoken language and to what degree. Third, as Montgomery (2001: 95) admonishes, the reference point in the British Isles must 'be understood within proper sociohistorical contexts' to which he adds that much more information is needed from 'specific communities'.

Bake turf[4]

They done what they call bake turf. Did you ever see bake turf? [Interviewer] No. [018] Well, the bake turf is er- they cut a big hole. And 'tis filled with water, you know what I mean. And they shovel this stuff in till it, do you know what I mean, like. Til it's like a slurry. Then it's lifted out. It's shovelled out on till a flat surface. And a man goes across like that and he shapes it, like that there. Makes like a track, like a trough. Then when it's all dried in the summertime, it can be lifted in a real turf ... They dig them out with it, with the spades ... But they were very very hard and long burners too like, you know. Like one of them calls flow turf and this other's bake turf, you know what I mean, the bake turf. (Alec Murray, 88 CLB 018)[5]

There is already an extensive body of work on northern Englishes. Indeed, innumerable dialect studies have been conducted of communities in Scotland (e.g. Dieth, 1932; Macafee, 1992b; Miller, 1993), Ireland (e.g. Corrigan, 2010; Filppula, 1999; Harris, 1993; Hickey, 2006), and England (e.g. Beal, 1993; Dyer, 1891; Hedevind, 1967; Masam, 1948; Shorrocks, 1998a, b; Wright, 1892). A corresponding wealth of information can be found on dedicated websites.[6] Nevertheless, the available literature contains some key lacunae. There is still relatively little comprehensive data from dialects in the specific source regions of North American migrations (Montgomery, 2001: 90). This gap is telling, especially since many of the linguistic features that have figured prominently in the North American literature can still be observed in Northern Ireland and Britain. The presence of archaic forms in the existing dialects presents an invaluable opportunity to bring new evidence to bear on the transmission of language in time and space. In addition, the nature of these materials as community-based projects using sociolinguistic interviewing techniques offers a substantial body of materials for analysis. Finally, there is the intrinsic value of adding these regions to the available pool of traditional dialects before they are gone forever.

In summary, the *original* source dialects of emigrants out of Ireland, Scotland and England no longer exist, and the fragments that remain are often insufficient for large-scale comparative analyses. However, the descendant dialects endure, spoken widely and proudly in the homelands of many of the early migrants. Most importantly, they retain many of the same features they had at earlier points in time. This means that analysis of the contemporary varieties may provide insight into the original source dialects that were transported to other places in the world.

Words from the wise

'Old English and old Norse were so closely related that there were no significant differences in the inventory of morphological categories between the two languages.' (Trudgill, 2010:25)

Background

Youse go paddle your ain canoe. (Robin Mawhinney, 55, PVG)[7]

In historical linguistics, the study of peripheral dialects is considered to be one of the most informative means to shed light on the origins and development of languages (Anttila, 1989: 294; Hock, 1986: 442). Because of their geographic location or isolated social and/or political circumstances, dialects tend not to be affected by some of the changes that their cohorts in mainstream communities undergo. Conventionally, however, data from regional dialects has been the province of the dialectologist, and traditional practice has been heavily descriptivist, with a focus on word choice and traditional vocabulary items. In contrast, historical and comparative linguists have typically resorted to historical written sources and formal theories for their interpretation, while focusing on syntactical phenomena. However, recent research suggests that dialect data can contribute fruitful evidence for many types of linguistic inquiry – the study of language structure and meaning (Henry, 1995, 1998), language contact (Chaudenson, 1992; Mufwene, 1996) and dialect endangerment (Mufwene, 2001: 145–66; Wolfram and Schilling-Estes, 1995), in addition to the more common studies relating to linguistic change over time and space (Labov, 1994b; Trudgill, 1983). Moreover, researchers have shown that dialect phenomena provide ideal evidence for viewing intralanguage variation in universal grammar (Trudgill and Chambers, 1991: 294) and the effects of competing linguistic systems (Labov, 1998), and can reveal important insights into the links between diachronic and synchronic linguistic inquiry (Labov, 1989; Trudgill, 1986, 1996). All these studies highlight the important contribution that dialects can make to ongoing developments in a number of diverse fields of linguistics. Such materials can be useful to much current research whose ability to address many of the new questions (more) adequately has been handicapped by the absence of large corpora of synchronic dialects.

Norwegian

Because it was always said, you know, round here that a lot of our dialect was Norwegian, you know, I mean, a lot of words as 'flate', and 'flay' and 'yam' and all this sort of stuff. (Andrew Meyers, 63, MPT)[8]

2 Dialects as a window on the past

Aye, you know, it's good history here.

(Harry Caddell, 83, CLB)

In this chapter, I deepen the argument that dialects in Northern Ireland, Lowland Scotland and northern England are a particularly important and interesting test site for the study of English. They also have implications for the study of language variation and change more generally. For simplicity, in this book I will refer to these dialects as 'northern' following a long line of researchers who have considered the northern climes of England, Lowland Scotland and Northern Ireland to be a broadly cohesive region in terms of language use (Beal, 1993, 1997; Wales, 2000).

There is extensive discussion in the literature about the so-called 'north–south divide' in Britain. The boundary where north begins and south ends differs depending on the point of view of the beholder and the chronological year. Moreover, the location of this watershed has changed from one time to the next (for lively discussion, see Wales, 2006). This is due, at least in part, to the fact that the dividing line between north and south is not definitive. Dialectologists differ in their views and so do laypeople. Moreover, the boundary seems to have moved further north in recent decades (Trudgill, 1990: 33–4, 63–5). This highlights the complex cultural base for any claims regarding a north–south dichotomy (Wales, 2006). Nevertheless, a general consensus arises suggesting that a gross southern British vs northern English distinction is reasonably valid (Montgomery, 2001: 145; Wales, 2006). As Weinreich (1954: 397) cogently argued, the study of borders and centres in dialectology is imminently linked to 'culture areas' and as Wales (2006: 24) contends, 'Northern English is as much a cultural construct as it is a reality.'

Miners

But whippets and greyhounds, these were the kind of things miners had. (William Burns, 82, CMK, 037)

Thus, the long history of the British Isles presents a strong case for believing in a north–south dichotomy for the use of one form or another, or more important, as we shall see, a distinction in the relative frequencies of one form or another. An ideal means to test this is to conduct a comparison across representative dialects. The Roots Archive along with the British Dialects Archive permit investigation of north–south differences since they comprise two communities situated in the south and six in what can reasonably be construed to be 'north'.

One of the fundamental axioms of language change as well as an 'essential ingredient of most work in historical linguistics' (Hopper and Traugott, 1993: 38) is the Uniformitarian Principle – the idea that 'knowledge of processes that operated in the past can be inferred by observing ongoing processes in the present' (Christy, 1983: ix). Contemporary dialects offer an important adjunct to this, particularly those spoken in isolated communities. Such communities, because of their peripheral geographic location or isolated social and/or political circumstances, tend to preserve features typical of earlier stages in the history of a language. They are essentially relic areas as far as the process of linguistic change is concerned (Anttila, 1989: 294; Hock, 1986: 442), and their use in tracking historical change follows from a long tradition begun in Germany and continued by dialectologists in the twentieth century (Kurath, 1949; Orton and Halliday, 1963).

Words from the wise

'The most acute problem of all language historians … [is] the lack of evidence of the spoken language of the past.' (Rissanen, 1994)

British roots; American soil

During the eighteenth century, at least 275,000 people left the British Isles for North America (Bailyn and DeWolfe, 1986; Fischer, 1989: 609; Montgomery, 2001; Wood, 1989). Although these migrants came from many different locales, the vast majority who immigrated between 1717 and 1775 originated from Northern Ireland (Ulster in particular), the Lowlands of Scotland and the northern counties of England (Campbell, 1921: 51; Fischer, 1989: 619; Landsman, 1985: 8).

American transplants

And I think when they were going to America they had to bake enough oatcake to keep them going on the boat, hadn't they? [008] Oh aye, them days it was desperate getting to America. You see with that long in the boat, six-to-eight weeks in the boat, you know. Mind they suffered something them'uns went away there too. And there's Irishmen and Irish people everywhere in America. (Rob Paisley, 78, CLB, 003)[1]

The main North American destinations of these emigrants were southwestern Pennsylvania, western parts of Maryland and Virginia, North and

South Carolina, Georgia, Tennessee, Kentucky and the Appalachian Mountains (Crozier, 1984: 315; Fischer, 1989; Leyburn, 1962: 184–255). While many areas involved British settlers from a wide range of other dialect regions (McDavid, 1985), census data reveals that the emigrants from Northern Ireland and northern Britain – groups referred to as 'northerners' – (Fischer, 1989) often vastly outnumbered other population groups. In fact, in some regions these emigrants were so numerous that they are said to have established a 'cultural hegemony' (Fischer, 1989: 635). Montgomery, in particular (Montgomery, 1997; 2001: 128, 134), notes 'the Scotch-Irish element is quite broad and deep'. In Montgomery's extensive study of verbal –s in third person plural contexts he argues strongly for linguistic lineage:

the remarkable retention of linguistic patterns and constraints across more than four centuries and two continents in the evolution of Scottish English into Scotch-Irish English into Appalachian English. (Montgomery, 1997: 137)[2]

Such large-scale demographic trends suggest that there are socio-historical links between Northern Ireland, Lowland Scotland and northern England and the mid- to southern United States (Fischer, 1989). Indeed, Montgomery (2001: 145) argues that the speech of the Ulster Scots emigrants 'is responsible for much of the diversity of present-day American English grammar'.

Muck, scunner

Having been born and raised in Scotland, two of the words were dear to my heart. The first was 'muck' as in to muck out a room or closet etc, meaning to give it a good cleaning. The second was 'scunner', meaning a pest or nuisance, or to take an aversion to something. Both of these were common words in the part of Scotland in which I grew up, and I was astounded to learn that they are used in northern Ontario. I can't help but wonder if they are remnants of language from Scottish settlers in the area. (email from a listener, Northern and Southern Expressions, *Ontario Today*, CBC Radio 1, Canada 18 October 2011)[3]

Muck out

Aye, used to get up early on a morning and feed up and then er if I was back in reasonable time on a night, which wasn't very often, I used to muck out. Feed on a night and then muck out, you see. (Harry Stainton, 59, YRK, 013)[4]

Muck in

We just built it with lads out ot club. 'Cos there's plumbers and electricians and builders. And they all just mucked in together and that was it, aye. (Janice Mortimer, 60, MPT, 012)[5]

Tangled roots

Unfortunately for the enterprise of transatlantic comparison, the relationship between Northern Ireland, Lowland Scotland and English locales and particular dialect regions where the varieties of English was transported is complicated by extreme dialect mixture. In the United States in particular, some researchers have argued that the contact from so many disparate varieties makes comparison virtually impossible (see Montgomery 2001: 86–151). This is because the early colonial days of settlement in the United States not only had in-migration from England, Scotland and Northern Ireland, but also indigenous populations and migration from Europe. Most importantly, there was also the mass importation of African slaves (Wood, 1974). This language-contact situation has led to the most heated sociolinguistic debate of the last century. Among the varieties of English that arose from the colonial southern United States is that spoken by the contemporary descendants of the African populations – often referred to as African American Vernacular English or by its abbreviation AAVE. This variety is quite distinct from Standard North American English. One of the most vexed questions of modern North American sociolinguistics is why this is the case. Early African American slaves would have acquired their variety of English either en route to the United States or more likely on the plantations and homesteads of the American South. But it is necessary to determine the nature of the varieties to which they were exposed. The fact that AAVE is so different has often been traced to the dialects from Northern Ireland, Scotland and England. However, they have as often been traced to African and Caribbean creoles. There is a long history of overly simplistic dichotomies on this issue which can be summarized as follows: (1) a 'creole origins hypothesis', based on linguistic parallels between AAVE and Caribbean creoles; (2) an 'English dialect hypothesis', based on linguistic parallels with the Irish and British dialects spoken by early plantation staff. In reality, the answer probably lies somewhere in between. Many arguments prevail based on one line of evidence or another. Perhaps the most damning is the lack of evidence of which populations were where and under what circumstances.

The debate over the origins of AAVE still rages on with no consensus in sight (see, e.g., Rickford, 2006). It is therefore both timely and relevant to present the language materials from the Roots Archive and the British Dialects Archive since they offer a crucial piece to the puzzle: robust linguistic evidence from people who currently live in the original dialect regions of the migrants to North America in the early settlement days. Of course, it is necessary to question whether the language spoken by elderly individuals from these dialect regions today can be taken to represent the language of their ancestors two or three hundred years ago. Moreover, due to the complex settlement patterns and contact situations of the early colonial days, now remote in time, it becomes critical to carefully scrutinize the linguistic evidence that remains. I now consider a case study as a model for exploring dialect affinity across time and space.

Digging deep

Harris (1986: 193) once asked what predisposed certain salient nonstandard British features to became widely established in Atlantic contact vernaculars while other dialect features from the same locales did not. In this case, he was referring to preverbal *do*. Subsequently, other regionally delimited dialect features have been discovered which offer key insights into the links between and across dialects.

Definition

'Vernacular' is a term that is used to describe the basic language of a population – 'real language in use' (Milroy, 1992: 66). It is the way people talk when they are not paying attention to how they *should* be talking.

The use of *did* in affirmative periphrastic constructions came to light in a study of Samaná English (SAM), a variety spoken in the Samaná peninsula of the Dominican Republic, as in (1) (Poplack and Sankoff, 1987; Tagliamonte, 1991):

(1) a. They had a little road way out there what they *did go* over. (SAM/S)
   b. I *did like* to eat the sugar. I used to like to eat the sugar. (SAM/J) (both from Tagliamonte, 1991)

Some time later, the same rare and fading dialectal feature was found in Wincanton (Somerset), as in (2) (Jones and Tagliamonte, 2004).

(2) a. And mi husband always used to tell me I *did* always *speak* before I *did think*. (WIN/d)
   b. 'Cos the nineteen-twenties and thirties was, well like 'tis now, farming *did* hardly *pay*. (WIN/g)

Further scrutiny of these two dialect corpora revealed that Somerset and Samaná shared numerous conservative features including perfective *be*, as in (3), pronoun exchange and *have* regularization, as in (4), bare past temporal reference verbs, as in (5), irregular verbs, as in (6), existential *it*, as in (7), *for to* complementizers, as in (8), and invariant *be*, as in (9).

(3) a. I'm glad I'*m not got* that sort of worry. (WIN/e)
   b. You see coffee, I'*m got* it there by the bag, look at it there. (SAM/M)

(4) a. And *her* have the pointer. She used to use it instead of a cane. (WIN/001)
   b. She lives in the central street, number nine, though in the same street *her* have number nine. (SAM/S)

(5) a. I used to catch 'em with a stick and a rope, put on their horns, and once you held 'em a couple times they *fell* down. They'd stop soon as they *see* you coming. (WIN/g)

b. Well when that sugar *come* down *come* and *fall* down in a big bag. So many kettles. Well when it *fall* in there and then *have* a machine *run* right on 'em. *Sew* up it up at once. Well then that sugar *dry*. (SAM/E)

(6) a. If we seen him in the street, we used to have to go up and doff our hats to un and if he *come* by on his horse. (WIN/I)

 b. Well we can't say direct if that is their title neither because somebody *came* and brought them – each person what *come* out they takes somebody's child. (SAM/A)

(7) a. So *it was*, you know, quite a few of us. But most now, 'spose are gone, really. 'Cos of the age. (WIN/d)

 b. *It was* two of us in the house, my eldest sister and myself. But I was the smallest one, the youngest one. (SAM/H)

(8) a. They got arms ready *for to* fight again, you see. (SAM/M) I think there was six to seven bus loads of girls come in there *for to* pack, you see. (WIN/i)

 b. He used to throw– throw 'em right up high, you know, take he about ten minutes *for to* go up and down. (WIN/j)

(9) a. The church *bes* crammed down with people. (SAM/D)

 b. But this one, it *bes* disused. (WIN/g)

A feature by feature comparison, as in (1)–(9), makes it look like Somerset and Samaná share the same grammar. However, shared forms are not the most critical factor when it comes to assessing comparability of linguistic systems. It is possible that there is a mismatch between form and function. This phenomenon became apparent when English-based creoles and AAVE started being compared in the 1970s and 1980s. Researchers noted that the same forms occurred across varieties – unmarked past tense verbs, e.g. *they dance*; *she work*, etc. In creoles the bare verbs patterned according to the aspectual nature of the verb (stative vs non-stative) and relative temporal relationship (anterior vs. non-anterior) rather than according to the phonological context (pre- and post-consonant vs vowel) as they did in AAVE (Bickerton, 1975: 28–9). In other words, varieties could have the same *form* but different *functions*. In subsequent research, the same mismatch has been found across a wide range of linguistic features, including plural marking, use of conjunctions, relative pronouns and many other variables. Thus, the key fact of importance for the present undertaking of dialect comparison is that forms may be parallel across varieties, but the functions they encode may differ.

Going back to the case of Somerset vs Samaná, we can observe that they share many correspondences. However, the forms illustrated in (1)–(9) can also be found in many dialects in Britain, Northern Ireland and Ireland. This makes a definitive answer regarding direct historical relationship between the two locations moot. More detailed linguistic information is necessary to determine whether forms are used in the same way in each locale. Just as in the case of the creole vs AAVE comparison mentioned above, one dialect may deploy a form quite differently from another dialect (see also Henry, 1995). This is why the analyst must be able to unscramble nuances within language behaviour. These patterns can serve as clues to sorting out deeper similarities and differences. Indeed, many misunderstandings in communication happen because forms mean something different from one dialect to another. What does *pinkie* mean to you?

Pinkie

We were working at Fairburns. The manager of it, he was broad Scotch. And he says to Joe Downs, he says, 'When you're putting that door up,' he says 'I want a wee latch on it.' 'What sort of a latch?' Joe says. 'Something you can open wi your pinkie.' And I says 'Joe, you don't know what he's talking about, do you?' [004] Wee finger. [008] 'Aye. No, I do not,' he says 'I thought he was being obscene!' he says. (laughter) Says to Joe, says 'No, it's your wee finger.' I'll never forget that. (Michael Adair, 74, PVG, 008)[6]

Deeper form-function discrepancies may be so subtle that they will pass unnoticed, at least most of the time. Consider the use of *whenever* in (10). Are they all the same?[7]

(10) a. But *whenever* I hear that siren or even hear it on old television films, your stomach turns over because it brings back all those memories of air raids. (Derek Burns, 60, YRK, 068)
   b. Before we arrived over she would go away through the scullery and bake a chocolate cake or something. And that was for a cup of tea. And when we went in she would say I baked a chocolate cake so just make your tea *whenever* youse want. (Angus Milroy, 66, CMK, 023)
   c. We moved like up to the Clough area *whenever* I was about twelve or thirteen. And then I were changed to Clough school, and lived in Clough village. (Jack Nesbitt, 78, CLB, 020)

In sum, close analysis of linguistic forms and their patterns of use are required in order to conduct dialect comparisons. A method that can extricate the underlying grammar is vital.

Definition

The term 'conservative' when used to describe dialects, language or features therein, refers to historical time depth, for example maintenance of structures from earlier stages in the history of the variety (Lehmann, 1992: 104), or maintenance of earlier patterns of grammar (e.g. Bynon, 1977: 82).

Disentangling the roots

As I have been arguing, a reasoned methodological approach is necessary in order to unravel the complex histories of dialects, one that can delve deep into the linguistic evidence. First, systematic comparison of frequency, distribution and patterns of use of the forms in the grammar is undertaken. Second, an exhaustive assessment of each point of comparison must be made. This has come to be referred to as Poplack and Tagliamonte's 'strong hypothesis' for comparative sociolinguistic assessment (see Clarke 1997a, b; Montgomery, 2001). However, this so-called strong hypothesis is actually the set of procedures and methods of comparative sociolinguistics (Tagliamonte, 2002a). Let us consider this method in more detail, since it is the cornerstone of the comparative methodology I will use in this book.

Comparative sociolinguistics rests on the assumption that whenever a choice exists among two (or more) alternatives in the course of linguistic performance, and where that choice may have been influenced by linguistic context or social situation, then it is appropriate to invoke statistical techniques (Sankoff, 1988a: 2). Taking a quantitative approach offers numerous advantages, in particular the ability to model subtle grammatical tendencies and regularities in the data and to assess their relative strength and significance when all possible factors operating on them are treated simultaneously. The combination of factors exerting an influence on a given linguistic feature will often be extremely complex. Moreover, dialects can and do differ both dramatically and subtly in the way these multidimensional factors operate. The task for the analyst is to identify those factors that are the most meaningful, to interpret them and then to compare them across dialects.

Measures such as form, frequency and pattern offer the analyst the ability to infer whether the data sets under comparison share more than simply the same word, but also the underlying patterns that govern the way that word is used in running conversation. Then, if the analyst can establish that one or more patterns are shared by a set of dialects, she can use this information to argue that they have a common source. If one or more patterns are parallel, but operate at varying strengths in different dialects, this must be explained in a different way. For example, the dialects may differ in ancestry, they may have developed with varying influences, they may be positioned at different stages of evolution of the system under investigation, etc. If the patterns differ in quality or nature, then here too a different explanation can be offered. The interpretation rests on the nature and depth of the correspondences in conjunction with the broader context.

Witchel

His wife says to me this day I was coming in, 'did you see the witchel about?' Sie 'what you mean the witchel?' This is the youngster, that's what they call the wean, the witchel. Did you see the witchel about here? (Bob Cottell, 85, CLB)[8]

Going back to the example of Somerset and Samaná, the two corpora were subjected to a point-by-point comparative analysis of multiple contextual constraints operating on the use of pre-verbal *did*. Each constraint had been extrapolated from both the historical record and from the creole literature. Not only did the two varieties exhibit the same form (as in 1 and 2), but they also used the forms according to the same set of structural and semantic constraints that are reported in the history of the English language. This result offered substantive evidence of parallel grammars for this feature and therefore common origins. Thus, based on occurrence of form, frequency of form and a set of complex linguistic constraints underlying the use of the form, the two varieties were argued to have a common linguistic root (Jones and Tagliamonte, 2004: 118–19).

Indeed, as Poplack and Tagliamonte (2001) argued, shared retention of features are the critical criterion for establishing common ancestry. Only where comparable, robust linguistic data exists can appropriate linguistic analysis be performed that can determine the character of a 'diagnostic' form and its functions. Indeed, it is abundantly documented that the sociohistorical record is fraught with ambiguous interpretations (Montgomery, 2001), making it nearly impossible to disentangle population mixes, proportions of different dialect speakers, and the myriad of different social influences that could have operated in distant eras of time. This is why being able to sort out and make sense of the linguistic evidence is critical. In essence, the procedures for discovering underlying patterns in dialect data are akin to linguistic detective work. I will return to a discussion of these methods in Chapter 4.

Stuff from America

They used to send stuff from America to mi mother's people here, but there never was nothing for boys, was all for girls. And I remember, the first zip fastener ever I seen. It must have been in the twenties. I never seen one before and we were fascinated with it. (Alec Murray, 88, CLB)[9]

Linguistic 'woolly mammoths'

The research tradition in dialectology, historical linguistics and sociolinguistics has demonstrated that researchers can gain access to the way English was spoken at earlier points in time. In the absence of a time machine, how is this possible? Consider the case of something from the distant past that has been preserved in the present – a woolly mammoth frozen in a glacier, for example. We can use evidence gleaned from this find to gain remarkable insight into a completely different time. In fact, linguists have been employing various methods for 'using the present to explain the past' for years (Labov, 1994a: 600). First, the general processes of language change are well known and can be extrapolated from one situation to the next. Linguistic innovations tend to originate in 'focal areas' that have cultural or political dominance. Thereafter, changes spread through a process of gradual diffusion across populations, progressing from the core areas outwards to more peripheral locations (Bynon, 1977: 214; McMahon, 1994: 229; Weinreich, Labov and Herzog, 1968: 153–5). Areas that are geographically remote, socially isolated or set apart from the rest are slow to adopt new changes, or are missed entirely. Such areas are referred to as 'relic' or 'peripheral' (Andersen, 1988) and tend to preserve older features (Anttila, 1989: 294; Hock, 1986: 442). Relic areas provide prime evidence about an earlier stage (or ancestor) of a language and play a key role in reconstructing earlier stages of a language's development. Thus, critical evidence for determining the antecedents of a variety can be found in remote, inaccessible or otherwise isolated areas. There is perhaps no place more akin to these descriptions than the north country of Britain and Northern Ireland:[10]

The prevailing view of the North in its early and medieval periods of history was of its isolation, geographical and political, its alien-ation and its alien-ness. (Wales, 2006: 62)

My own prediction for the future would be that, whatever the degree of levelling towards regional standards, there will be the maintenance ... of variety within Northern English symbolic of the distinctive regions within the North ... (Wales, 2006: 210)

In historical linguistics, dialect areas are characterized according to type. Focal areas are places at the social centre of a language or dialect, places that individuals consider to be areas of prestige. Innovations in language are accepted by surrounding areas only as far as the prestige of the focal area extends. Transition areas are places at the limits of well-defined speech areas. Relic areas are found in locations that are difficult to access for any number of reasons, cultural, political or geographic (Lehmann, 1973).

In the air

[008] Why the change o dialect inside a few hundred mile? What brought that about? [003] My own answer to that is there's something in the air. Like a grit or a granite or something, you know, in the air. That – that – [008] Aye, that changes things ... [003] That we breathe in, changes the accent. (Michael Adair, 74 and Pete Dennet, 69, PVG)[11]

Evidence from other peripheral communities

In the late eighteenth and early nineteenth centuries there was a mass exodus of African Americans out of the southern United States. They went to far-flung locales in Canada, the Caribbean, Africa and South America. The communities they established tended to be isolated, both geographically and socially, and have often remained so up to the present day. These communities have been shown to provide insights into what AAVE was like at an earlier point in time. Two of the communities African Americans established in the early eighteenth century were in Nova Scotia, Canada (North Preston and

Guysborough). Analyses of these varieties have demonstrated linguistic parallels with British dialects (Poplack and Tagliamonte, 2001). This has led to the conclusion that the language of these early African Americans can be traced to Northern Ireland and Britain.

The results of this research are suggestive; however, other scholars have found just the opposite, namely that there are linguistic parallels with creoles (Rickford, 1997, 1998; Singler, 1991, 1993; Winford, 1992). This has led to the conclusion that the language of the early African Americans can be traced to the creolization of African languages during the time of slavery.

Pullen

Pullens. Used to get pullens, aye, that's right. No you wouldn't get the pullens now. Very little, very little. There was a few years ago, used to come round. All the fishermen'd come round selling them. But you wouldn't see them now like you know what I mean. (Alec Murray, 88, CLB, 018)[12]

There are a number of possible reasons for the extreme differences between these claims. One reason is that many investigations of early varieties of AAVE have relied on secondary source materials (dialect grammars and literary works) for comparison. These reports are notoriously selective and tend to record what their authors happen to notice rather than to provide a more reliable structural analysis. However, an even more important gap is that there are very few accountable studies of *comparably isolated* dialects in the appropriate source regions in Northern Ireland, Scotland and England. Montgomery (2001: 145), in discussing the importance of British and Irish antecedents of American English, argues that:

It is not too much to say that the speech of Ulster emigrants is responsible for much of the diversity of present-day American English grammar. Kurath [an Austrian-American dialectologist] suspected such an influence on Midland [American] speech but was unable to detect it … because his linguistic atlas survey was designed to elicit few grammatical patterns. Solving 'Kurath's puzzle' requires focusing more intensively on morphology and syntax and including possible source varieties in Ireland and Scotland only partially accessible in the EDD[13] and not at all in the SED.[14] (Montgomery, 2001: 145)

In some cases, in fact, features considered to be creole elements in AAVE could as easily have been traced back to Northern Ireland, Scotland and England. In early research, for example, the 'irregular and unsystematic character' (Labov, Cohen, Robins and Lewis, 1968: 167) of verbal –s in AAVE was attributed to a creole-like system. Pitts (1981: 307) considered it a relexificaiton of habitual *de* found in Gullah and Bickerton explained as a hypercorrected version of creole *doz* which reduced to –s or –z in rapid speech and transferred from pre- to postverbal position. It was not until Schneider's (1981, 1989) research on the WPA Slave Narratives (Leiby, 1985) that northern British and Northern Irish dialects were considered to be another plausible source.

Another example, not as prominently studied, is the 'associative plural' as in (11), which is reported in Gullah, an AAVE variety spoken on the Sea Islands off the coast of Georgia and South Carolina

(11)   Da's where Viola *dem* live. (Rickford, 1986: 46)

According to some researchers, the form has 'clear creole roots' (Rickford, 1986: 47) and is a feature that AAVE 'shares with creoles rather than other varieties of English' (Mufwene, 1999a: 73). Yet a notably similar construction is found in the southern US, as in (11), as well as across certain British and Northern Ireland dialects, as in (12), and also with a tendency of occurring with proper nouns.[15]

(12)   a. An' my mother *and 'em* had done got to the house. (Feagin, 1979: 331)
         b. And all the ones round there, the Neelys and the Johnsons *and all them*, they all fished. (CLB/008)
         c. Aye, it would start at the Warnick's Road, Sean. And go on a wee bit fae the Warnick's Road. Where Shirley *and them's* at, there. (PVG/008)
         d. How's your Paul *and them* getting on? (WHL/007)

These two examples demonstrate that, without the perspective from the source dialects, the North American debates suffer from lack of historical and comparative linguistic evidence. Thus, it is crucial to gain access to this type of evidence.

She come to school on a pony and trap at that time. (Lily Trimble, 86, CLB, 012)

Back to the roots

The areas from which most Northern Irish and British migrants to North America originated between 1717 and 1775 were the counties of Derry, Antrim and Down in Northern Ireland; Ayrshire, Dumfries and Wigtown in Scotland; and Cumberland and Westmorland in northern England (Fischer, 1989: 622; Leyburn, 1962: 94). Crucial for purposes of linguistic comparison is the fact that these regions can be described as having 'a common border culture which was unique in its speech' (Fischer, 1989: 786). The dialects of Lowland Scotland and northern England both have their origins in the Northumbrian dialect of Old English (Murray, 1873). This, coupled with proximity to Scotland, is reflected 'in the linguistic characteristics of the area' (Beal, 1993: 187–8) which shares many of its features with Scots. Similarly, Lowland Scotland has strong linguistic links with certain parts of Northern Ireland. The Ulster Plantations between 1605 and 1701 (Gregg, 1985: 9; Leyburn, 1962: 94) were a political scheme whereby settlers from Lowland Scotland were granted land in Northern Ireland. This led to a dominance of Scots migrants in certain areas and the development of a unique dialect called Ulster Scots (Barry, 1981:.59).

Petticoats

In my young days, now young people, boys and girls wore petticoats until they maybe four or five years of age, you know what I mean, like. And some of them went till school in their bare feet, you know what-I mean. They had nae money to buy them. And some of them went in clogs. (Alec Murray, 88, CLB, 018)[16]

Words from the wise

'The use of *till* for "to" is an indication of Scandanavian origins.' (Wakelin, 1988)

According to the Founder Principle (Mufwene, 1996:122–3), the language to emerge in contact situations would be influenced by the frequency and nature of the linguistic features of the varieties spoken by the dominant founder population, as these will have 'selective advantage over competing alternatives'. Similar processes are invoked for dialects in contact (Trudgill, 1986, 1999; Trudgill, Gordon, Lewis and Maclagan, 2000). The connections between these source linguistic regions and the magnitude of their relative proportion in certain regions in North America in the colonial period suggest that varieties of English that emerged in these locales may be somewhat 'northern' in nature.

Furthermore, strong socio-cultural and historical links unite the three dialect areas. First, the dialects of Lowland Scotland and north-west England have a common origin in the Northumbrian dialect of Old English (Murray, 1873). This, coupled with proximity to Scotland, 'is reflected in the linguistic characteristics of the area' (Beal, 1993: 187–8) which shares many of its features with Scots. Lowland Scotland is intimately connected with Northern Ireland. The Ulster Plantations of 1610 (Gregg, 1985: 9; Leyburn, 1962: 94) led to a dominance of Scottish migrants in certain areas of Northern Ireland. This formative founder population led to the development of a unique variety – Ulster Scots (Barry, 1981: 59). This variety is notably different from other varieties in the Republic of Ireland, which, in contrast, developed out of contact with settlers from (southern) England. It should be noted that in Northern Ireland too there are areas that were predominantly settled by English migrants (e.g. Gregg, 1985), thus there is no monolithic Northern Irish variety. However, the specific locales from which these data come (County Antrim and north-east County Down) were settled predominantly by Scots (Gregg, 1985; Harris, 1993).

County Antrim

But here in County Antrim we're the plantationers, we're all broken Scotch, every one of us, we're all Scotch. (Bob Cottell, 83, CLB, 002)

Our ancestors all – we were planted here. Time o' plantation, our folk come here down along this coast. ... We come fae Galloway and the Ayrshire coast. You know, my granda ... arrived at Portglenone, aye. That's where mi granda and them landed. (Robin Mawhinney, 55, PVG, 002)

In sum, these regions are special. First, they represent one of the primary source counties of immigration at a key point in the early colonization period. Second, the dialects spoken in these communities are significantly different from the varieties that would set the norms for Standard English in the nineteenth and twentieth centuries. Indeed, there are strong arguments for a separate 'Northern English'. Third, the north has a large amount of internal consistency across regions that is deeply cultural, historic and linguistic. Indeed, one could argue that northern dialects of England, Scotland and Northern Ireland are as distinct from southern Standard English as AAVE is from Standard American English.

The North-South divide … is deeply embedded in the nation's cultural history in a variety of manifestations, including the linguistic; … the opposition itself helps to determine the 'meaning' of the North and being Northern. (Wales, 2006)

Transatlantic links

We cannot recreate Northern Irish, Scots and northern English dialects exactly as they were spoken in colonial days whether in the British Isles and Northern Ireland, or in North America, India, Australia or New Zealand.[17] Indeed, cautionary measures must be taken in extrapolating contemporary evidence to earlier varieties (Montgomery, 2001). However, there are still many communities that are geographically separate and socially and/or politically isolated in the source regions in northern Britain and Ireland. People living in such small, peripheral communities tend to speak a dialect very unlike that spoken in contemporary cities, either the standard or the vernacular form. In the case of northern English this is even more poignantly true since the history and culture of isolation in these regions is centuries old. Most importantly, these dialects have preserved linguistic features of much earlier stages in the history of the language. Taking the quintessential northern vowels of the lexical sets BATH [æ] and FOOT [ʊ] as exemplars, Wales (2006: 29) describes how linguistic features serve to identify an accent:

Linguistic features, like cultural artefacts such as caps and braces, leeks and whippets, serve again as metonyms or synecdoche, standing for the whole image, and this is clearly the case for the short vowel in words like *bath*, *grass*, and *laugh*, and the vowel in *butter*, *up*, or *bugger*, which are mentioned time and again in characterisations of Northern English.

As mentioned earlier, the dialect regions in which the varieties under investigation are situated also have historical connections among themselves with common roots in centuries past. Therefore, the perspective afforded by a cross-variety comparison amongst them and, where possible, with other dialects in the UK, will provide a comprehensive view of a unique dialect landscape as well as a window on the distant past.

Definition

English pronunciation was classified into 24 lexical sets by Wells (1982). Each set is based on the pronunciation of the vowel in two reference accents, Standard British English and General American English.

Leeks, Onions and Cabbage[18]

There wasn't any fancy puddings nor no fancy cake nor biscuits. It was loaf and jam … but you know, you sliced your loaf in them days. You had a slice. And we would have had that … And then the next night she would have had a big pan of onions. And the next night it would have been a big fry of leeks. She had something different every night. But we never got any beef to Sunday and that was broth. You got a big pot of broth. (Lily Trimble, 86, CLB, 012)

We had greenhouses like and we grew tomatoes and that you know. And then we'd gardens that we'd grow tatties and leeks, onions, all that. (Phil Stephenson, 84, MPT, 022)

Oh everybody had a vegetable garden. My granny would go out and get parsley and leeks and er – kale and things out the garden for soup. (daughter, Ester Hamilton, 88, CMK, 025)[19]

No, no. It was all good plain food made- baked at home. Home baking. Oh plenty of spuds and cabbage and leeks, everything like that. Oh yeah. (Jack Nesbitt, 78, CLB, 020)

Then you know we had to muck in and help her, you see. We would have scrubbed the potatoes. She would have boiled a big pot of cabbage the night er – was a fire in the hearth, you know, er – one big great pot. And she would have filled that with cabbage and took that off and strained it and put on a big black pot of these potatoes. And when my father came in, he had to work to six, and when he came in, the pan went on and the bacon was fried and lifted out, and she fried this great big pan of cabbage. And we all sat round that table with that big pot of potatoes emptied out onto a great big dish. (Lily Trimble, 86, CLB, 012)

Where the roots still show

In the late 1980s a British writer journeying northward arrived at a northern landmark, Scotch Corner,[20] and mused that:

Beowulf and the monster Grendel[21] might have been out there somewhere fighting their legendary battles for bog and moor … *the north is another country.* [italics mine] (Chesshyre, 1987: 48; cited astutely by Wales, 2006: 26)

In order to have the greatest chance of finding the history of English in the wilds of this 'other country', it was necessary to target the most peripheral and isolated communities situated in the relevant counties of Northern Ireland, Lowland Scotland and north-west England. The first challenge was to locate just the right communities. The selection criteria were the following:

1. located in the key dialect areas of relevance to migration;
2. geographically remote;
3. relatively isolated from mainstream developments.

It was also important to achieve coverage of each of the main geographic areas implicated in the early exodus out of Britain and Northern Ireland. I targeted four towns: Maryport in Cumbria, Cumnock in south-west Scotland, and, in Northern Ireland, Cullybackey and Portavogie. I selected communities that had all the characteristics of the traditional historical linguistics 'relic area' (Hock and Joseph, 1996: 355), the smallest, most cohesive, most rural and peripheral communities I could find. Due to the characteristics of these communities, I hypothesized that they would stand the best chance of preserving linguistic features of the traditional dialects of the area, at least amongst the oldest generation. Then, I specifically sought out the elders of these communities, the people whose voices would be most likely to retain the traditional dialects of the region. In the end, I recorded 1 million words from over 110 individuals in these four small communities, north-west from Scotch Corner, across three countries around the Irish Sea, as indicated in Figure 2.1. I will refer to these materials as the Roots Archive.

Words from the wise

'The real life of language is in many respects more clearly seen and better studied in dialects.' (Sweet, 1900: 79)

In addition, I will discuss a number of other communities, which together comprise what I will refer to as the British Dialects Archive. Included in this archive is the large-scale community-wide York English Corpus from York, the traditional county town of Yorkshire (Tagliamonte, 1998). The archive also includes several smaller community-based studies collected by my students and collaborators: Buckie (Smith, 2000, 2001a, b; Smith and Tagliamonte, 1998), Wheatley Hill (Martin, 1999), Tiverton (Godfrey and Tagliamonte, 1999), Wincanton (Jones and Tagliamonte, 2004) and Henfield (Ashcroft, 1997). Each of the communities represented in these archives is indicated on the map in Figure 2.2.

As mentioned earlier, these materials may also provide a worthy backdrop for broader comparative studies of varieties of English worldwide, an enterprise that has garnered considerable attention (e.g. Bauer, 1994; Hickey, 2004; Trudgill, 1999, 2004; Trudgill et al., 2000). Indeed, any study of varieties of English elsewhere in the world must be attentive to what the source dialects in Britain may have been like during the early founder period of the colonial setting (Mufwene, 1996, 1997, 1999b, 2000, 2001; Trudgill, 2004).

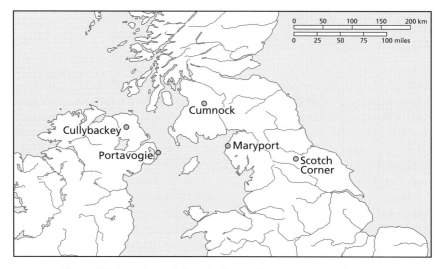

Figure 2.1 Location of Scotch Corner in context with the Roots Archive Communities

[T]he evidence for the presence of a mixture of British Isles English dialects in 19th century New Zealand and Australia is overwhelming. (Trudgill, 2004: 23)

Depending on the population mix of the colonial setting, the varieties under investigation are particularly germane. In the case of New Zealand, as documented by Trudgill (2004: 13, 16), the dialects in contact originated in England, Scotland and Ireland, but the dominant group was England, but not the north. In contrast, North American migrations favoured the counties of Derry, Antrim and Down in Northern Ireland, Ayr, Dumfries and Wigtown in Scotland, and Cumberland and Westmorland in north-west England. These are the regions of Britain from which the vast majority of British migrants to North America originated between 1717 and 1775 (Fischer, 1989: 622; Leyburn, 1962: 94). While more southern regions of Britain figured in the input populations to North America (e.g. Kytö, 1993b; Le Page and Tabouret-Keller, 1985; Wright, 2004), the vast majority of settlers who immigrated between 1717 and 1775 originated from the Lowlands of Scotland, Northern Ireland and the northern counties of England (Campbell, 1921: 8; Fischer, 1989: 619; Landsman, 1985: 51). The communities from which these data come are all within these very counties. According to Mufwene's (2001) concept of 'feature pool', the nature of the dialect that arises in the contact setting will depend on competition and selection among this mix of features.

Family in America

Mi mother's sisters all went to America, just before the first world war. There was six or seven of them. All went till America. (Alec Murray, 88, CLB, 018)

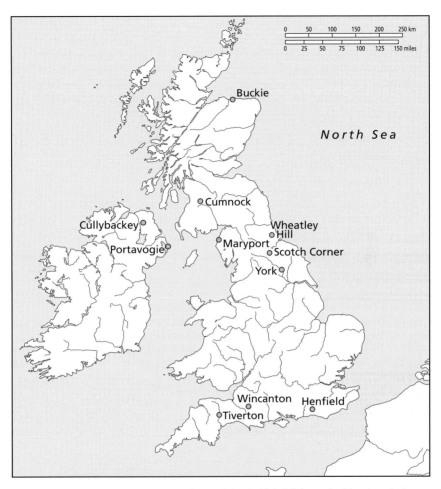

Figure 2.2 The Roots Archive and the British Dialects Archive in relation to Scotch Corner

I had a younger brother died in infancy. But the rest are all – aye, one in America, a brother in Kendall, a sister in Luton and a sister in Doncaster and a sister in America, a brother in Manchester. I'm the only one actually here... (Graeme Nesbitt, 69, CMK, 024)[22]

Aunt Margot Mam used to call her, and Liz, Aunty Lizzie. They went to America and it must have been early nineteen-hundreds. (Lou Fitzgerald, 73, MPT, 021)

The socio-historical circumstances through which these communities evolved from that period onwards and their ongoing separation from the mainstream have created ideal circumstances for the maintenance of conservative features. Indeed, the dialects contain a plethora of archaisms. Consider the causal connector *for to*, as in (13), which is said to be one of the shared grammatical features between Northumberland and Scotland (Beal, 1993: 193). The deictic *yon* is from Old English with cognates in Germanic and Norse as in (14). Note the use of *thon*, (14b), which was a nineteenth-century alternate combining *this/that* and *yon*. The preposition *till* 'to' is also noted as an Old Northumbrian word reinforced by Norse (Wakelin, 1988: 50), as in (15), and there are numerous conservative past tense forms of common verbs, such as *go, teach, take, have*, as in (16).[23]

(13)   a. In the early stages I was pleased *for to* have the support that I did get. (MPT/¢)
       b. I needed to have a bike *for to* get the job. (CMK/O)
       c. Them was boilt *for to* feed everything. (CLB/a)

(14)   a. He says, '*yon* silly bugger. [laughs]. *Yon* silly bugger.' (CMK/013)
       b. And see *thon* wee woman that was his wife. (CMK/037)
       c. There were *yon* horses tied on to the other like that behind. (CLB/015)

(15)   a. I said, 'if you know any different *till* what I know' I said 'just let me know'. (MPT/031)
       b. I used to be able *till* eat a bar of chocolate, you know. (CLB/014)

(16)   a. I should have *gied* when the wife died. (CMK/037)
       b. Horseman in front *teached* them what to do. (CMK/017)
       c. Well this door was *taen* off and it was papered up. (CMK/025)
       d. And I would've *haen* to have *haen* the floor scrubbed and everything cleaned for him coming. (CLB/001)

Both Lowland Scotland and north-west England have a smattering of double modals, as in (17). The form *yan* for 'one' is shared by the Northern Irish and north-west England communities, as in (18). Note too that Portavogie in Northern Ireland retains velar fricatives such as *nicht*, as in (18b). North-west England has *thee/thou*, *yam*, *ga*, *gas*, etc., as in (19).

(17)   a. You *used to could* go through the estate from Auchinleck side. (CMK/o)
       b. So I say – you *won't can* read it lass. (MPT/d)

(18)   a. I was youngest and first *yan* to be married. (MPT/001)
       'I was the youngest and the first one to be married.'
       b. We were coming haim to a dance *yan nicht*. (PVG/008)
       'We were coming home from a dance one night.'
       c. His wife aie gien him two hard-boiled-eggs in his box, you see. And he took *yan* at the first break. (CLB/002)
       'His wife gave him two hard boiled eggs in his box, you see. And he took one at the first break.'

(19)   a. And where*'st thou* gan next? (MPT/011)
       'And where are you going next?'
       b. He said 'Will you *ga yam*, lass!' he said 'You look terrible.' (MPT/032)
       'He said "Will you go home, lass!" he said, "You look terrible."'

c. And if you were outside you done something wrong and somebody says 'I'll tell thee father' … you thought, 'oh if he *gas yam* and tells my father I's in for it'. (MPT/025)

'And if you were outside and you did something wrong, and somebody says "I'll tell your father"… you thought "oh, if he goes home and tells my father I'm in trouble".'

Definition

A modal is a type of auxiliary verb, such as *must, can, might, may, could*. Note that modals do not have inflections, e.g. **she musts*, or an infinitive, e.g. **to must*, at least not in the standard language. A 'double modal' is a construction that contains two modals instead of one, e.g. *might can, may could*.

Thus each community in the Roots Archive retains numerous features recorded in the history of English, which have since disappeared from mainstream varieties. This conservatism in the linguistic inventory of the varieties together with the ecology of their socio-cultural settings, alongside that evidence from linguistic analysis, may shed light on the origins of transported varieties, which developed out of population influxes from these areas.

In sum, these data are foundational and critical to the study of any variety whose roots could potentially be traced to Scots, Northern Irish or English origins. More generally, the book draws on this rich, comprehensive evidence to support the exploration of dialect history.

Definition

An obsolescent or moribund form is a feature of language that is passing out of use, e.g. 'for' as a conjunction, *I have a cat for I need company.*

Dialect puzzle 2.1

Spot the following dialect features in the examples of Chapter 2:

Questions

a. Use of a possessive pronoun to encode familial association or kinship term.
b. An ancient morphological form of *be*.
c. A term used for a female.
d. A nonstandard verb with 1st person singular.
e. Contraction of 'it is'.
f. Two words for 'relatives'.
g. A nonstandard past participle.
h. Two words for 'potatoes'.
i. How many nonstandard preterits can you find?
j. A dialect word that means 'a few'.

Answers

a. *How's your Paul and them getting on?* (WHL/007)
b. *And where'st thou gan next?* (MPT/011)
c. *Lass*
d. *I's in for it.* (MPT/025)
e. *'Cos the nineteen-twenties and thirties was, well like 'tis now, farming did hardly pay.* (WIN/g)
f. *Folk* and *people*, e.g. *Our folk come here*; *mi mother's people.*
g. *I never seen.*
h. *Tatties, spuds, we'd grow tatties and leeks; Oh plenty of spuds and cabbage …*
i. Six. *Come, boilt, gied, teached, taen, haen*
j. *Wheen, there's a good wheen of young'uns*

3   The Roots Archive

It's roots. You get your roots down, you know.

(Samuel Clark, 85, YRK)

In this chapter, I detail data-collection methods and procedures, fieldwork experiences and corpus compilation. I also introduce the communities and the individuals as well as provide many lively examples of the fascinating features of the dialects.

A well-known fact of historical linguistics and sociolinguistics is that certain dialects tend to be more conservative than others. Crucially for the sociolinguist, the dialectologist and the historical linguist, they do not participate in ongoing linguistic change at the same rate as others. This may simply be due to their geographical separation from the mainstream, but it can also be due to some combination of social and/or cultural separation as well. Meillet (1967) observed that 'very often it is sufficient to arrange facts geographically to understand their history'. Although synchronic dialects cannot exactly replicate varieties of English as they were spoken in earlier days, they provide at least a partial 'snapshot' of earlier stages in the history of the language.

All told, the data on which this book is based comprises a rich compendium of British dialects totalling 3 million words of natural speech, including the Roots Archive itself as outlined in Table 3.1 as well as the British Dialects Archive as outlined in Table 3.2, all illustrated on the map in Figure 2.2. Crucial for the comparative socio-historical enterprise is that each of these corpora comes from communities that exist in varying situations of contact with mainstream norms.

See, we use thous and thoos and thys more out at villages than what they did in town, didn't they? (Andrew Myers, 63, MPT)

Dialects in the British heartland

A critical goal of sociolinguistic fieldwork is to gain access to the naturally occurring speech of a representative sample of individuals in a particular speech community (e.g. Sankoff, 1974). In order to accomplish this, it is particularly important to be able to record the type of speech people use when they are not concerned about how they sound, what sociolinguists refer to as the 'vernacular'. In other words, representation of the typical conversational interchanges of a community is required. However, when traditional dialect speakers meet up with speakers of Standard English, they tend not to use local dialect features. There are unavoidable socio-cultural reasons for this. Dialects tend to be ill-regarded, not only by people from outside the communities in which they are spoken, as in (1a), but also by the people who speak dialects, themselves, as evident in (1b) and (1c). Note especially the irrepressible clash of generations and opinions in (1d)!

(1) a. [3] If you use your dialect they look down on you. [1] Oh they definitely do aye. (MPT/003 and 001)

   b. His language was disgusting, my father's. But that was what we called cattle market language. (YRK/002)

   c. Jack Manning always says to me, says I murder the English language. Say I cannae help it! (PVG/002)

   d. When I was on the train going off home to Brechin – was it Christmas time? And this granny and granda obviously came in with their grandchild and she said something to them and the kid said 'Aye'. And she said 'It's not aye, it's yes.' And I thought 'No! it's "aye". Say aye.' [012] That's it eh. [*Local Interviewer*] And he was told off about four times for it. [012] Really? [*Local Interviewer*] Aye, the wee kid, for saying aye. [012] Oh no I don't think you should. [*Local Interviewer*] Aye, I thought there was nothing wrong with 'aye' at all. (MPT/012)

These factors make it almost impossible for outsiders to hear the 'real' dialect. To obviate these problems, local community members were engaged to assist in data collection. This method ensures access to the naturally occurring speech of a community, the community's vernacular.

Definition

The 'vernacular' is a term used to describe the variety spoken by people when they are at their most natural – unmonitored, typically informal, language.

Sociolinguists enter a speech community in such a way as to optimize observation of the vernacular (e.g. Labov et al., 1968; Milroy, 1987; Trudgill, 1974). This is crucial in the study of dialects such as those in the Roots Archive and the British Dialects Archive, which to an outsider's ear are quintessentially nonstandard. In order to tap this type of discourse, the fieldworker must either be an in-group member, or have some affiliation with the community so that he or she can be perceived as a legitimate presence in the local milieu.

Back from America

[003] And mi father was in America. He had went to America but mi mother had been pregnant at the time and whenever I was born he come home fae America, for I was the first boy you see and then that brought him home. (Adam Majury, 91, CLB, 003)[1]

The Roots Archive was collected in just this way, either by an ingroup field-worker or by a research assistant with ties to the community. The materials contain rich language data with a wealth of rarely heard features of the English language. There are innumerable dialect words and expressions. There are odd sounds. There are unexpected twists in the arrangement of sentences and in the way sentences begin and end. There are arcane conversational rituals. There are many things that are peculiar and exotic; there are some things that are entirely unknown and yet others are hauntingly familiar. In many cases, features long gone from mainstream varieties of English endure – the voices on the audio record echo with the sounds of the past. All the examples in this book are orthographically transcribed from the audio-recordings.[2] In the next section I discuss each of the communities in turn.

No, we don't beep out any bad language. (Interviewer 001, Roots Archive)

Words from the wise

'Those who have tapped the real resources of the speech community find that field work is a rich pursuit that is never exhausted. I have found that there is no greater pleasure than to travel as a privileged stranger to all parts of the world, to be received with kindness and courtesy by men and women everywhere, and to share their knowledge and experience with them as it reappears in their language.' (Labov, 1972b: xviii)

Lowland Scotland

Cumnock

Cumnock is a small ex-mining town in Ayrshire in south-west Scotland with a population of about 11,000. A railway link established Cumnock as a growing mining community in the nineteenth century. When the mining industry collapsed in the 1980s, the town suffered considerable out-migration, leaving behind a core of long-time residents.

The fieldworker in Cumnock was Jennifer Smith, who was also a research assistant on the project. As it happens, Jen is a speaker of a relic Scots dialect, having been born and raised in Buckie in Banffshire, Scotland. Given this general 'northern' Scots identity she was able to make contact with the locals with relative ease. Upon arrival she was soon in contact with a wide and diverse group of residents. Many of the individuals in this corpus are ex-miners who had a host of stories to tell about conditions in the 'pits'. In all, 41 people were interviewed.

The Pits

I seen a lot of men get killed in the pits, ken, aye. Aye, getting carried out ken. It's maybe just as well they're shut. Because between putting men into bad health wie the stour. And I mean I used to work in sections down the pit where the water was pouring down on top of you. Aye, and you had to wear skins and you had to tie your sleeves ken so the water, when you worked up there, the water was nae going down your sleeve. And tie your neck, ken. They kind of things ken. And then, where there was water coming down on top of you it was usually a bad roof! (Alec Campbell, 70 CMK, 004)

They had trains running you know to the seams. To give you an idea some of the roads were twenty feet high and twenty feet wide. And then there maybe er further in they were maybe fourteen by ten. But the height of these roads and er all with the girders erected, you know, at er three feet intervals … But it did nae reduce the amount of dust in the air. And this is the thing er creates all the trouble. But it was better than what it was in the old pit. Because sometimes you wondered how you was able to breathe. Because the ventilation was that poor in the old pits. But there were plenty ventilation in the modern pits. In fact it was like a hurricane, the force of it. (William Burns, 82, CMK, 037)

The modern mining, you know it had to be seen to believed. In the old pits a man and er his drawer, that was the man who pushed the tubs out and in the roadways, they came from what we called the lye, taken into the face and the two of them would start and fill these hutches … And er they says it was like er some of these things that was shown for … the future. The machines that come up with picks, if you'd've gotten in its way and er been caught and dragged into it you would've come out like mince. There were … great big picks, bigger than my hand, and they could cut in you know to the coal and that. But it's very difficult – in fact the old miners who never ever seen that type of work, it was hard for them to understand it. (William Burns, 82, CMK, 037)

North-west England

Maryport

There's nothing in the town for to bring people in. (Grace Kenway, 74, MPT, 023)

Maryport is an ex-trading port on the north Cumbrian coast, approximately 27 miles from Carlisle with a population of 11,500. The traditional industries were coal mining, fishing and ship building. Unlike some areas of Cumbria, Maryport did not benefit from the tourist boom of the last century. This has helped Maryport to retain its own special character.

There are those people who would argue that Cumbria is … 'forgotten', a 'blank space' on the Northern map. (Wales, 2006: 26)

The Maryport data was collected by an in-group community member. The man was a natural conversationalist, who tapped into his own social networks in order to facilitate data collection. He was able to record much of the local culture and history through stories and reminiscences from forty-three members of the oldest generation.

Maryport

Maryport was always poor, people were poor. I mean it wasn't a wealthy place, but it was happy place. Everybody mucked in and you know if you wanted anything and the next-door-neighbour had it, you only had to say and it was there. (Helen Phillips, 79, MPT)

Yokel

[3] Well this is what annoys me. If we go down south they think we're yokels. If we'd to talk broad Cumbrian down in London, say, or down south they just look at you like that. We have to change our dialect so they can understand us. [1] But they would nae change theirs. [3] Do the Cockneys change theirs or the Geordies or the Scousers? [001] No, they don't, that's right. [3] It's the Cumbrian, he has to change his accent to be understood. [1] And it is annoying as well that they instantly think you're stupid. [3] Well they think you're below them because of the dialect.(Andrew Myers, 63, and James Irwin, 72, MPT)[3]

Northern Ireland

In Northern Ireland, I specifically sought out old Ulster-Scots communities. We ended up with two – Cullybackey in County Antrim and Portavogie in County Down.

Cullybackey

The village of Cullybackey, with a population of 2,500, is situated 30 miles north-west of Belfast in County Antrim. The main industries are agriculture, retail and manufacturing. Critical, for our purposes, is the fact that, despite its picturesque setting, Cullybackey has not developed as a tourist destination.

   The Cullybackey data was collected by an in-group community member. She was engaged on site by the project fieldworker. This woman worked through her own social networks in the community to record local culture and traditions through stories and reminiscences from twenty members of the oldest generation.

Cullybackey

You'll find that the dialect down here wouldn't be the dialect that you would get if you went over to Stranraer. To get something similar to the dialect here you need to go to Aberdeen. (Dan James, 64, CLB, 001)

I says 'it's very warm the day' and I talk about a het day. And I says, 'if it was a cold day I'd talk about a caul day'. And I says, 'if it was snow on the ground I talk about snaw. And if it's raining I talk about a wat day.' And that the way I talk. (Rose Donovan, 89, CLB, 001)

Portavogie

Portavogie is even smaller than Cullybackey, with a population of only 1,500 situated on the Irish Sea coast of the Ards Peninsula, 21 miles south of Newtonards. It is a small fishing village, still wholly reliant on the herring industry for its livelihood.

A port in the bog

'Bally' in Irish means 'village' and a 'mull', M-U-L-L means a low rounded hill, you know, like that type o' hill, right? Like that hill. Like Billy's Hill … Portavogie was once called Ballymullochmoor. Right? And then of course the Vikings come. They changed it to Portavogie, and 'Portavogie' means 'a port in the bog'. (Pete Dennet, 69 PVG, 004)[4]

A herring station

Portavogie started off as a herring-station for fisher – Scotchmen came here, there was herrings in abundance, they caught herrings and they didn't go home. That's just what it boils down to. So they eventually brought their wives and families to Portavogie, and – well it became a little colony of Scotland. (Michael Adair, 74, PVG, 008)[5]

The Portavogie data was collected by a research assistant, Helen Lawrence, in conjunction with a local interviewer who was a 'friend of a friend'. Participation of the in-group member in the interviews enabled us to record eight elderly residents on community events and stories.

Finding old friends

Well, I just heared a story last night fae Shirley. Shirley's in a place up about your road. And they takes a day wi all the er [inc][6] in the hospital. She's on call there all the time. If there's anything say heart-machines or something goes wrong with them, they ring her and she sends mechanics out to fix them. Big money business, you know. And this woman always rung her, forget what they called her. And she [inc] first, and went on it was, something was wrong with this and the mechanic was there yesterday and it's broken again, and all this carry-on. And two days ago, yan o' mechanics come in. And he says to Shirley, he says, 'I took a photo o' the girls up there.' And Shirley looked at the three – three women that was on at them. And she says to the girl that's in the office wi' her. She says 'I know that woman. I used to work wi her.' So she rung her up, and sure enough … (Dan James, 64, PVG, 001)

These stories typify the Roots Archive – informal discussions with a 'grass roots' perspective on community life and times. The interactions range from a minimum of one hour to a maximum of three hours and focus on local history, cultural practice, and all aspects of people's experiences during their lifetime.

Grass roots

You know the Americans are always looking for the real grass roots. (Interviewer, MPT, 001)

Table 3.1 *The Roots Archive*

	Male	Female	Total individuals	Total words
Cumnock [CMK]	17	22	39	349,428
Culleybackey [CLB]	15	5	20	223,693
Maryport [MPT]	20	23	43	401,376
Portavogie [PVG]	7	2	9	92,803

Nature of the data

The result of the fieldwork is an archive of considerable breadth and volume. It comprises 115 hours of audio-recorded conversations, ranging in length from thirty minutes to three hours with 110 individuals, all over the age of 50, and divided among men and women. The sample constitution of the Roots Archive is shown in Table 3.1. Each community is listed with the abbreviation used to identify it in the examples.

The data is informal and interactive; it contains personal reminiscences, gossip, reflections on life, folk wisdom, and stories of all kinds. Many excerpts are interspersed throughout the book; however, here are several that are particularly colourful.

The clucker ghost

Well, it was in this barn where we got wind there been a ghost … And er it turned out to be that it was a clucker, which is a hen sitting on eggs. And when folk were coming past it was fluttering and flying about, you see. And of course there was nae lights and 'twas pitch dark with this white thing fluttering about… (Lou Fitzgerald, 73, MPT, 004)

Never sell hay

Aye, that was another thing Daddy said to me too. Says, 'Never sell hay. Don't sell hay' he said, 'or sell anything like that,' he says, 'if a neighbour comes till you just and needs a lump of hay,' he says, 'throw it till him,' he says, because he says, he says 'at the end of the day,' and he says, 'you'd a lump of hay left over and not do any harm yet,' but he says, 'at the end of the day,' he says, 'there'll be some time you need something too. Don't ever forget that.' Daddy told me that. (Mike O'Leary, 53, CLB, 013)

Muck for tatties

The biggest laugh I got, we were doing story of Barnabus in Sunday school. And I said to them now Barnabus was the man who wanted to give summat to the poor. And he had nae money you know and he had nae animals to sell. So what could he do? So he decided he would his bit of land. He had a bit of land. So he selt his bit of land. Well in due course – and he give the money to the poor. But in due course when spring come round of course he had no – nowt to grow yet – there was nae where – so I says, 'What would he miss now? What might he have grown on that bit of land that he hasn't got now?' And they said sugar and er corn and er wheat. And I said 'Aye, it could be, it could be.' And then one laal lass said 'tatties' – that's potatoes as you know – and afore I could speak another laal lass said 'Don't be daft. He couldn't grow tatties.' And I didn't know why so I kept quiet which is best way. And this other laal lass says, 'Why couldn't he grow tatties?' And I can see her yet, she says 'Hasn't Mrs. Fitzgerald just telt you he had nae animals. Now where's he gan get his muck frae to grow tatties?'(Lou Fitzgerald, 73, MPT)

How do you churn butter?

Mi uncle kept two cows and you know he only had them two cows for him and me. What I had to do through the week was churn. Some nights we churned – some weeks we churned twice, you know. You were sort of sick. And a woman said to me, her fella was just the same, he kept two cows. Says, 'You go and buy yoursel' a wee churn and keep just the cream of the milk, the top you know, and the bottom'll do your calves.' And I did that and then I only had to churn one day in the week. But I hated churned butter. Oh I hated churned butter. [Interviewer] Then I suppose you had to make the butter. [012] Oh aye. You churned it. That was a night's work, you know. You churned it and you had to hae everything perfectly clean. And you churned your butter and then you lifted out your butter and you made it and, put it – [Interviewer] Was that just rinsing it out in water? [012] Oh you had to rinse it three or four times and then salt it and rinse it again and then you salted it and put it into a great big ball.(Lily Trimble, 86, CLB, 012)

Within the social and cultural information contained in these materials are dozens of linguistic features worthy of investigation. Many are common to vernacular dialects across Britain. These include the ubiquitous lack of agreement with preterit *be*, as in (2), particularly in existential constructions (3), with simple present *be*, as in (4), variation in verbal endings in the simple present tense paradigm, as in (5), a variety of different complement markers, e.g. *for to*, as in (6), regularized *don't*, as in (7).

(2) a. In that picture of me with those cats, they *was* all ginger ones. (TIV/07)
     b. And then, but we *was* going out through there um, with the donkey the first time. (WHL/002)
     c. When we *was* kids it was good, really good fun. (HEN/004)

(3) a. There *was* railway cottages up on the bank. (HEN/005)
     b. There *was* two of them. (WHL/007)
     c. There *was* a lot of good players there. (WIN/036)

(4) a. There*'s* not many round here. (HEN/008)
     b. During the week, she comes now because weekends *is* no good because that's out for her, you see. (HEN/001)

(5) a. We don't call them Old Aged Pensioners, we *calls* 'em Senior Citizens. (TIV/002)
     b. So I *goes* down to Mr. M which was the welfare-officer. (WHL/002)

(6) a. God gien the people the earth *for to* rear their families. (CLB/017)
     b. I sold my clothing coupons *for to* spend on the boys' clothing. (CMK/034)

(7)   a. She *don't* know what a hoop is, do you? (HEN/005)
      b. He *don't* have everything. (WIN/009)

Another advantage of the Roots Archive is the perspective it affords of numerous dialects simultaneously. Unlike research that focuses on specific features in individual dialects, the breadth of these data sets enables exploration of dialect parallels and contrasts across a range of different northern dialects. In so doing, it is possible to answer questions above and beyond those that are particular to individual communities. The types of change found in one community may not be found in others, nor will the same change manifest identically across communities. However, it is possible to situate any change more broadly, as part of ongoing grammatical change in Britain. From this broader perspective, it will be possible to assess whether the external influences on grammatical change in one community are similar to that of another. If so, then the similarities and differences may be uncovered. Further, it then becomes possible to compare grammatical changes observed across British dialects to what can be found in other dialects of English. How broad and deep will the similarities go?

Various levels of connection can be posited for the four communities. Obviously, the two Irish communities should be similar simply based on their geographic proximity and regional affinity. Moving to a slightly broader perspective, we can compare Northern Ireland with Cumnock in south-west Scotland. The connection between certain Northern Ireland locations and Cumnock should be quite close. This is because Ayrshire, where Cumnock is located, was the source area for the Ulster plantations in Northern Ireland, and both Cullybackey and Portavogie were settled by Ulster Scots. Comparison between Maryport and Cumnock should expose a Scots vs English contrast. Finally, since there are also arguments for the overarching commonality between Northumbria and Lowland Scotland (Beal, 1993; Wales, 2006: 50–1), there should be at least some correspondences across all of the Roots Archive communities. It will be interesting to discover what features are similar across the board and which differentiate communities. In this way contrasts between universal and local linguistic features will become possible.

Ulster-Scots

My sister gan off at me, she's 'Wish you'd stop speaking that old broad Bally French dialect.' I says 'Beg your pardon, wait a minute.' I says 'I'm no speaking broad Bally French dialect, I'm speaking Ulster-Scotch. Or Old-English, as it's come fae.' I says 'Go on there, I'll get you a dictionary,' I got a Chambers English Dictionary, and I looked it up. And we were talking about a 'stane' for 'stone'. You know, a stone it would be. We would call it a 'stane', and I looked up 'stone', and it said 'origin, Old-English, "stane"'. S-T-A-N-E and a 'rape' for a 'rope'. (Kate Devoy, 62, PVG, 004)[7]

Stane

These men does nae want ice in my fish, my fish is fresh. I says 'they're no wanting a stane o' ice in the box, for they'll be a stane o' fish less in it'. And I says 'They're no gonna pay me for ice,' and I says 'and they dinnae want them ice.' (John Abbott, 67, PVG, 007)[8]

Definition

The term 'broad' used to describe a dialect refers to a way of speaking that is marked by strong and regionally demarcated features.

Tapping the vernacular

In each locale we interviewed the most insular individuals from the oldest generation at the time of the fieldwork. Each corpus comprises tape-recorded conversations representing in many cases hundreds of thousands of words (see Table 3.1). While there are undoubtedly formality effects operating within the context of the interview situation, these are within normal parameters of conversational interaction. There are sometimes metalinguistic comments about pronunciation and perceptions of dialect. However, none of the material contains dramatic style shifting or performed narrative speech that appear to be present in fieldwork sites where the interviewers were alien to the community (e.g. Schilling-Estes, 1998). Instead, we went to great lengths to ensure that the interviewers were either local or shared some salient extra-linguistic characteristic. The interviews reflect this in their jocular tone and unselfconscious style. Indeed, the broad dialectal quality of these materials along with their generally informal tone makes me confident that the speech faithfully reflects the typical discourse found in each community and is as close as possible to the vernacular norms of the regional dialects.

Good English?

When I got off the plane in Toronto I looking for London, for the plane for London, you see … And I seen this girl at this desk and she was a white girl like miself. And I went up to her and as I thought I was speaking good English and asked her where I would get the plane for London and some other questions. And she says, 'do you speak English?' (Laughs). And I was speaking what I thought very good English! (Adam Majury, 91, CLB, 003)[9]

Prittas

They were good prittas if you were able to have seventy baskets in the day. [4] That was good? [001] Seventy baskets that was about what? Thirty-five pound eh? And that was if the prittas was good. And you … put the wee'uns into a bucket. And they were boilt for the hens, pigs, beasts or whatever you were feeding. There were a wild lot of feeding then with prittas … I can mind when prittas was one bare pound for a ton. A shilling a hundred. And I can mind as well I was working in Montgomery's so it must've been either the late twenties or the early thirties. And I washed nine baskets of prittas every day and them was boilt for to feed everything. (Rose Donovon, 89, CLB, 001)[10]

Table 3.2 *British Dialects Archive*

	Male	Female	Total individuals	Total words
Buckie, Scotland [BCK]	4	5	9	198,086
Wheatley Hill [WHL]	12	13	25	206,320
York [YRK]	43	54	97	1.2m
Wincanton, Somerset [WIN]	17	17	34	205,783
Tiverton, Devon [TIV]	7	2	9	96,472
Henfield, Sussex [HEN]	4	4	8	128,421

Comparison dialects

In the course of exploring the Roots Archive, there are times when it will be important and relevant to compare the results with a wider range of British dialects, including those in the south. Fortuitously, I have compiled a rich compendium of different British dialects, which I will refer to as the British Dialects Archive. Most of the materials consist of sociolinguistic interviews conducted by York University students between 1997 and 2001. In each case the students were local to the community under investigation, and the corpus is typically made up of their family and friends. In addition to the students' training in sociolinguistic methods, this familiarity with the individuals goes a long way to ensuring the vernacular nature of their speech.

The British Dialects Archive is in some ways comparable to the Roots Archive and in other facets presents a range of divergent extra-linguistic characteristics. As Wales (2006) argues, when it comes to British and Northern Irish dialects, the distinction between non-standard, peripheral and mainstream becomes blurred. This is why it is critical to have the consistent cross-variety perspective that these corpora permit. Triangulation of many varieties and multiple linguistic features from different levels of grammar will help to overcome these problems (see Poplack and Tagliamonte, 2001: chapter 5).

Buckie

Buckie is a town on the far north-east shore of Scotland with a population of 8,172 in 2001. At the time of data collection (c. 1997), the population was almost entirely Scots (92%). It was once a thriving fishing and ship-building port. Despite the decline in the traditional fishing industry, the community has been able to maintain its cultural cohesiveness due to the maintenance of local employment provided by the oil industry (Smith, 2000).

Working in Buckie

[002] Yes, he got a good job … He was working on the docks. He was on the boat building and that, workit at the docks. Quite a nice job … Then the family grew up. There

was two boys. One's got a deer farm, but he's a builder. He's a good builder, he could build houses, but he actually startit the deer farm. (John Jappy, 88, BCK, 002)

The Buckie English corpus was collected by Jennifer Smith and is documented in her PhD dissertation (Smith, 2000) as well as in numerous publications (e.g. Smith, 2001a, b; 2004). Research focusing on particular northern linguistic features includes extensive use of nonstandard *was* (Smith and Tagliamonte, 1998), as in (8), negative concord, as in (9) (Smith, 1999), and negatives with *do,* as in (10), (Smith, 2001b).

(8)   a. We *was na* getting a house at the time. (BCK/GF)
      b. If I kent you *was* coming I would have taen it out. (BCK/AC)

(9)   a. We've *nae* got a shower or *nothing* like 'at. (BCK/371.51:1)
      b. She *wouldna* ging wi' *naebody* else. (BCK/94.31:3)

(10) a. I *dinna* mind fa taen it. (BCK/a)
         'I don't remember who took it'
      b. I *na* mine fa come in. (BCK/a)
         'I don't remember who came in'

Each of these studies has exposed extensive variation in the community. Despite being stigmatized elsewhere, many of these highly conservative features are stable across generations.

Definition

'Negative concord' is a term that refers to the occurrence of two negative markers in a sentence, a negative indefinite pronoun, e.g. *nothing*, along with a marker which negates the whole sentence, in the standard language *not.* A sentence with negative concord has both, e.g. I did *not* know *nothing.* Negative concord can also be referred to as 'double negation' in the literature.

Wheatley Hill

Wheatley Hill is a village in County Durham in north-east England with a population of 3,181 in 2001. It was once a thriving mining community, but in the last few decades many of the mines have closed down, forcing the inhabitants to find work in nearby urban centres. The village itself has become depleted as well, and inhabitants must go into the city of Durham to shop.

Wheatley Hill

The pit was just down at the bottom. There was the Miner's Hall, there was the Royalty, there was the Regal … there was shops right the way along … the shops and the store-garage and the pork shop and everything was right away along to the end … From the school we used to go over and into garage fruiters and get a carrot or get a teacake and munch away like. The schools used to play football, the school teams and what have you and there used to be crowds on an afternoon er – when the local football team used to be, there used to be crowds there. Now there's nothing. There's nobody. (Jimmy Greener, 69, WHL, 023)

In a sense we're more like a Scotch – a bit of a Scotch accent in the Durham accent, I think. In fact there's that much Scotch in it they take you for Scotch when you go up there. Even the Scotch lads take you for Scotch so. (WHL, 015)

A study of variation in the copula in the community (Martin, 1999; Martin and Tagliamonte, 1999) revealed that there was a small amount of copula absence, as in (11).

(11)   a. Amanda Coulson over the road from us. Got lovely long hair. She [Ø] gonna have it all shaved off … totally bald for a role she[z] doing in Macbeth. (WHL/018)
         b. I think it was thinking 'God they [Ø] great, them'. (WHL/021)

Martin (1999) discovered that patterning and conditioning of the copula variants in Wheatley Hill was parallel to reports for this feature in North American varieties. Furthermore, the patterns of use for the zero variant were comparable to both European and African varieties in the southern United States. The zero copula has also been reported for Yorkshire (Giner and Montgomery, 1997) as well as for some varieties of Scots (Macaulay, 1991). This study offered additional evidence that copula absence is a minor variant in northern England.

York

York is a small city in north-east England with a population of 137,505 in 2001. It is unique amongst English cities for at least two reasons. First, the industrial revolution somewhat passed it by. York did not undergo the massive economic upheaval (e.g. population growth, rebuilding, etc.) found in other English cities. Second, the predominant in-migrations in the nineteenth century were from local (north-eastern and Yorkshire) dialects (Armstrong, 1974: 145). Indeed, the majority of local inhabitants have come from the immediate surroundings for at least the last century. For both these reasons, York has retained a somewhat conservative character.[11]

The city is relatively self-contained. Despite its relatively urban context (compared to the other dialect data), its insular history until recent times and particularly its northern population base have led to the retention of many conservative features (Tagliamonte, 1998, 2001).

York

York has a dialect of its own … Because it's made up of everything around about. This guy he was in Cornwall of all places and we was only on about it the other night. We were sat in this pub and he sat down, was talking to him. Cornish chap. And he says 'Oh you're from Yorkshire.' Which is pretty obvious, you know. He says 'You're not from

Barnsley, you're not from Leeds,' he said 'But you're not far off Leeds.' 'You're not from Dales side, and you're not from moors side,' he says 'All I can say is er' and he got it, he says 'You're from York.' He's only one that I know who's actually got us bang on where we're from. (Robin Jones, 50, YRK, 019)[12]

The York English Corpus is the largest body of materials in the British Dialects Archive. It was collected with the goal of modelling the entire speech community from late adolescents to octogenarians (for further discussion, see Tagliamonte, 1998) and is intended to be a representative sample of vernacular York English speech at the turn of the twenty-first century (c. 1997). Each individual in the sample was required to meet the sampling criteria of having been born and raised in York. Following the techniques developed by Milroy (1987), we entered the community through three independent social networks: (1) acquaintances in the University service personnel, (2) neighbours and friends of the interviewers and (3) a community church in the inner city. Because one of the main goals of the project was to track linguistic change in the community, we made every effort to stratify the sample by age and sex. Moreover, due to the three-pronged network strategy, the individuals represent a diverse range of occupations and education levels.

The corpus consists of ninety-two individuals, ranging in age from 15 to 91 years of age and divided among forty men and fifty-two women. This broad age range makes it unique among the other British Dialects Archive communities as well as the Roots Archive, both of which focused on the oldest generation in each community. Moreover, the York Corpus represents a range of education levels. Most had been educated at least to the age of 14. Of the individuals educated beyond the age of 16, there is a range from technical college to university, although those in the latter category are a minority.

Yorkshire

[002] It is nice, though, the soft, Yorkshire accent. A lot of the youngsters I think speak with quite a broad Yorkshire accent as well. [5] Some of them do, yes, yes. Because they've lived in York. But it was the war really that changed York completely. [2] Changed everything, though, didn't it? [5] Yes. But you still get quite a lot of people who are broad Yorkshire and proud of it, and wouldn't change. (Mrs Tweedle, YRK, 5)[13]

Numerous studies of the local dialect have been conducted on the corpus, including variation between *was* and *were* (Tagliamonte, 1998), as in (12), *come* and *came*, as in (13) (Tagliamonte, 2001), the definite article, as in (14) (Tagliamonte and Roeder, 2009), the so-called 'Yorkshire cleft' (Durham, 2011), as in (15), the habitual past, as in (16) (Tagliamonte and Lawrence, 2000).

(12)   a. She *were* a good worker. She *was* a helluva good worker. (YRK/092)
       b. There *was* a lot of us that *were* sort of seventeen. (YRK/004)

(13) a. Well I *come* home a few cuts and bruises but then I used to think nowt to them. (YRK/076)
      b. And I was coming along Skeldergate Bridge, and on the bike, and a car *come* straight in front of me. (YRK/g)

(14) a. *The* main thing is be happy. And if I get a bit miserable with miself, I go *t'*top *t'*garden and talk to mi tomatos. (YRK/076)
      b. *T'*only thing – only way you'd find *t'*well would be to follow *t'*pipe from where *t'*pump was. (YRK/092)

(15) a. Teelee run – he had a good milk business, *had Teelee.* He did all Fulford area and roundabout. (YRK/092)
      b. He'll do anything for anybody, *will Cliff.* (YRK/035)

(16) a. Well, *we used to go* every week. It was one of those things we *did* every week. (007/524–5)
      b. I *used to swim*, but GCSEs came up … Yeah, I *swam* for York. (030/228–30)
      c. On Monday it *would be* mince, on Tuesday it *was* chicken. (044/198–9)

It is interesting that Mrs Tweedle in the excerpt above mentions that 'it was the war that really changed York'. In virtually all the research studies that have been conducted on the corpus, I have found that the Second Word War is a distinct watershed in the community. This suggests that an examination of different generations in York will expose the direction of change in contemporary British English, at least in the relatively mainstream context of a small city in the north.[14]

Wincanton

Wincanton is a village in south Somerset with a population of 4,803 in 2001. There is no railway link, since the station was closed in the 1960s. The main road between London and south-west England built in the 1970s bypasses Wincanton and there is little to attract people to come into it. Like many towns in south-west England, Wincanton suffered depopulation in the late nineteenth century. Once an important market town, the milk industry is now its major industry. The locals complain about the advent of large retail parks that bring people into the area, but not into the town centre.

Wincanton

You know, people talk about it's gonna, you know, ruin the centre of Wincanton and all that sort of thing. But that to a degree has already happened, you know. I mean the people that are complaining now should have complained about Safeway years ago. Because you know, like we've just said. Had a bad effect on the town … 'Where can you buy a jacket or a pair of trousers in Wincanton?' Well, you can't, can you? (David Smith, 76, WIN, 013)[15]

A longstanding feature of this region is the use of pre-verbal *did* in contexts of past habitual, as in (17).

(17)   a. And mi husband always used to tell me I *did* always *speak* before I *did think*.
          (WIN/d)
       b. 'Cos the nineteen-twenties and thirties was, well like 'tis now, farming *did*
          hardly *pay*. (WIN/g)

A study of this feature showed that even though pre-verbal *did* is dying out, it was still conditioned by a complex of linguistic factors that have been reported for this feature throughout the history of the English language (Jones, 2000; Jones and Tagliamonte, 2004). This demonstrated that even features on the brink of extinction can still preserve the grammar of centuries. It also corroborates the hypotheses that these peripheral communities provide a window on the past.

Taken together, the British Dialects Archive represents the state of the English language among the eldest generation in each community c. 1997–2002.

Tiverton

Tiverton is a small town in mid-Devon with a population of 18,621 in 2001. The major industry from the sixteenth century was the wool trade. In the 1800s it become a lace-making town and the industrial centre of the south-west with a rail link and thriving industry. Like most small towns, however, it suffered decline in the twentieth century, with closing factories and removal of the railway. In the twenty-first century there has been something of a revival with the addition of a local museum and the development of footpaths and country parks; nevertheless, the major industry continues to be agriculture.

Tiverton

[001] Went in a hotel in Tiverton to work. The Lime Hotel, it was down by the old Blundell's Garage, it was. Some old lady and that used to take in guests there and that. And then I went to Punchard's out Hay Park. Went up there and worked for so long. Then Miller's, you know, I expect you've heard of them. Um what's the name of the hill again? Isn't it Newt's Hill? ... Wonder why they called it Newts? Like there was newts up there. (Rose Harris, 64, TIV, 001)[16]

A prominent feature of rural Devon is the widespread use of verbal *–s* across the grammatical paradigm, as in (18), even in contexts that would never occur in the north, as in (18f), *they calls 'em*.

(18)   a. Her *gives* me a hug and a kiss, when I *comes* in and one when I *go*.
          (TIV/007)
       b. People *says* 'yeah but look at your weather, you *gets* it freezing cold in the
          winter, you *get* all the rain'. (TIV/002)

   c. He *comes* every – three times a week he *come*. (TIV/001)
   d. We *belong* to Senior Citizens, we don't call them Old Age Pensioners, we
       calls 'em Senior Citizens. (30196)
   e. Kiddies *come* over … and they'm talking to the animals and that. And the
       animals *looks* down, you know. (TIV/002)
   f. Funny big head he got. They *call* 'em something like a battlehead or some-
       thing they *calls* 'em, don't 'em? (TIV/010)

A study of this feature in Tiverton revealed that verbal *–s* did not have the pattern of the Northern Subject Rule (Ihalainen, 1994: 213), but instead comprised a slightly reorganized system in which all the constraints were in place (Godfrey, 1997; Godfrey and Tagliamonte, 1999). Where the Northern Subject Rule predicts a categorical split between personal pronouns and noun phrases, in Tiverton use of *–s* was variable in both. This suggests that when verbal *–s* diffused southwards from the northern regions of Britain between 1500 and 1700, the constraints on its use reorganized in subtle ways. Such changes are to be expected when linguistic systems diffuse across time and space and across diverse dialects and sociolinguistic circumstances (Labov, 2007). This underscores that it is critical to tap into the subtle weight and constraints on variable linguistic patterns.

Henfield

I wouldn't live anywhere else but Henfield. (Jane Dawson, 79, HEN, 001)

Henfield is a village in the far south of West Sussex, 33 miles south of London. In 2001 it had a population of just over 5,000. It maintains a vibrant community culture with a good selection of shops, restaurants and pubs. From the mid-nineteenth century the village became favoured by moneyed people for retirement and residence; some are even described as 'gentry'. This profile suggests that the variety of English spoken in Henfield is likely to be a relatively standard variety.

Henfield

I don't consider that Henfield is spoilt. I love it still. It's the friendliest village in this part of the world … People strangers are welcomed always. And anyway, everybody that I know that has come into the village into a new area that's been built, they're delightful and fit in so well, and do an awful lot things to help. They've taken over er what we older people built up and er one is proud of it, you know. Very nice people. (Dora Hedges, 85, HEN, 006)[17]

Proxies for historical change

In order to determine how language changes, it is necessary to compare two points in time. Ideally, the type of language data from two points in time should be the same, in terms of its representativeness, social make-up, ancestry, etc. In reality, two data points in time from entirely comparable data sources are impossible to find. This means that analysts must use some other means to study historical change.

Peripheral to mainstream

The premise underlying the comparative cross-community analyses in this book is that characteristics of the communities under investigation and the fact that the individuals represented in the corpora are the oldest generation at the time of recording (1997–2001) together provide the necessary conditions for potentially extreme conservatism. The main proxy for time depth is varying states of regional conservatism. On the assumption that language change progresses across space, I use the range of conservative and progressive dialects in the Roots Archive and the British Dialects Archive to mirror change in progress. York is a substantial urban centre with a thriving internationally renowned university. It is also an extremely popular tourist destination, with thousands of outsiders on the streets and in the pubs all the time. Therefore, despite the longitudinal local conservatism, the younger generations in York may be rapidly assimilating to supra-local norms. The other communities range from small rural hamlets to modest-sized villages. They range from highly isolated and conservative to relatively urban and proximate to the mainstream. There are varying degrees of movement in and out of these communities. The Roots Archive communities were purposefully sought out for their peripheral characteristics. Moreover, the people who were interviewed in each community were the very oldest individuals we could find. In early twenty-first-century Britain and Northern Ireland, these individuals tend to be less educated and have typically spent their lives in traditional jobs and close-knit social networks. In the words of the individuals themselves, the dialect has not yet been 'hammered out of them'.

Losing dialect

Well, it's watered down over the years and then everybody gointa secondary school and it's hammered out o' them. (Kate Devoy, 62, PVG, 004)

When I went to Crediton school you know you wouldn't talk Devon. Well it got – not knocked out of you – but you automatically associated with town boys and that, who didn't talk so broad as we did, so yeah. (Phil Dunster, 69, TIV, 009)

My aim is to use these materials to tap the underlying cycle of loss and renewal in various systems of grammar. I speculate that a cross-dialectal perspective will encompass (some of) the 'later recorded steps' in the historical change (quoted in Christy, 1983: 84; Whitney, 1867). In essence, these synchronic dialects offer a window into diachrony.

An afternoon out

They comes along – sometimes there's only two there, and then the next minute you sees six there. Then a couple of them will go away and come down again. And then there's people who's out for like the bank holiday. When they was out for walks they would er, lot of them goes up from Sampford. Parks the car at Sampford, walks up to Westleigh, um, up to Burlescombe on the canal. Gets off the canal, walks down to Westleigh. Comes down past my place. They sees the animals there and they comes in, spends you know maybe twenty minutes or so there with the animals, rabbits and that and then they walk back again. And 'tis is a nice afternoon out. (Ivor Thom, 67, TIV, 002)[18]

Speaker age

Everyone notices that older people and younger people do not sound the same. A person who was born in 1900 will not speak the same way as a person born in 2000. Individuals of different ages in the same community will have different ways of speaking.

You'd plenty more places who have a local accent … probably with the introduction o' television and all has died out quite a bit, you-know. It's only the real people – and the old people o' the village who speak it [the dialect] now. (Michael Adair, 74, PVG, 008)[19]

Sociolinguists refer to these differences as differences in 'apparent time' and use it as a means to understand the progression of change. The construct of apparent time is an important and useful analytical tool for the analysis of variation (Bailey, Wikle, Tillery and Sand, 1991). In an apparent-time study, generational differences are compared at a single point and are used to make inferences about how a change may have taken place in the (recent) past. Age differences are assumed to be temporal analogues, reflecting historical stages in the progress of the change. The technique has been in use since the early 1900s (e.g. Gauchat, 1905; Hermann, 1929) and has become a keystone of Variationist Sociolinguistics (Bailey, 2002; Bailey et al., 1991; Labov, 1963, 1966). A gradually increasing or decreasing frequency in the use of a linguistic feature when that feature is viewed according to speaker age can be interpreted as change in progress (Evans Wagner and Sankoff, 2006). This pattern has provided the basis for a synchronic approach to language change. Analytically, apparent time functions as a surrogate for chronological (or real) time, enabling the history of a linguistic process to be viewed from the perspective of the present.

On the assumption that language change is represented among people of different ages, I will sometimes use the generational perspective of the York English Corpus, which comprises individuals from nineteen to ninety-two in order to consider how the changes in question may be progressing among the younger generations in England.

Definition

In linguistics, 'real time' refers to the chronological progression of time. 'Apparent time' refers to the progression of chronological time in the generations of a community. Change can be inferred from the linguistic behaviour of people at a single time and place arrayed from childhood to old age.

Dialect puzzle 3.1

A. Here is a story told by Bruce Donaldson, aged 68 from Cumnock:
The Dram

I always remember John Smith. This was a chap – he was an engineer that I worked a-side and he – he had a grandmother that stayed up oh, up near Killun, you know, direction. And er the – they were great churchy people and the minister – I think the minister that had been in the parish had been there for about oh, I think nearly all his lifetime. Ever since he was a young minister and he was an old man by this time but when – he came as he did in those days certain days er, did his parochial visits. Anyway, he came – she always had a dram for him, you see. And it was always quite a good dram and topped up with a little water. However the old man retired and a new minister came just straight from theological college. And she thought 'now I wonder if this young man'll like a dram?' So she was nae too sure but eventually she said to him 'do you take a dram minister?' And he says 'oh yes, I do'. And er she says 'oh that's fine'. So she thought she'd be careful so she just put in some – a wee whisky and a lot of water. And John always says that the minister had his cup of tea and his bit of bun and then he started this whisky. And er she was sitting away fine and the old woman says 'is the whisky to your liking minister?' He says 'Well, I just want to ask you one thing' he says. 'Did you put the whisky in first or did you put the water in first?' 'Oh' she says 'I put the whisky in first and then I topped it up with the water.' Ah he says 'that's alright I like that' he says. 'I was beginning to wonder as it says in the good book if the good things were going to come at all' (laughs). John used to always say this. 'Are the good things going to come at all.' So she learnt a lesson. Can you tell what a 'dram' is?

B.

According to Heslop (1892) the form *I's* in Northumberland can mean *I am*, *I shall* or *I have*. What does this data from Maryport tell us?

a. I was twelve when I left. I's telling you now when I started work.
b. 'I's ganna retire.' I says
c. I's the sidesman so I's just behind them.
d. I's ganna – I is ganna phone her.
e. I's alright.
f. [*Interviewer*] I've enjoyed our crack. [028] Well I's pleased to see you James.
g. He says, 'that's thee wages'. So 'Is that all I's getting, like?'
h. I's no coming back down.
i. 'I thought you were working away.' I said, 'Aye, I's finished.'

j. Folk'll say eh 'Are you happy with it?' Aye, I's happy.

k. Next yan's gan to be better. I-mean, I expect I's coming down here.

l. I's famished.

m. 'If I don't get owt t' eat afore long I's gana die.'

n. I's dying now.

o. After that I've been retired up 'til now, but I's still here e.

p. No, I's okay.

q. Don't know what I's gan to do with that shed now.

r. Oh if he gas yam and tells my father I's in for it you know.

s. Then there was Mary and then me, I's baby.

t. I don't know whether I's gonna come back yam or not.

u. So I said 'Oh no I's not gan.'

v. End of this month I's eighty-five.

w. I's only fifty.

x. And I says 'I know what I's gan to do then.'

y. I's gan nae police-station with it.

z. I's seeing Mary tomorrow.

aa. Oh, John says 'I'll ga anyhow, I's here.'

bb. [032] Oh aye, I admit, I used to sulk for nae reason at all. I still do, divn't I? I – I still think I's about sixteen.

cc. I's tensed up and – and I weep bucketsful.

Answer: Every token is a context for 'I'm'; however, the meaning differs depending on context. Note that the simple present tense can also be used for future temporal reference.

a. present progressive

b. future

c. present

d. future

e. present

f. present

g. present progressive

h. present progressive morpoholology; future meaning

i. present or perfect? (ambiguous; meaning could be either)

j. present

k. present progressive morphology; future meaning

l. present

m. present progressive morphology; future meaning

n. present progressive

o. present

p. present

q. present progressive morphology; future meaning

r. present morphology; future meaning

s. present

t. present progressive morphology; future meaning

u. present progressive morphology; future meaning

v. present morphology; future meaning
w. present
x. present progressive morphology; future meaning
y. present progressive morphology; future meaning
z. present progressive morphology; future meaning
aa. present
bb. present
cc. present

4   Methods of analysis

Aye, folk gets fed up with folk wie long faces, hen, ken.
(Joan Dewar, 67, CMK, 007)

The analyst must take these materials – words, reminiscences, stories – and analyse them in such a way as to characterize the grammar of the dialects. In this chapter I outline the methods used to analyse the linguistic features. Methods for analysis of language differ quite substantially from one area of linguistics to another. For example, the standard practice of dialectology is to map words to places. The methodological approach I will take to the dialect data in the Roots Archive and the British Dialects Archive is instead modelled on the comparative method of historical linguistics (Baldi, 1990; Hoenigswald, 1960; Meillet, 1967) married with the methodological innovations of sociolinguistic analysis (Poplack and Tagliamonte, 2001: 7–8). In so doing, I integrate insights and techniques developed in fields that have seldom previously collaborated: historical linguistics, sociolinguistics and dialectology.

Words from the wise

'The comparative method is the only one which permits us to do linguistic history.' (Meillet, 1967: 25)

Dialects under the microscope

The analytic procedure employed in this book is quantitative. Whenever a choice exists among two (or more) alternatives in a conversation, and where that choice may have been influenced by any number of factors, then it is appropriate to take into account how often one form occurs in comparison with another (Sankoff, 1988a: 2). Quantitative methods are based on the premise that the features of a given speech community vary in systematic ways and that this system can be discovered. The advantage of this type of analysis lies in its ability to identify subtle regularities in the data that are well beyond the scope of intuition. These measures then provide the basis for comparative linguistic research.

The analytic method I will utilize is designed to examine complex patterns of language use in conversational data. In this case, I will not simply identify forms, but also calculate their proportion out of the total number of contexts in which that form, or another one like it, could be used as well. Further, I will consider the grammatical and discursive contexts that are hospitable to one variant or the other. This will expose not only the state of grammatical developments, but also the patterns underlying the process. Variation among the main forms used for each of the linguistic features under investigation will be the foundation of analysis.

Traditional dialectology focuses on words and/or expressions or on pronunciation. For example, the word 'fuzzok', discussed in the excerpt below, is a word found only in the York Corpus. This is not surprising since it is known to be an old Yorkshire word. Dialect words are often rare because the contexts for their occurrence are so highly circumscribed, such as the word for 'marble' attested in Durham, *muggle*. It is often the case that dialects have their own words for common, everyday items. For example, the word for 'potato' varies considerably from one place to another in the north, where potatoes have long been one of the foremost food staples. In this way, words and expressions can identify dialects.

Fuzzok

My husband's very broad Yorkshire, I mean, he even calls donkeys 'fuzzoks', which is a Yorkshire word for donkeys. (Maureen Londry, 62, YRK)

Muggles or marbles?

[015] A marble a muggle, aye. A muggle. [016] And he says to him, 'Get the muggle.' And he's stood looking at him, he says, 'It's a marble.' (Mr and Mrs Adams, DUR, 015, 016)

Potatoes

If you talk the Irish, potatoes, prittas. Down in Portavogie they'll call it pootas. Other places they call it prootas, with an r in it. (Jim Baird, 66, PVG, 005)

However, there are deeper patterns of language that can be tapped by a more linguistically informed, scientific approach.

Accountability

Sociolinguists have long argued that it is critical to take an accountable approach (Sankoff, 1988a, b). This is fundamental to quantitative methodology and one that sets off this study from most dialectological research. In typical dialectological reports, dialect features would simply be reported as present (or absent) in one dialect or another. In contrast, accountable analysis has consistently demonstrated that it is not sufficient to simply note the interesting dialect features and expressions. Instead, each form is tallied up and treated as an instance within a composite system of the grammar. I will illustrate with two examples: (1) a typical northern feature, such as the use of *–s* in 3rd person plural present tense contexts, as in Example (1); and (2) a nonstandard dialectal verb form, *heared*, as in Example (2).

(1) a. *Them boys goes* out and *they lift* up maybe a ton or maybe two-ton and that and *they drop* into a hole in the boat. (CLB/018)
     b. You never *heared* word of the like in your life … No, never *heared* people talking about money. (CLB/017)

(2) a. She went to the post-office and she left her. You will hae *heard* this before. (CLB/017)
     b. He was in a wheelchair the last time I *heard*. (CLB/017)

In (1a), the three verbs are 3rd person plural with the same pronominal subject and in the same tense. They represent the different possible forms used for this function in the grammar of the dialect. Examining this feature accountably means taking into account all the instances of 3rd person verbs, the ones that have an *–s* ending, as in *goes*, as well as the ones with no *–s* ending, as in *lift* and *drop*. Without the perspective of *all* the forms, it would be impossible to (1) determine exactly how often the *–s* marked verbs are used and (2) compare the use of verbal *–s* consistently across dialects. In (1b), the two verbs are encoded with the regular past tense suffix *–ed*, *heared*. However, without checking for use of the alternative (standard) form *heard* the analyst cannot discern the system in the data. Examining this feature accountably means taking into account all the instances of the verb 'to hear' used in past temporal reference whether *heared* as in (1b), or *heard* as in (1c) or some other form.

In the analyses in this book, use of the form(s) under investigation will always be reported as a proportion of the total number of relevant constructions in the data, i.e. the total number of times the same function (i.e. meaning) occurred (Wolfram, 1993: 206). For example, in (1a), the proportion of *–s* is 1/3, or 33%. Had the analysis taken into account only the *–s* marked verbs, the majority part of the system (the other 2/3) would be left unknown. Similarly, in (1b), the individual in question (Molly Ellis, aged 89) used the verb 'to hear' twice in the example. However, she actually used the verb 'to hear' 18 times in her two-hour interview. Of these, 15 were *heared* and 3 were *heard*, 15/18 or 83.3%. Molly's use of the form *heared* dominates her system. However, accountability also requires examination of individual and community patterns. Molly's use of *heared* must be put in context with the community to which she belongs by comparing her use of the verb 'to hear' with its use by other individuals. It is important to know how often the form *heared* is used overall, also how often it is used by each individual The next step is to compare how the overarching community norm compares *across* communities. The rate of use in Cullybackey must be compared systematically to its rate of use in the other communities. The only way to do this is by a consistent and accountable analysis.

Note

Variation may also be referred to as *layering*. This refers to the fact that, as language change progresses, there may be more than one form for the same meaning at the same time, e.g. *I have a cat*; *I've got a cat.* Layering refers to the combination of older and recently evolved forms co-existing in the language simultaneously.

This is perhaps one of the most fascinating facts of linguistic variation – features of language are variable not only in the community's grammar, but in each person's grammar. Language is inherently variable. This story called *Knitting* provides a good example.

Knitting

Manys a time I wondered how in the goodness that I could have come in you know. When I went to Fraser and Houghton's them women was all sitting at their dinner hour in the winter time sitting in there, and I thought they were daft. They were all sitting there. There was a woman she was knitting lace … and some of them were sitting crocheting, some of them was embroidering and some of them was knitting. And there was another girl in it, she was married … neither her nor me could knit off a pattern. And this girl, she had terrific hands 'If youse get the wool and a pattern, I'll show youse how to knit off a pattern.' And she showed us the way to knit. (Lily Trimble, 86, CLB, 012)[1]

Definition

Inherent variability is convincingly illustrated by what I call a 'supertoken' (Tagliamonte, 2006), which is alternation of two or more variants by the same speaker in the same stretch of discourse, e.g. 'He's *got* bad breath'; 'he *has* smelly feet'. (YRK/I)

Constraints

A speaker of any language is always under the influence of external social and cultural influences as well as internal contextual influences. When investigating dialects, prescriptive norms become highly influential. The idea of 'speaking proper' vs 'speaking broad' becomes an overriding dichotomy. In such circumstances the frequency of nonstandard features will vary markedly depending on an individual's age, sex or education and even more dramatically on the situational context, who the person is speaking to, i.e. the interlocutor (a stranger vs a close friend), the type of discourse event the person is engaged in (a joke vs a question), the situation (a conversation with friends vs a meeting with a boss) or any number of influences. It is particularly acute across northern varieties of English, where centuries of prejudice and stereotyping have stigmatized the dialects. The analyst interested in the grammar of dialects must find some way to access the underlying grammar despite these ingrained behaviours.

A well-established finding in language variation and change is the distinction between frequency of usage and patterns of use. Forms will vary in frequency by context. For example, an informal variant may occur often with friends but rarely with strangers. However, the patterns of use of that form will stay stable in an individual's language, regardless of context, even if the frequency of use of that same form varies dramatically from one context to the next. This is how sociolinguists tap into the grammar of individuals and communities and dialects. They look underneath the forms themselves to find the grammar of usage that underlies them. Take, for example, a common northern feature – verbal –*s* in 3rd person plural. The –*s* ending tends to occur more in casual situations and less often in formal situations. However, the fact that –*s* will occur more with NPs than pronouns stays constant regardless of the context. The type of subject is the constraint; the fact that –*s*'s occur with more than pronouns is the pattern.

Definition

A 'constraint' is a pattern that underlies the use of a linguistic form such that the form occurs at a consistent greater or lesser level of frequency from one context to the next, e.g. NP > pronoun; subordinate > main; consonant > vowel > pause, etc. Note the patterning of the Northern Subject Rule in the *Knitting* story above, *The women was* vs *They were*.

In order to tap into the underlying systems of the dialects, I also incorporate into the comparative analysis the Principle of Diagnosticity (Poplack and Tagliamonte, 2001: 100). In substantiating any claim for origins or relationship of linguistic features across dialects, Poplack and Tagliamonte argue that it is important to establish how that feature functions in a non-trivial way. Moreover, not all features are equally useful in establishing correspondences. Some features will categorically distinguish one community from the next (e.g. one dialect will use *pootas* for 'potatoes' and another dialect will use *prittas*). Other features may be more general, and in some cases there may even be pan-English features found in the data (e.g. use of *there was* for existentials). This is where cross-variety comparison of the hierarchy of constraints on the occurrence of variant forms becomes pivotal. While the dialects may use plural existential *was* with different degrees of frequency, patterns of use, e.g. a contrast between affirmative and negative contexts, may stay the same. These expose the underlying grammar of the linguistic features in the dialects, whether they are the same or different.

The variationist notion of constraint hierarchy or conditioning of factors on the linguistic features is a key element in the analyses. Thus, if these four communities share a feature, for example a verbal –s ending in 3rd person plural, then this will be the first step in the analysis. The next step will be to determine the frequency of verbal –s across dialects. However, a critical third step will be to examine the details of its patterning in each dialect. If the dialects share the same pattern, then this will be evidence that they share the same grammar. If they do not, then this will require further consideration and explanation. Of course, there is also the possibility of varying degrees of parallelism.

(3)   a. 1st, occurrence of the form/feature
       b. 2nd, frequency of the form/feature
       c. 3rd, patterns of use of the form/feature

Constraints are found by searching the existing literature, both synchronic and diachronic, which often report patterns of use that can be tested in data. When observations come from historical sources, these help to determine the origins of the synchronic variability found, which can be traced to earlier stages in the history of the language. When observations come from contemporary studies, these help to situate the distribution and nature of the variability with respect to other dialects and/or standard uses. A constraints-based analysis offers an added layer of evidence analysis to test for similarities or differences across dialects. For example, maybe one dialect will use verbal –s considerably more frequently than another, but the two dialects may have the same pattern of use. Alternatively, frequency *and* pattern may be parallel. In a broad-based comparison, the latter would be deeper evidence for similarity than the former. As systems of grammar evolve, the grammatical constraints can be expected to be constant (Kroch, 1989). This is referred to as the Constant Rate Effect, the 'constant' being the parallel pattern in the operation of constraints over time. For example, the subject type constraint on verbal –s has remained constant over time.

As we shall see, many nuances of frequency, constraints and comparison will come to the fore using comparative sociolinguistic analysis (Poplack and Tagliamonte, 2001: 93–4; Tagliamonte, 2002a: 733). Each bit of evidence adds to the depth of the comparison.

Comparison

In historical linguistics, the comparative method is used to establish genetic relationships amongst languages by reconstructing earlier forms based on evidence (typically cognate forms) found in descendent languages. The success in this endeavour is dependent upon preservation of earlier forms in those languages. This possibility is, of course, hampered by any number of developments, including independent linguistic changes in one variety or the other, or differential external change – cultural, social, political, demographic or any other.

Sociolinguistic practice adds a critical supposition – namely, the notion of inherent variability. Inherent variability refers to the fact that language at any time or place is variable. There will be more than one way of saying the same thing. Thus, for example, 3rd person plural may be encoded with a verb ending in –*s* on one occasion and without an –*s* ending on another, without any change in meaning. This 'inherent' variability is taken as given, and it is the distribution and condition of these variants (–*s* and nothing) that are relevant. In comparative sociolinguistic analysis, the focus of investigation is dialects instead of languages, and the goal of the comparison is to determine the constraints that underlie linguistic features in one dialect as compared to another so as to understand their origins (Poplack and Tagliamonte, 2001: 17; Tagliamonte, 2002a). In this type of analysis, neither the existence of a form nor its frequency is sufficient to assess its source. Instead, the status of a form is evaluated based on an examination of its patterning according to variable constraints on its occurrence in the dialect or variety. As we shall see, there is a clear and highly demarcated system for the appearance of –*s* marked verbs in northern dialects (Chapter 5).

Where the dialects preserve features as well as patterns, and further, if it can be established that there are a significant number of these parallels (e.g. same form, same frequency, same pattern) across different linguistic features, then genetic affinity may be more successfully established than with a single measure. As argued by Poplack and Tagliamonte (2001: 95), 'the basis for reconstruction, in historical linguistics, as in evolutionary biology, is shared retentions'. Comparative sociolinguistic methodology requires assessment of all such parallels across the dialects (e.g. Tagliamonte, 2002a). The nature of the correspondences may lead to an explanation of direct carry-over of linguistic patterns or there may also be evidence for the dynamic processes of change typical of dialect contact such as simplification, levelling and reallocation (Trudgill, 1986).

Bampton Fair

Went to Bampton Fair and always remember it. I was in the ring watching them selling the ponies. Suddenly one of the auctioneers said 'Sold'. He said 'name?' So he says 'John Peters'. I said there's not another John-Peters beside me. So he'd mentioned my name. A small pony about this high, he was. Brought home on the back of a car. [Interviewer] Gosh! So what did you do with him? [006] Had him home and I put him up behind my mother's in a chicken run. Had fed and grassed it for a while. And kept him for about two years. And couldn't do nothing with him. He was like a lion. He used to just come running towards thee. Had to feed the thing, you see. But daft thing, isn't it. I think I sold him for five pound in the end. Got rid of the damn thing. (John Peters, 72, TIV, 006)[2]

Grammar and discourse

Innumerable dialectological treatises have been written on lexis, pronunciation and phonological aspects of British dialects. Comparatively little has been done on morphology, even less on syntax and discourse. Perhaps this is due to the unfortunate portrayal of dialect grammars as relatively uniform (Biber, Johansson, Leech, Conrad and Finegan, 1999: 20–1). In addition there is a common idea that dialectal grammar is a simplified version of the standard; however, this is definitely not the case. For example, the Standard English pronominal system has a two-way contrast between proximate *this* and *that*; however, in traditional dialects, the system is more typically three-way with the additional *yonder* (or *thonder*, also a later assimilation), pointing to something more remote in place or time (Melchers, 1997: 83; Wales, 2006: 186).

(4)   a. Their wives put their clothes on the hedge over the back lane, along *yon* hedge. (CLB/15)
      b. Harry, he just sits *thonder*. [Interviewer] Harry's quiet. [006] Er very quiet. (CLB/006)

Another example is the use of 2nd person *thee* and *thou*. Researchers have claimed it is receding (Tidholm, 1979), but it is still reported in everyday use in the north (Wales, 2006: 182).

(5)   a. Where's *thou* frae? Down York or summat? (MPT/001)
      b. I don't want to talk like *thee*. It's as simple as that. (MPT/001)

Some accounts of northern dialects argue that it is clearly evident from any cursory inspection or eavesdropping that English, Scots and Northern Irish dialects vary greatly at the morphological and syntactic levels (Shorrocks, 1997; Wales, 2006: 179). Indeed focusing attention on grammatical and discourse factors in vernacular conversational data opens up a considerable number of new perspectives for understanding the history of dialects:

Grammatical features have many potential advantages for investigating antecedents, however, not the least of which are that grammar generally changes more slowly than vocabulary or pronunciation … and that grammatical features often permit more sophisticated types of comparison. (Montgomery, 2001: 145)

Yet the existing literature is still relatively sparse on discourse and syntactic features. Traditional dialect surveys tended to focus on phonology, lexis and morphology (e.g. the *SED*). In the 1990s and 2001s researchers have gone a long way toward remedying this traditional lacuna in knowledge (e.g.

Beal and Corrigan, 2002; Cheshire, 1994, 2007; Cheshire and Milroy, 1993; Corrigan, 1997, 2000); however, large-scale accountable studies of morphological, syntactic and discourse features are still relatively rare and are particularly lacking in northern dialects (but see Pichler, 2009; Pichler and Levey, 2011; Pietsch, 2005). Therefore, in the spirit of Montgomery's assertion, I will focus the analyses on these lesser-known phenomena in this book.

The Roots Archive is replete with grammatical and discourse-pragmatic features particular to Scotland, northern England and Northern Ireland. It also contains an abundance of features that are common across nonstandard varieties of English (Milroy and Milroy, 1993). Due to this fact, it is even more important to employ a comparative sociolinguistic approach in order to tease apart the differences that may exist across dialects that – for the most part – employ the same nonstandard forms.

How to use 'thee' and 'thou'

Dinna *thou* anybody older than thisel' (Informant from Cumberland, Survey of English Dialects, cited in Wales, 2006: 184) [3]

Types of change

The questions of how language changes and why are necessarily multiplex. One possibility is 'drift', which is the essential, internal change that comes from the grammatical system itself (Sapir, 1921). However, there are many external influences on language change. Sociolinguistic studies tend to focus on speaker age, sex, social class (Labov, 1972a, b, 2001; Trudgill, 1974) and social network (Milroy, 1980). Dialectology often focuses on contact (e.g. Trudgill, 1986). In historical linguistics contact is examined in terms of dialect borrowing or foreign influence (e.g.Thomason and Kaufman, 1988) or as abductive vs deductive change (Andersen, 1973). Spatial characteristics are also critical, including urban vs rural (Chambers and Trudgill, 1980) and centre vs periphery (Andersen, 1988). Yet all these influences must also be put in context with the nature of the community itself (Kerswill, 1996, 2009a, b).

Moreover, a critical dimension of change is its type: *transmission* from one generation to the next within the same community or *diffusion* from one community to another (Labov, 2007). A key gauge for identifying these distinctions comes from the details of linguistic patterning: in transmission, complex grammatical conditioning is preserved; in diffusion, these tend to be lost or modified. Yet the grammatical patterns can sometimes *diverge* across a population. This means that individuals within the same community may not preserve the same grammatical constraints, and individuals across communities can share them. These questions can be reconciled by comparing features from different levels of the grammar and examining them across diverse geographic contexts. Another critical component to consider is ongoing grammatical change and crucially whether or not people of different ages in the same community might actually have slightly differing constraints on the use of a feature of grammar. In rapidly changing systems this can happen.

Definition

When change comes from within the community grammar it is called 'change from below'. It arises systematically and unconsciously. When change comes from outside the community grammar it is called 'change from above'. This type of change comes about more consciously, driven by factors such as prestige of the new form (Labov, 1972b).

Grammaticalization

As innovating linguistic features enter a language or dialect and spread, they do not remain stagnant, but often undergo grammatical development. Indeed, the trajectory of change for many morpho-syntactic and discourse-pragmatic features is the result of grammaticalization – a type of linguistic change in which lexical forms evolve into grammatical markers (e.g. Hopper and Traugott, 1993). Building on recent developments in grammaticalization theory (Brinton, 1996; Traugott and Heine, 1991a, b) research has shown that the trajectory of a grammaticizing form can be observed in the detailed (variable) constraints on its distribution (e.g. Poplack and Tagliamonte, 1999; Tagliamonte, 2003, 2004). Thus, the stage of development of a linguistic feature offers a key nuance for interpreting complex constraint patterning in transmission and diffusion across diverse community types.

Information from nonstandard vernacular data can shed light not only on community-based, regional norms, but can also be used to situate linguistic change at a particular point on its trajectory. Thus, an important consideration will be the extent to which the dialect data reflects grammatical changes in the history of English. As time moves on, a language evolves by undergoing incremental change. Grammaticalization is a type of change that involves the development of content words into grammatical (or function) words. The standard example is the change undergone by the verb *go* from a lexical verb into a future marker *going to*. However, there are innumerable other examples at all levels of grammar (e.g. Heine, Claudi and Hünnemeyer, 1991; Hopper and Traugott, 1993; Traugott and Heine, 1991a, b). In order to assess the grammatical function(s) of forms and their status in the community, I test the effects of linguistic features associated with the linguistic change. I then correlate these contextual factors with the different variants in the data using quantitative techniques such as distributional analysis to assess their patterning.

The comparative method is then used to assess similarities and differences across age groups in the community (for further discussion, see Poplack and Tagliamonte, 2001: chapter 5; Tagliamonte, 2002b). Internal linguistic constraints (or correlations) on variable forms can be traced to constraints attested in the history of the English language, and thus can be interpreted as 'persistence' (Hopper and Traugott, 1993). This provides some insights into what earlier points in the trajectory of development of these areas of grammar may have been like. Similarly, as forms take on new grammatical functions, we may observe shifts and re-weighting of contextual effects pointing to 'specialization' (Hopper, 1991). Indeed, differences in inter-variety distributions across generations may reveal the pathway of such change. As we shall see, a community represents its own 'slice in time', reflected not only in the varying frequency of forms, but more strikingly in their patterns of use (distribution). In this way, synchronic dialect data provides a means to illuminate these processes. Finally, I demonstrate the utility of Variationist Sociolinguistic methods in the analysis and interpretation of linguistic patterns and the critical role it serves in their evaluation (Poplack and Tagliamonte, 2001: 88–112).

Words from the wise

'Grammaticalization theory and variation theory have traditionally made uneasy bedfellows, but in many ways they are natural allies.' (Poplack, 2011)

Linguistic change is often conceived of as a pathway in time (Hopper and Traugott, 1993). Historical linguists have determined that the details of a form's history from lexical item to grammatical marker will be reflected in constraints on its current distribution (Bybee, Perkins and Pagliuca, 1994; Hopper and Traugott, 1993). The interesting question is whether different dialects are following the same path and, if so, whether they are at the same or different places on that path. Although grammaticalization is thought to be a phenomenon that has broad typological tendencies, it can also be influenced by social factors (Hopper and Traugott, 1993). Therefore it would not be surprising for local anomalies to develop along the same grammatical path and thus for divergent tendencies to be visible in dialects. Such possibilities will inform my interpretation of trends in one locality compared to another.

Definition

'Typological' in this sense refers to the idea that languages or language families that have derived from some common source continue to evolve linguistically in similar directions and undergo similar linguistic changes. A good example is the *go* future. Many related languages show evidence of grammaticalization pathways towards more use of *go*, although they may be at differing points in the trajectory of change (Bybee et al., 1994).

In order to assess the grammatical function(s) of forms and their status in the dialects, I examine the effects of linguistic features that have been reported in the historical record or are known to be associated with one form over the other as the linguistic change progresses. For example, verbal *–s* endings in 3rd person plural have long been associated with pronominal subjects in northern dialects (Ihalainen, 1994; Murray, 1873). I then test these contextual factors in the data using quantitative techniques, frequency and distributions, to assess their patterning. The comparative method is then used to assess similarities and differences across communities (for further discussion, see Poplack and Tagliamonte, 2001: chapter 5; Tagliamonte, 2002a).

The information from cross-variety comparative analysis sheds light on community-based *and* regional norms. However, the *relative* frequency of variants and their distribution in the data situates linguistic change at a particular point in its trajectory. In this way, the constraints on variation in comparative perspective provide an indication of the contemporary status of the grammatical system (Poplack and Tagliamonte, 2001: 95–100). The internal linguistic constraints (or correlations) on variable forms can then be used to infer the underlying grammar of variant choice, and in particular, the point of development of the areas of grammar in its trajectory of change (see also Poplack and Tagliamonte, 1999; Tagliamonte, 2003).[4] For example, if a pattern is attested for the early stages of development of a linguistic form, then a dialect that exhibits this pattern can be taken to be at an early stage in that form's pathway of change.

Long-term evolution of forms for the same function, yet historically documented takeover by one construction, presents an interesting subject for a study of grammaticalization processes in corpus data. First, because the forms entered the language at very different points in time, their frequency can shed light on the stages of development of the system in a given corpus and thus the nature of linguistic change (particularly grammaticalization) in this area of English grammar (Bybee et al., 1994). Thus, for example, low frequency of usage would indicate an earlier stage in the development of a feature or, alternatively depending on the context, a very late stage in a feature's demise. Second, comparisons with patterns extrapolated from the historical and synchronic literature can be used to track varying trends in corpus data and illuminate the underlying mechanism involved in the grammaticalization process, for example, if a pattern attested (or documented) from 1512 still exists in 2012.

The shop

Well it was um Mrs Porter's. She was a confectioner. She was in High Street opposite the post office. And how I come to get in there, you see, mi mother used to get her bread and that there, her cakes or whatever. She always baked her bread but she would get her cakes and maybe something there, you know. And um, she took me on and like my mother would say 'Our Grace wants to be in a shop.' But I had to help in the confectionery place as well and scrub their boards down. Oh no I didn't like it. There was more water in t'buckets, I tell you, when I finished with crying because I didn't like it. So I hadn't a good set off at all. (Grace Kenway, 74, MPT, 023)[5]

Putting dialect features into social and historical context

A number of areas of English grammar have been the locus of extensive reorganization in the last several hundred years. Contemporary British dialects offer an incredibly rich layering of these forms in every area of grammar. Some examples of layering in the same speaker in the same stretch of discourse include the deontic modals in (6a), relative pronouns (6b), adverbial –*ly*, as in (6c).

(6)   a. '*I've got to* cycle all the way back and then this afternoon I'll be cycling back up again!' You *have to* keep those thoughts er thoughts to yourself. (YRK/X)
      b. It was a job *that* I always wanted … It was a job Ø I've always enjoyed. (CMK/x)
      c. I mean, you go to Leeds and Castleford, they take it so much more *seriously* … they take it so *serious*. (YRK/T)

This variability is often attributed to external factors, often the difference between major varieties of English (e.g. British vs North American). Other explanations have been grounded in dialect origins, social class, age, etc. However, the variability may also be viewed as the product of grammatical change and reflecting the characteristics of grammaticalization (see, e.g., Hopper and Traugott, 1993).

   Indeed, each of the systems of grammar represented in (6a–c) embodies a scenario of long-term evolution of forms for the same function. These variable changing systems present interesting cases to study for a number of reasons. First, because the forms (variants) competing in each sub-system entered the language at different points in time – *must* for deontic modality; Old English, *have to*: 1579, *have got to*: nineteenth century – their distribution across dialects sheds light on the stages of development of the system itself and thus the nature of linguistic change in this area of English grammar (Bybee et al., 1994). Second, because the evolution of these subsystems often involves cases in which a vernacular feature – *gotta* for deontic modality; *'ve got* for possession; the zero adverb marker, etc. – has won out over erstwhile standard competitors, the developments in these areas may be useful in tracking the lag between written and spoken data in language change. On the other hand, some changes are precisely the opposite, involving the evolution of forms from formal registers into the vernacular, e.g. the WH relative markers *which* and *who*. Comparison of these different trajectories of change across features will further elucidate the forces driving them. Finally, information on linguistic patterns of variability, trends, constraints etc., extrapolated from the historical and synchronic literature, can be used for comparative study to track the varying trends across dialects and thus to tap into the evolving linguistic processes of the language.

Definition

A function word encodes some type of grammatical information, relationship, speaker attitude, etc. A lexical word has a specific meaning. Whether it is a noun, verb or other part of speech it refers to a specific item, e.g. *cat, dream, pout*, etc.

The comparative method I adopt also incorporates information from historical sources.[6] Examination of these records enables me to assess whether the origins of the variability I find in the data have derived from earlier stages in the history of the language. I also incorporate information from available synchronic data sets in order to assess the distribution and nature of the variability in other dialects. Taken together, such information can disentangle which patterns result from influences from outside the community, which to internal mechanisms of linguistic change, or both, and will lead to a fuller understanding of the mechanisms underlying changes in English more generally.

Dialect puzzle 4.1

In the Roots Archive data, the form *heared* is only ever found in the Northern Ireland communities of Cullybackey and Portavogie. Every token of the verb 'to hear' from two individuals, one male (cM); one female (aF) are listed below. Conduct an accountable study of the variation between *heared* and *heard*.

I HEARD that they were conversing. They were like sisters. (aF)
And mi da HEARD them and he said 'You – you girls are a good bit.' (aF)
She says 'I HEARD you speaking German there.' (aF)
And they HEARD a car coming. (aF)
I HEARD a – a boy there, the feller's a Christian there. (aF)
I HEARED them talking about it. (aF)
I never HEARED the word – never heared the word 'nap'. (aF)
Never HEARED the word 'nap'. (aF)
Well I never HEARED that. (aF)
And I never HEARED her talking about her ma. (aF)
You ever – you ever HEARED them talking about the tailor? (aF)
And I HEARED them yelling at me, and they waving at me. (aF)
If you HEARED a motorbike coming. (aF)
I HEARED this bike coming. (aF) I HEARED this thing coming. (aF)
I HEARD this yan went over a whole lot o times. (cM)
He could hae preached the best sermon ever you HEARD. (cM)

I know, I HEARD this yan! Aye (cM)
I've HEARD of them all. (cM) Glen-Churley, I HEARED mi ma and them talking about Glen-Churley. (cM)
Sheila has HEARED this a few times. (cM)
Now HEARED Robert-MacPherson, (cM)
He was yan o smartest mens he e – he ever HEARED on the Scriptures. (cM)
I HEARED that, you know! (cM)
I HEARED all this before. (cM)
If you'd hae HEARED two – two Portavogie men talking on the radio (cM)
You would hae HEARED yan saying. (cM)
If it had been a good day, you would hae HEARED them speaking a bit o English. (cM)

Questions

a. How many tokens are there?
b. What is the proportion of use of the nonstandard variant *heared*: (i) overall and (ii) by speaker?
c. Who uses *heared* more, the man or the woman?
d. Can you identify any pattern to the use of *heared*? Hint: Look for features of the context that are present for *heared* but not for (or not as often for) *heard*.

Answers

a. 28
b. (i) 32.1%; (ii) aF = 33.3% cM = 30.8%
c. They use the nonstandard form at about the same rate.
d. The nonstandard form is used much more often in contexts that have the adverbs 'never' or 'ever' (85.7% compared to 61.9%).

5   Word endings

Them times is not the same as now. ... Them times was hard times.

(Kate McBridge, 88, CLB, 005)

In this chapter I examine a number of variable features that involve word endings. Word endings are affixes, features that add grammatical meaning to a word, such as 'plural', 'grammatical person', etc. The study of words, word stems and affixes is referred to as morphology. Variation in morphology is a common feature of language. Endings may differ from one community to the next and there tends to be considerable variation as to whether the endings prescribed by Standard English grammar are present or not.

> **Note**
>
> A stem is a word to which affixes attach. A stem can be a simple word, e.g. *cat* + *s* = *cats* or a word that already has an affix attached to it, e.g. *helpful* + *ness* = *helpfulness.*

The history of the English language is at least partly to blame for the variation in endings in some situations. This is because English evolved from language contact with other languages at various times in its history, Germanic and Scandinavian varieties at the early stages and French from 1066, as well as dialect mixture between the north and the south (see, e.g., Wales, 2006). Let us see how variation in this area of grammar operates across the Roots Archive.

Nicht

There was a German girl ... and somebody spoke to me ... and I turned round quick and just answered her mi own way of speaking. The German looked at me, she says 'Kate, I didn't know you could speak German.' I says 'I'm no speaking German.' She says 'You are,' she says 'I heard you speaking German there.' I says 'Why, what did I say?' It was something I'd been talking to someone about the 'nicht' ... (Kate Devoy, 62, PVG)[1]

Endings on verbs

A verb is a part of speech that describes an action, state or occurrence. In many languages, verbs are inflected (i.e modified in some way, such as with endings or suffixes) to mark tense, aspect, mood and voice. Verbs often agree with the person, gender and/or number of their subjects or objects, e.g. *I was* vs *you were*. Although English is relatively impoverished with respect to verb morphology, in the contemporary standard language there are three contexts where verb morphology is variable: (1) lexical verbs (other than 'to be') in the present indicative, (2) the verb 'to be' in the present indicative and (3) the verb 'to be' in the past. In standard contemporary English the simple present tense 3rd person singular takes an *–s* ending, e.g. *she says, she goes*. Everywhere else the verb is bare, e.g. *I say, I go*. For the verb 'to be' the same pattern holds, e.g. *he/she is* but *you/we/they are*. In the past tense the verb 'to be' also has a differentiated paradigm; the standard forms are *I/he/she was* but *you/we/they were*. However, this prescription has not always been the case, and even in the twenty-first century there are still dialectal variations reported all over the English-speaking world.

In the next sections, I will consider each of these contexts of variation in turn. Because we are dealing with verbs and the ending *–s* in each case, we may wonder whether the patterns of variation across lexical verbs and the verb 'to be' will be the same.

Definition

A lexical verb simply refers to a verb that is not an auxiliary verb; in English these are the verbs *have* and *be*. The word 'lexical' in general refers to content as opposed to function words, i.e. words that have grammatical roles in the linguistic system, e.g. *boy* is a content word, a noun; *him* is a function word, a pronoun.

Synchronic perspective

Use of an *–s* ending on verbs other than the 3rd person singular has been widely reported in British, American and antipodean varieties of English. Notice the *–s* ending on present tense lexical verbs, as in (1), in simple present and past tense 'to be', as in (2) and (3). In each case, I illustrate the most prominent context exhibiting this variation – 3rd person plural.

(1) a. Youngsters *gets* far too much and they've no manners. (CLB/e)
     b. Four men from Auchinleck *works* in that factory. (CMK/D)

(2) a. I think the big farmers *is* no making a lot of money now. (CLB/p)
     b. That's where he keeps his van there, just where them wee houses *is*. (CMK/ç)

(3) a. Mi mother's folk *was* all fishermen and mi father's folk *were* more farmers. (PVG/2)
     b. The old shafts that caved in *was* wooden shafts, ken. (CMK/d)

No baths for naebody

And in these days in the pits there were no baths. You come home fae your work and you got washed in the middle of the floor. There was a tin tub. And you'd all the old towels and everything all round about the tub to catch the water. And you sat in the middle of the floor. And my brothers would maybe be home fae the pit afore my father and they had to sit there 'til my father got the first of the water. [Interviewer] Naebody got any? [022] Naebody got washed. [022] He got priority. (CMK, Iain Ferguson, 72, IF 021, Elspeth Ferguson, 70, 022)[2]

Historical perspective

Alternation among inflections of the present indicative has been a longstanding, well-documented feature of English since the Old English period (Brunner, 1963: 70; Curme, 1977: 53; Holmqvist, 1922: 15; Jespersen, 1909/1949: 16; Wakelin, 1977: 119). In Old English *–th*, marked present indicative in 3rd person singular and all persons in the plural. One of the chief characteristics of the transition between Old English and Middle English is the gradual loss of many of the older verbal endings. By the Middle English period, inflection in the present indicative was basically uniform across the paradigm, though the choice of marker varied across dialects. In the north, for example, it was used with all persons and numbers but 1st person singular (Jespersen, 1909/1949: 16; Strang, 1970: 146; Wright, 1900: 175–6). The original 2nd person singular verbal ending *–s* spread first to 2nd person plural, then to other persons of the plural, and finally to 3rd person singular (Curme, 1977: 52). This variation originated in colloquial speech and subsequently passed into the written language (Curme, 1977: 53; Jespersen, 1909/49: 17–18; Holmqvist, 1922: 159; Wyld, 1927: 256). By Middle English, *–s* appeared throughout the paradigm. At this time it spread geographically to the Midlands where it coexisted with *–th* in the 3rd person singular and occurred variably in the plural. Later the *–s* inflection became established in London and in the south more generally, first affecting only the spoken language, and subsequently penetrating written styles. In contrast, *–th* was used categorically in the more serious style required for Bible translations (Curme, 1977: 53). By the early seventeenth century *–s* gradually became established in all styles of literary language, but was restricted to the 3rd person singular as it is in the contemporary language.

Competing marking patterns in the indicative present-tense paradigm have long been considered regional variants. In fact, the verbal *–s* inflection has been considered one of the safest criteria in determining the dialectal origin of a Middle English text (Barber, 1976: 242; Curme, 1977: 53; Holmqvist, 1922: 72; Wakelin, 1977: 119; Wardale, 1937: 102). Until at least the early seventeenth century *–s* was a marker of popular, colloquial or dialectal speech (Barber, 1976: 239; Curme, 1977: 53; Holmqvist, 1922: 183; Strang, 1970:

146). However, it continues to be attested in many dialects in Britain (e.g. Cheshire, 1982; Milroy and Milroy, 1993) and the United States (e.g. Cukor-Avila, 1997; José, 2007; Schneider, 1995). Specific patterns of use have long been associated with northern dialects (Pietsch, 2005); however, the phenomenon is known to have spread to southern dialects of England and Ireland (McCafferty, 2003, 2004). The relevant fact is whether or not the dialects are the same in terms of constraints.

A pervasive pattern that has come to be referred to as the 'Northern Subject Rule' (Ihalainen, 1994: 221) has been reported for centuries (e.g. Giner and Montgomery, 1997, 2001). Its nature is unmistakable: 3rd person plural nouns take –s, but their corresponding pronouns do not, as in (4).

(4)   a. The cattle all goes to, to the big markets, these days … they go straight to the slaughterhouse. (TIV/008)
       b. *Them boys goes* out and *they lift* up maybe a ton. (CLB/b)

A minor part of this pattern is the proximity of the subject to the verb. When the noun and verb are separated, pronouns also take an –s ending, as in (5).

(5)   They *all plays* duets. 'Tis jolly nice, really. (TIV/00X)

The problem is that contexts where the subject is not adjacent to the verb are very rare in these spoken-language materials.[3] It thus becomes critical to examine the use of –s according to the characteristics of the subject.

Peery

[031] Did you have a peery? [030] Oh Aye, I had peeries. [1] What's a peery then? [031] A spinning top. (Angus Milroy, 66, CMK, 031)

Methodology

In order to focus on the most propitious contemporary environment for the –s ending, only 3rd person plural subjects (existential, pronominal and nominal) were extracted for analysis. In the case of lexical verbs, of course, only pronouns and noun phrases were extracted. Coding protocols developed in earlier research (Poplack and Tagliamonte, 1989, 1991, 2004) were followed. Each token was coded for the choice of –s or zero, the community, individual and type of subject, whether the subject was a full noun phrase or pronoun and the type of clause (affirmative, negative, question).

Distributional analysis

Figure 5.1 shows a cross-variety distributional analysis of lexical verbs in the present indicative according to type of subject, whether pronouns or noun phrases.[4]

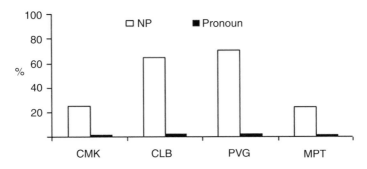

Figure 5.1 Lexical verbs, –*s* ending in 3rd person plural by type of subject

Figure 5.1 reveals that all the communities exhibit –*s* endings and in each one the pattern expected of the Northern Subject Rule (where only full noun phrases are marked with –*s*) is in operation. In these northern varieties, the 3rd person plural pronoun (*they*) virtually never gets an –*s*. This result is entirely as predicted. Notice that the cross-variety comparison reveals a nuance to the dialect situation. The Northern Ireland communities – Cullybackey and Portavogie – have a much higher frequency of –*s* in nouns than either Maryport or Cumnock.

Another place in the grammar for variable use of verb endings is the verb 'to be'. Variable realization of present (6) and past tense forms, as in (7), is often considered a vernacular 'universal' of English (Chambers, 2000, 2001, 2004) because this variation is so widespread across varieties of English everywhere in the world.

(6)   a. There*'s* some of the boys *are* really broad. (PVG/001)
      b. Even those that *are* left and there*'s* very few left now ... (PVG/003)

(7)   a. The dry-irons *was* hard to work with but steam-irons *were* terrific. (CLB/012)
      b. Well, the ones that *was* in the farms *were* the same. (CMK/003)

This is, of course, not prescribed in contemporary Standard English where strict subject-verb agreement according to person is required. However, the historical record confirms that this type of variation has existed for a long time (e.g. Curme, 1977; Forsström, 1948; Jespersen, 1940; Pyles, 1964; Visser, 1963–73). Indeed, use of –*s* endings (*is* and *was* instead of the alternative *are* and *were*) has been reported in every century of the English language. Descriptions of English usage from the sixteenth and seventeenth centuries confirm that this type of variability was 'frequent' and 'regular' (Traugott, 1972; Visser, 1963–73).

Figure 5.2 shows the proportion of –*s* endings on the present tense of the verb 'to be', i.e. *is*, according to the type of subject, whether pronoun or noun

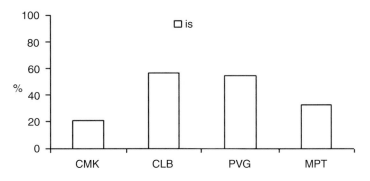

Figure 5.2 Proportion of *is* in 3rd person plural noun phrases in the present tense of the verb 'to be'

phrase. Notice that there are no instances of *they is/they's* in this data; therefore the figure shows only 3rd person plural noun phrases.

The Roots Archive shows the same frequency of use of the *–s* ending form (in this case *is*) as with the lexical verbs. In this context too the Northern Ireland communities – Cullybackey and Portavogie – have a much higher frequency of verbal *–s* than either Maryport or Cumnock. Indeed, the rates of use are nearly identical to that of lexical verbs in the present tense.

Figure 5.3 shows the proportion of *–s* endings on the past tense of the verb 'to be', i.e. *was*, according to the type of subject, whether pronoun or noun phrase. In this case, *was* occurs with both pronouns and noun phrases so constraint ranking between noun phrases and pronouns is visible.

Remarkably, the communities show the same frequency of use (in this case for *was*) as with the lexical verbs and present tense *is*. The consistency of the patterning is striking, both in terms of frequency and in terms of the hierarchy of constraints between pronoun *they* and noun phrases.

Constraints analysis

The use of *was* in plural contexts is so frequent and diffused across varieties of English (despite being nonstandard) that several constraints on its use have been reported. We can put these constraints in broader contexts by comparing the Roots Archive with the British Dialects Archive (Tagliamonte, 2009, 2012).

Existentials The constraint that has been most heavily studied with regard to verbal *–s* endings is the grammatical person of the subject. Chambers refers to 'the remarkable regular hierarchy of subject-types' (Chambers, 2004: 141). Among the grammatical persons, existentials stand out in virtually every

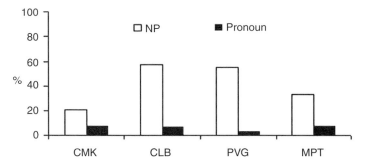

Figure 5.3 Proportion of *was* in 3rd person plural by type of subject in the past tense of the verb 'to be'

study that has been conducted because they are widely known to promote the –*s* ending: '*was* is most frequent after *there*' (Britain and Sudbury, 2002: 19–20; Chambers, 2004: 132). Britain and Sudbury (2002: 19–20) refer to this correlation as 'the existential constraint'. The consistency of this ranking (in addition to the worldwide diffusion of the phenomenon) has been used to bolster the argument for interpreting default agreement as a universal (e.g. Walker, 2007).

Figure 5.4 shows the effect of existentials vs other plural subjects across communities. It reveals that the use of *was* in contexts of existential *there* is indeed a pervasive pattern. Every locale shows the contrast between high rates of verbal –*s* with plural existentials as opposed to other plural subjects. The one exception is Cullybackey, where plural existentials (N = 142) overwhelmingly take *were*, as in (8).

(8) a. And we made the tea in a teapot, Elizabeth, on the fire on the moss and there *were* eggs sent to boil. (CMK/å)
     b. Aye, there *were* some of them in the Mounties in Canada, them Wilsons. There *were* big families in them days. (CMK/ʃ)

Negation Another constraint reported for default agreement is the effect of negation (e.g. Anderwald, 2002; Britain and Sudbury, 1999; Tagliamonte and Smith, 2000). Several different patterns have been reported in the literature. The first is what has been referred to as 'Vernacular Pattern I'. This is where the –*s* ending occurs regardless of type of sentence. This pattern is said to be the simpler and more basic pattern. A second pattern, labelled 'Vernacular Pattern II' is the case where –*s* occurs in affirmatives but not negatives (Chambers, 2004: 131). This pattern is attested in south-west England (Reading) (Cheshire, Edwards and Whittle, 1989) and in the Fens in south-east England (Britain and Sudbury, 2002), as well as elsewhere in Britain

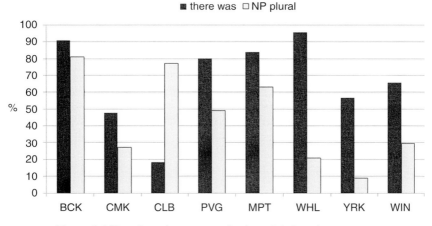

Figure 5.4 Use of *was* in contexts of existential *there is*

(Anderwald, 2002). The third pattern is the opposite pattern, where the –*s* ending is preferred for negatives over affirmatives, i.e. *wasn't* (Tagliamonte and Smith, 2000: 160–1).

(9)   Vernacular Pattern I
       Use of *was/wasn't* for affirmative and negative, no constraint ranking

(10)   Vernacular Pattern II
       More *was* for affirmatives, *weren't* for negatives

(11)   Vernacular Pattern III
       More *wasn't* for negative contexts; *were* for affirmatives

Figure 5.5 reveals that all three patterns are present. Vernacular Pattern I is identifiable by an equal proportion of default agreement for negative and affirmative contexts. This exists in Wheatley Hill (marginally) and Wincanton. Vernacular Pattern II is identifiable by a contrast between a higher proportion of –*s* for affirmatives than negatives. This constraint ranking is visible in four communities – Culleybacky, Wheatley, York and Tiverton. Vernacular Pattern III is identifiable by a contrast between a higher proportion of –*s* for negatives than affirmatives. This constraint hierarchy is found in Portavogie, Cumnock and Maryport. In sum, all three of the so-called vernacular patterns are visible. It is important to note that the negative contexts are relatively rare, and thus these results must be interpreted with caution. Nevertheless, the communities that pattern together suggest norms in certain regions. Note the common constraint ranking across Cumnock, Portavogie and Maryport: negatives consistently have more –*s*.

It is important to explain the idiosyncratic behaviour of Cullybackey, where *were* is the predominant form in existentials, unlike all the other communities.

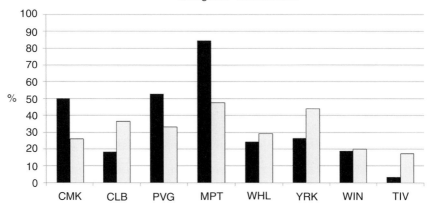

Figure 5.5 Distribution of *was* according to negative vs affirmative

As it happens, some dialects in Britain and Northern Ireland have an alternative pattern across negative and affirmative contexts. In some dialects, instead of the *–s* ending, the *–r* ending occurs across grammatical persons. This is often referred to as '*were* regularization' because the same form, in this case *were*, occurs across all the grammatical persons, as in (12).

(12)   a. I *were* just thinkin' that. (CLB/ɪ̂)
       b. Aye, oh then you *were* all right. You *weren't* so bad now. (CMK/é)
       c. She *were* a great worker mi mother. (CLB/ʃ)
       d. There *were* a wee alarm-clock sat on the window. (CLB/å)
       e. Their two cars *were* sitting out in the yard but they *were* locked. (CLB/é)
       f. There *were* no doors locked. There *weren't* even a lock on mi Granny's door. It was just a bar. (CLB/ʃ)

What does the use of verbal –s tell us about dialects?

The accountable analysis of the verb ending *–s* and the forms *is* and *was* offers a consistent assessment of patterns across the Roots Archive and the British Dialects Archive. The Roots Archive communities both retain the ancient *–s* ending and respect the Northern Subject Rule. However, the communities do not retain its use to the same degree. In Cumnock and Maryport it has receded dramatically, whereas in Northern Ireland it is much more frequent. The fact that the underlying patterns are the same but the frequency differs suggests that the communities share the same underlying system. This means that the differences in relative frequency are more likely to be the result of differential obsolescence rather than a difference in grammar. It would be interesting to determine how frequent the *–s* ending is in these communities among the younger generations. I suspect there would be a significant decline in the use of –*s*. If so, there may come a time when the Northern Subject Rule will be gone forever.

Definition

When a dialect or dialect feature is *obsolescent*, this means that it is no longer used. This does not mean that the dialect or feature is not adequate. It still conveys the same function as it always did; however, some replacement is perceived to be more appropriate or desirable.

Adverbs with –*ly* or zero

Ballywalter and Portavogie are alike at each other in that they both speak slow. But they speak different. But Ballyhilbert speaks quick. (Kate Devoy, 62, PVG, 004)

An adverb is a part of speech that modifies another part of speech other than a noun (modifiers of nouns are adjectives or determiners). Adverbs can also modify clauses or sentences. Adverbs are easily identified because they typically provide information about how, in what way, when, where, to what extent (i.e. manner, place or circumstances) of some activity. In contemporary Standard English most adverbs take the ending –*ly*; others do not, e.g. *hard, late, well*. However, in vernacular usage, some adverbs can take either a –*ly* ending or no ending at all. These are often referred to as 'dual form' adverbs because they may have two different forms. Of course, sociolinguists recognize this as inherent variability, or layering.

Synchronic perspective

In the late twentieth century, adverbs with no –*ly* ending (i.e. zero adverbs) were widely reported (e.g. Milroy and Milroy, 1993; Tagliamonte and Ito, 2002; Trudgill, 1990: 86), as in the quote from the Roots Archive above, *slow, different, quick*.

Not surprisingly, these forms are associated with nonstandard (Quirk, Greenbaum, Leech and Svartvik, 1985) or colloquial language (Christian, Wolfram and Dube, 1988; Poutsma, 1926: 634; Zettersten, 1969). They are often considered features 'of the illiterate' (Poutsma, 1926; Pulgram, 1968) and are sometimes even considered 'vulgar' (Van Draat, 1910: 97). Thus, the two forms partition according to a standard/nonstandard dichotomy (Hughes and Trudgill, 1987; Macaulay, 1995; Trudgill, 1990). This is echoed in most descriptions of this variation in contemporary grammar books (Leech and Svartvik, 1975; Quirk et al., 1985: 404). Zero adverbs can also be associated with certain genres. Alford (1864: 203), for example, suggests that 'this adverbial use of adjectives is entirely poetical and not ever to be allowed in prose'. Similarly, Poutsma (1926: 632) observes that zero forms are used when accommodating metre or rhythm in poetry, but 'literary English would hardly tolerate [them]' (Poutsma, 1926: 385).

The zero adverb has also been associated with pidgins and/or creoles, presumably due to the fact that pidgins at least are known to have reduced inflectional and derivational morphology as compared to the source languages (Arends, 1995: 31). According to Crystal (1995), in creoles 'adjectives are routinely used in adverbial function'. Yet Crystal (1995: 327) also lists the zero adverb as a characteristic of 'Estuary English', a variety of British English held responsible for ongoing dialect levelling throughout the UK.

The zero adverb is widely reported in the US (Mencken, 1961; Pooley, 1933; Ross, 1984), where it is considered geographically and socially diffused (Mencken, 1961: 388; Wolfram and Schilling-Estes, 2006: 378). However, it is attested most often in southern dialects of American English, particularly Appalachian and Ozark English (Christian et al., 1988: 168–9; Feagin, 1979; Wolfram and Schilling-Estes, 2006: 378). There is also evidence for zero adverbs in widely separated locales elsewhere in the world, e.g. Tristan da Cunha (Zettersten, 1969: 80) and the Channel Islands (Ramisch, 1989: 161). Given the ubiquitous nature of these reports, it seems that the zero adverb is widely diffused across English dialects. It then becomes a point of curiosity to find out where it came from.

Historical perspective

In Old English, adverbs were formed by simply adding the ending *–e* to the adjective. However, some adjectives already ended with *–e*, which led to many adverbs and adjectives looking the same, as in (13).

(13)   a. *blide* 'joyful' or 'joyfully'
       b. *clæne* 'clean' or 'cleanly'

Between the late Old English and Middle English period final unstressed *–e* ceased to be pronounced in English. This led to even further ambiguity between adverbs and adjectives. This ambiguity is thought to have prompted the use of another ending, *–lice* (and its descendant *–ly*), to form adverbs in order to distinguish them from adjectives (Mustanoja, 1960: 314; Robertson, 1954: 134–5). This led to *–lice* and later *–ly* becoming 'the real indication of adverbial function' and it was thereafter used 'to an ever increasing degree' (Jespersen 1961a: 408).

Nevertheless, the zero adverb is reported to be 'common' throughout the Elizabethan period (Abbott, 1879) and many authors cite examples from the prevailing literature, particularly Shakespeare (c. 1564–1616), who clearly varied in his usage, as in (14)–(16) and also Milton (c. 1608–1674), as in (17) (Emma, 1964: 80).

(14) a. Which the false man do's *easie*. (*Macbeth*, II, 3.156)
      b. How *easily* murder is discovered! (*Titus Andronicus*, II, 3.1040)

(15) a. 'Tis *noble* spoken. (*Antony and Cleopatra*, II, 2.805)
      b. As hotly and as *nobly* with thy love … (*Coriolanus*, IV, 5.2878)

(16) a. For though he comes *slowly*, he carries his house on his head (*As You Like It*, IV, 1.1843)
      b. Could best express how *slow* his soul sail'd on, How swift his ship. (*Cymbeline*, I, 3.286)

(17) a. … and to the' Eastern Gate/ Led them *direct*. (*Paradise Lost*, 12.638–40)
      b. And sits as *safe* as in a Senat house. (*Comus*, 388)

Such statements are supported by research tracking the use of these forms from 1350 to 1710 (Nevalainen, 1994a, b, 1997).[5] This study revealed that the 'zero-forms lose ground in the Early Modern English period' (Nevalainen, 1994a: 142) as they were gradually replaced by a –*ly* ending (Nevalainen, 1994a, 1997). It is important to keep in mind that this process was gradual (Nevalainen, 1997: 163): the zero form represented 21% of all variable adverbs in 1350–1420, but only 13% by 1640–1710. This downward trajectory suggests that contemporary varieties of English would have even less use of the zero variant.

Yet according to Van Draat (1910: 97), use of the zero form is 'of the most frequent occurrence in the eighteenth century'. Lowth's influential grammar book (Lowth, 1762/1775: 125) quotes Swift (c. 1667–1745), complaining that 'adjectives are sometimes employed as adverbs, improperly, and not agreeably to the Genius of the English language', e.g. *extreme* elaborate, *marvellous* graceful, etc. Yet Jespersen (1961b: 371–2) reports the following examples from Swift himself, as in (18).

(18) a. It rains *terribly*. (Swift, *Letter to Stella*)
      b. I did not go to town today, it was so *terrible* rainy. (Swift, *Letter to Stella*)

All this indicates that, despite the development of –*ly* as the standard adverb marker in English, variation between zero and –*ly* is still vigorous in the vernacular language. Indeed, notice the variation in the sentential adverb *rightly* in the *Twin Lambs* story below.

Note

Adverbialization refers to the process by which adverbs are formed. In this case, the ending –*ly* evolves to become the standard adverb marker in English and the use of unmarked, or zero, adverbs declines.

Twin Lambs

I knowed of a boy up by Larne, there. I don't know who he was now but there were a boy in Ballyclare told me this. You heard about it Tom? He had lost a set of twins. And they were two or three weeks old and he lost this set of twin lambs and, och the ewe's mad looking for lambs and she was only going to be wrecked for him keeping her, you know. She would go take a bad udder or something, you know and he thought he would get rid of her, you know. Maybe somebody else be looking for a foster-mother. And he went to Ballyclare with her and this boy that was staring at the lambs, he had a pair of lambs for sale, you know for boys that was looking for lamb. The minute she went into the place she was away two or three pens away. When she heard the lambs bleating, you know and she knowed her own lambs rightly. And some other boy said, 'Take her out of there,' he says, 'to see what she's looking for,' you know. And she out – flying down to the pen where the two lambs were. And the lambs was trying their best to get out and some other one of them let the two lambs out and they went flying till her and sucked away at their own mother. They knowed right. She knowed rightly. And them away from her for three or four days too! (CLB, Mike O'Leary, 53, 013)[6]

The Roots Archive

The Roots Archive has many zero adverbs and there is indeed substantial variation between the two endings, as in (19) and (20). Note that individuals use both variants; compare the (a) and (b) sentences from the same individual in (19, 21 and 22).

(19)   a. And he was *awful* homesick you know my Uncle John. (CMK/j)
       b. He worked *awfully* hard. (CMK/j)

(20)   a. That's *terrible* good for your blood. (CLB/1)
       b. I think if it's *terribly* bright, awful bright sun, it's no so good. (CMK/i)

(21)   a. He wanted to get as many finished as he could that night as *quick* as he could. (WHL/c)
       b. Be able to think twice as *quickly* as your customer. (WHL/c)

(22)   a. Aye, I could've passed it quite *easily*, you know. (CMK/A)
       b. Oh I could've had a job quite *easy* with him. (CMK/A)

We now examine how the zero form is distributed across communities and its patterns of use.

Methodology

Every adverb in the Roots Archive that could take either the *–ly* or Ø form without a change in meaning was extracted for examination following protocols developed in earlier research (see Ito and Tagliamonte, 2003; Tagliamonte, 2008). Pre-verbal contexts were excluded following Quirk et al. (1985) except in places where variability could be established, e.g. *near(ly)*. This provided

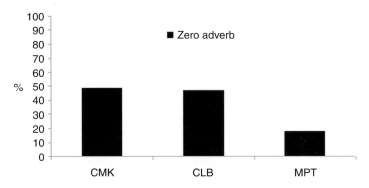

Figure 5.6 Proportion of zero adverbs by community

a total of 761 tokens across three communities in the Roots Archive. Each token was then coded for the type of adverb, the nature of its use as concrete or abstract and the specific lexical item.

The Policeman

And another time there was a policeman staying with him. And he had booked him. And then here he was coming along the road one night. And he saw his bicycle at the side of the road. He was actually investigating boys that had been stealing wood fae old folks. So my Uncle Robert got off the bike – the motorbike and he let down his tyres. And the big one had to walk back the whole road without his bike to Skares. And he come in and they were at their dinner in the kitchen. And my granny, of course, was an innocent. She saying, 'You're late, Sandy, you're awful late tonight.' He said. 'I had to walk the whole road back. 'Cos these young buggers that I was chasing must have come back behind me and let the tyres down on my bike!' (Bruce Donaldson, 68, CMK)[7]

Distributional analysis

Figure 5.6 shows the overall frequency of zero adverbs across communities. Despite the relatively vague observations in the literature that the use of zero adverbs is frequent (e.g. Edwards and Weltens, 1985), its rate of occurrence is rarely reported. In the Roots Archive proportions of zero range from a high of 49% in Cumnock and 47% in Cullybackey, to only 18% in Maryport. While all of these rates might qualify as 'frequent' there is a clear demarcation among the communities.

Function of the adverbs A widely held determinant of adverb form is the function of the adverb. Adverbs that can alternate between Ø and –*ly* have three distinct functions: manner, as in (23), which describes the nature of a verb (*carefully* or *easily* or *heavily*); intensifier, as in (24), which amplifies the meaning of an adjective; and sentential, as in (25), which modifies an entire clause. Notice again the within-speaker and within-community variability.

(23)   Manner adverbs
    a. He had to tread very *carefully* on a bad day. (CMK/o)
    b. They weren't just peas. And you could *easy* get a handful. (MPT/s)
    c. You did nae breathe too *heavy* on it. (CMK/u/)

(24)   Intensifying adverbs
    a. You could put on a *real* good show. (MPT/d)
    b. He was an *awful* nice boy, he was. (CMK/J)
    c. And like outside it was *absolutely* torrential rain. (MPT/u)

(25)   Sentential adverbs
    a. *Funnily* enough I did the garden for awhile. (CMK/d)
    b. *Funny* enough I had a big pot of jam on. (CMK/n)
    c. They took us about five mile inland and the only thing was where you got where you're going nothing was just as – just as you can imagine. *Obvious*. (MPT/n/M/82)
    d. *Surely* she's retired, she has. (CMK/e)
    e. *Sure* it's terrible isn't it? (CMK/e)

According to the literature, at earlier stages of English, the intensifier use of adverbs tended to be zero marked, while verb modifiers tend to be *–ly* marked (Nevalainen, 1997: 169; Peters, 1994: 284; Poutsma, 1926: 634). Yet when synchronic data is considered, the opposite tendency is reported. Opdahl (2000: 32) notes that alternation between Ø and *–ly* will generally not exist with sentential or intensifying adverbs in present-day English. These discrepancies suggest that there have been important changes in the nature of this variation.

Figure 5.7 shows the distribution of Ø adverbs by function across communities. There is no consistent pattern; each community has a different ranking of zero variants by function. In Cumnock, sentential adverbs stand out and in Cullybackey both sentential and manner stand out. Maryport has generally lower rates overall with a regular progression from intensifier to sentential with manner adverbs having the most Ø forms. This is exactly the same pattern found in York English (Tagliamonte and Ito, 2002). Because Maryport patterns more like the standard language with mostly *–ly* on adverbs, it may be that this is due to Maryport's location in north-west England with closer proximity to larger cities in Scotland and northern England. In such a locale we may surmise that zero adverbs have decreased over time just as has been reported in historical research. However, it also seems apparent that zero adverbs have declined most dramatically in intensifier and sentential functions, while manner adverbs retain more of the older forms.

Blackbird

There was a blackbird sung in one tree and a thrush in the other … That blackbird … sings on that same tree and especially early in the morning when I go out, that boy's

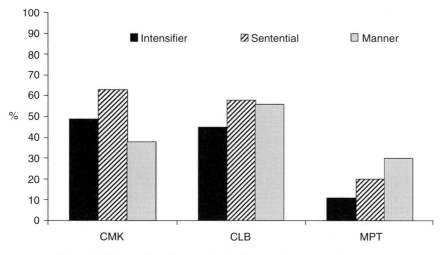

Figure 5.7 Proportion of zero adverbs by type by community

singing his heart out. Well says I, 'it's very strange,' says I, 'this blackbird that sung and sung and sung and has the one perch in this tree away down the back there. And still … on the very same perch that blackbird sings. And it's a lovely singer, you know.' (Daniel Binchy, 86, CLB, 014)[8]

Lexical effect The effect of individual lexical items may underlie these patterns. In the Roots Archive there are fifty-five different adverbs in the data. While nearly half of them occur only once or twice, the remainder are heavily weighted towards two or three frequent forms. Table 5.1 shows the frequency of zero adverbs that occur ten times or more.

There are substantial differences in variability. A number of infrequent adverbs, e.g. *tight*, *wild* and *powerful* (not shown individually in Table 5.1), as in (26), occur at 100% zero. More frequent forms, such as *awful*, are nearly categorical, 97%, as in (27). In contrast, some adverbs have less than 5% zero, e.g. *absolute* and *definite*, as in (28).

(26) a. It was a *wild wild* hot day, *powerful* warm. (CLB/a)
      b. She was *wild* fat. I think she was twenty-three stone or something. (CLB/017)

(27) a. It's a lovely run. It's an *awful* nice run, hen. It's an *awful* nice run down to Dumfries and the white sands, it's lovely. (CLB/007)
      b. Oh it was a beautiful ice-cream, it was that. Lovely oh it was good – it was *awful* good aye. (CMK/021)

(28) a. But she was *absolute* horse-mad at time, eh? (MPT/012/F/60)
      b. Oh it's a lovely place. Lovely. [*Interviewer*] The other side of life. [j] Oh aye, *definite*. (CMK/j/F/67)

Table 5.1 *Frequency of Ø adverbs by lexical item (N ≥ 10)*

Lexical adverb	%	N
Near	**10**	151
Sure	**45**	132
Real	**2**	102
Awful	**97**	68
Quick	**84**	38
Terrible	**82**	34
Absolute	**6**	32
Right	**36**	25
Fair	**31**	16
Definite	**5**	20
Funny	**75**	20
Easy	**64**	14
Proper	**0**	10
All other adverbs	**50**	116
TOTAL	**39**	761

Three frequent lexical items – *near, really, sure* – represent 19.8%, 13.4% and 17.3% of the data, respectively. Interestingly, they represent one of each of the adverb functions: *near* = manner; *really* = intensifier; *sure* = sentential. The adverb *near*, as in (29), is the most frequent (N = 151), but is virtually always –*ly* except in Cullybackey. *Sure* occurs 132 times and appears unmarked a good proportion of the time, as in (30). In contrast, the intensifier *really*, also a frequent form (N = 102), is overwhelming marked with –*ly*, as in (31).

(29) a. I put my hand in. I very *near* burnt my hand. (CLB/i)
      b. He was *near* down in Dungannon wasn't he? (CLB/f)

(30) a. He drives the bus *surely* and he's never off the road. (CLB/005)
      b. We had one, two, three, four, five, six, seven, eight, nine about eleven farms around our village. They've slowly but *sure* were swallowed up. I-mean there's two of them still left but er slowly but *surely* were swallowed up by building house, you know. (PVG/036)

(31) a. Forty-seven was a *really* bad winter, yeah. (MPT/021)
      b. And mi mother was *really* musical. (CLB/008)

We now consider whether these adverbs are used in the same way across communities.

Table 5.2 shows the three most frequent adverbs and their proportion within each community separately. Only two surface in the top contenders – *nearly* and *really*.[9] However, notice that several additional forms have now surfaced

Table 5.2 *The three most frequent adverbs by community and their proportion out of all adverbs used in each community*

	1st	2nd	3rd
CLB	*nearly*	*terribly*	*rightly*
	41.9%	13.3%	11.8%
CMK	*awful*	*really*	*nearly*
	33.0%	17.0%	10.2%
MPT	*really*	*nearly*	*absolutely*
	23.7%	21.7%	6.3%

as common features in certain communities, *awful* in Cumnock, *terribly* and *rightly* in Cullybackey and *absolutely* in Maryport. What this tells us is that different places have their favourite adverbs, and even when the same adverb is used, variant choice can be locally determined.

The use of *near* as *nearly* or *almost* is reported in the literature (1898–1905), as in (32), and singled out as common in Scottish and northern English dialects (Grant and Murison, 1931–76: 395).[10]

(32) a. Haddo's own Tenants, who could not *near* drink the Ale of a Boll. (Abd. 1758. Session Papers, Grant v. Farquharson (4 Aug.) 15)
      b. He near missed it: aye, age *near*. (Sc. 1887 Jam) (both cited in Grant and Murison, 1931–76: 395)

Next, let's consider how these patterns compare to other British dialects. Figure 5.8 plots the distribution of the two most common adverbs by six communities.

It is now even more evident that Maryport patterns with the other British communities, whether northern (Wheatley Hill and York) or southern (Tiverton), whereas Cullybackey and Cumnock are distinct. Both stand out as retaining the zero adverb in the large group of 'other' adverbs, as in (33). However, note that Cumnock uses *really* (rather than *real*), just like all the other communities.

(33) a. The moon was shining *bright*. (CLB/n)
      b. I like him, *terrible* nice young fellow. (CLB/b)

Examination of the internal constraints may provide a further perspective. In the trajectory of change from zero marking to –*ly*, concrete adverbs, as in (34), were said to occur more with the zero form than abstract adverbs, as in (35) (Donner, 1991; Nevalainen 1994a, 1994b, 1997; Schibsbye, 1965).

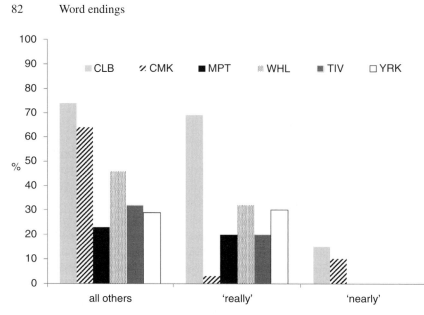

Figure 5.8 Distribution of zero adverbs isolating two common adverbs

(34) a. Food wise people ate so *simple* in them days. (WHL/c)
      b. They weren't just peas and you could *easy* get a handful. (MPT/s)
      c. Well my mother, she went quite *quick*. (CMK/M)

(35) a. He's involved *heavily* in that one. (TIV/h)
      b. I was never loved *properly*. (WHL/l)
      c. They were all very *closely* connected. (CMK/A)

An illustration of this can be found in Swift, quoted by Jespersen (1961a: 371–2) in the contrast in ''tis *terrible* cold … it has snowed *terribly* all night'. In the first case, the meaning is concrete whereas in the second it is abstract. Figure 5.9 tests this constraint by showing the proportion of *–ly* by these meanings across communities.

In every community, the zero adverb is more frequent with concrete readings. This means that despite the varying numbers and rates of use of the zero adverb, all these communities retain this older constraint.

What does the zero adverb tell us about dialects?

In considering the use of zero adverbs, we have discovered tracks of change but also stability of constraints. There are both local and universal patterns in the dialect data. From the overall distribution of zero adverbs across the Roots Archive compared to the British Dialects Archive, we might have reasonably

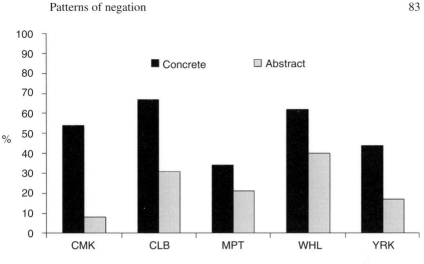

Figure 5.9 Proportion of –*ly* by meaning

concluded that zero adverbs were simply general nonstandard English grammar, since they exist to a greater or lesser degree everywhere. However, once
the individual lexical items were distinguished, it became obvious that certain
adverbs are popular in one place or another. Looking at manner adverbs only,
we tested for a well-known historical constraint (concrete vs abstract). Every
community has this contrast, exposing longitudinal systematic patterning in the
adverbialization trajectory (Nevalainen, 1994a, 1994b). The inter-community
stability of this constraint, regardless of overall frequency and across six centuries, provides a dramatic confirmation of the idea that morphological variants
change over time, and their patterning remains constant (Kroch, 1989).

Patterns of negation

A critical diagnostic for distinguishing British dialects is whether the auxiliary
in negative sentences is contracted or not, as in the supertoken in (36). Also,
compare the constructions in (37a) and (38a) with those in (37b) and (38b)
from the same individual in each example.

(36)   You *won't* see that now. You *'ll not* see that now at all. (CMK/n)

(37)   a. He *'ll not* be better again Margaret, no. (CLB/e)
       b. And you *won't* have the same interest. (CLB/e)

(38)   a. But she *'s not* that daft, though, Geoff. (MPT/%)
       b. I said 'I know it *isn't* gonna affect you.' (MPT/%)

(39)   a. And I *'ve no* been so mobile since. (CMK/A)
       b. I don't know her, I *haven't* seen her. (CMK/A)

Synchronic perspective

The full form of the auxiliary followed by a contracted negative particle, i.e. *n't*, is said to be more common in Southern British English (Swan, 1995: 159). In contrast, the contracted auxiliaries, e.g. *will* →*'ll*, *would* →*'d*, *have* → *'ve*, *has* → *'s*, *is* → *'s*, *are* →*'re*, followed by *not* are said to be more common in Scotland and northern England (Aitken, 1984; Beal, 1993; Haegeman, 1981; Miller, 1993; Quirk et al., 1985). Indeed, a commonly cited axiom is that the frequency of contracted auxiliaries increases 'the further north one goes' (Trudgill, 1978: 13). However, these statements tend to be based on observation rather than quantitative study (but see Hiller, 1987; Krug, 1994; Miller, 1993) and the literature generally is 'vaguely speculative' (Hiller, 1987: 532). In actuality, it is not 'known for sure which contractions are employed often and which are hardly ever used' (Krug, 1994: 1). Furthermore, little mention is made of phonological variation in the form of the negative particle, which can vary depending on the region, e.g. *nae*, *na*, *no* or *not*.

The propensity of auxiliary contraction in negative sentences is also said to differ according to the auxiliary. Scots dialects are thought to prefer AUX contraction for *will*, as in (40), and *be*, as in (41) (Aitken, 1984: 106; Beal, 1993: 199; Haegeman, 1981: 23; Quirk et al., 1985: 122). Further, Scots varieties are said to have a distinct ranking of the three auxiliaries with *be* most likely to occur with AUX contraction, then *will* and finally *have*, as in (42) (Miller, 1993: 114).

(40) *will*
      AUX contraction
      a. She*'ll no* touch it. I mind of that. (CLB/g)
      b. You*'ll no* get in at Cumnock. (CMK/n)
      NEG contraction
      b. The bloody thing *won't* start. (MPT/g)
      c. Covers your mistake, but *won't* cover mine. (CLB/o)

(41) *be*
      AUX contraction
      a. It*'s not* all shopping. (MPT/y)
      NEG contraction
      b. It i*sn't* in his book, then. (MPT/y)

(42) *have*
      AUX contraction
      a. It*'s not* cost him anything, like. (CLB/n)
      NEG contraction
      b. He *hasn't* time, like. (CLB/n)

However, the auxiliaries generally are not equally disposed to variation. With auxiliary *be,* the forms are said to 'vary freely' (Selkirk, 1981: 114). Yet *have* is said to have a distinct preference for NEG contraction, as in (42b) (Quirk et al.,

1985: 123; Selkirk, 1981: 114). This is corroborated by studies that have found that *n't* forms are favoured, both for *has* (85.37%) and *have* (91.04%) (Hiller, 1987: 536). It is also supported by acceptability judgements (Greenbaum, 1977: 99). *Will* is also said to prefer NEG contraction, i.e. *won't*. For example *I won't* occurs 99% of the time in the spoken data analysed by Hiller (1987: 536) and 95% in Kjellmer's (1998: 181) written data.[11] While these findings suggest that each auxiliary has 'its own preferences' (Selkirk, 1981: 114), it is important to note that the speech of the same speaker in (40), (41) and (42) shows alternation between AUX and NEG contraction with the same auxiliary in the same discourse. This means there must be some other explanation.

Historical perspective

According to most researchers, AUX contraction first appeared in the late sixteenth century. NEG contraction, on the other hand, does not appear until the middle of the seventeenth century (Barber, 1976: 254; Brainerd, 1989; Pyles and Algeo, 1993: 203; Strang, 1970; Warner, 1993: 208). The earliest attestations (c. 1621) of NEG contraction appear in representations of nonstandard English, and only later amongst the educated (Brainerd, 1989: 191). This suggests that it was a change from below that may have come from regional dialects.

A number of observations in the historical record also support the idea of long time differences among the auxiliaries. Murray (1873: 216) and Grant and Main-Dixon (1921: 116) cite the NEG contraction forms *wunna* and *winna*, as in (43a) for Scots. However, the same author produces AUX contraction with *will* as well, as in (43b), suggesting a long history of variability, at least in Scottish varieties.

(43) a. I *winna* insure ye, if you dinna mend yer manners. (1818, Scott, *Heart of Midlothian*, ch. 4)
      b. Weel, weel, neibor, I'*ll* no say that ye mayna be right. (1818, Scott, *Heart of Midlothian*, ch. 8)

AUX contraction with the verb *be* on the other hand seems to have always been high (or categorical) in Scots communities (Murray, 1873).

Old days

Used to talk about the good old days. They're no good old days Margaret. For Margaret I come through them and I know. They were hard old days! (Kate McBride, 88, CLB, 005][12]

Methodology

In order to examine NEG/AUX contraction, we extracted all contexts of negation with an auxiliary verb in Cumnock, Cullybackey and Maryport for a total of

3,795 tokens. In many cases, the northern dialects use an invariant negative particle, *no*, *nae* or *na*, as in (44)–(45). These were treated along with the standard negative contraction tokens as alternates to contraction of the auxiliary.

(44) a. He *would nae* wash or nothing. There *was nae* a farmer … (CMK/q)
      b. Some of the big yins *had nae* any more than I had. (CLB/f)
      c. I *would nae* know a flower fae a dandelion. (CLB/f)

(45) a. They*'ll no* be here long. (CMK/t)
      b. I *hae na* gotten an acceptance card. I *hae na* gotten a card. (BCK/a)
      c. Fishing*'s no* fishing nowadays. (CLB/b)

Once these contexts were tabulated, however, it became immediately apparent that many contexts had little or no variation. First person subjects with 'be' were categorically AUX contraction, i.e. *I'm* (N = 395). Instances of *amn't*, *ain't* or *aren't* were rare or absent.[13] Accordingly, all first person contexts with auxiliary 'be' were removed from the analysis. Cases of elided subjects, as in (46), were categorically NEG contraction (N = 53), so they too were excluded.

(46) a. [*Interviewer*] Was it a bike, you had? [014] *Hadn't* a bike, no, just a 'barrow. (MPT/ n)
      b. Covers your mistake but *won't* cover mine. (CLB/o)
      c. Sometimes folk*'ll* say, '*Wouldn't* live anywhere else for t'world.' (MPT/z)

The data also contained a large number of tag questions (N = 598), as in (47). These only ever appeared with NEG contraction, so these were excluded as well.

(47) a. You got to spend your money somewhere, *haven't you*? (CMK/u)
      b. It's about sixty mile up fae Banff and Macduff, *isn't it*? (CMK/k)
      c. So, that will be next week, *won't it*? (CLB/e)

Interrogatives (N = 111) were biased towards NEG contraction as well, 65%, as in (48). The other 35% appeared as aux + subject + neg, as in (49).

(48) a. *Isn't* that strange? (CMK/g)
      b. *Isn't* that scandalous? (MPT/@)

(49) a. *Are* they *not* ready for jam? (CLB/n)
      b. *Is* that *no* working now? (CLB/b)

In sum, a group of specific contexts are lexicalized to the AUX contraction forms. Removing all of them – questions, interrogatives, tags, first person subjects with 'be' – along with null subjects and uncontracted forms left 2,755 tokens in which NEG/AUX contraction was variable across dialects.

Distributional analysis

Given the widely cited geographical claims about this linguistic feature, the first step in the analysis is to ask how the communities behave with respect

Table 5.3 *Overall distribution of AUX contraction by community*

BCK		CMK		CLB		MPT		WHL		YRK		TIV		HEN	
%	N	%	N	%	N	%	N	%	N	%	N	%	N	%	N
38	216	**51**	382	**42**	422	**14**	608	**45**	121	**18**	549	**18**	198	**31**	259

to variant choice. Table 5.3 shows the overall distribution of AUX contraction across the eight communities under investigation.

Table 5.3 reveals that three of the northern communities have high percentages of AUX contraction – Buckie has 38%, Cumnock 51%, Wheatley Hill 45% and Cullybackey 42%. This is consistent with the idea that northern British locales will have more frequent AUX contraction than southern ones. However, Maryport and York, which are also northern, have substantially lower rates, 14% and 18% respectively, patterning along with Tiverton in the south (18%). Henfield in Sussex, where the community is known for its 'gentry-like' population, has an overall proportion in between, at 31%. Thus, the expected north–south divide is non-existent. Moreover, the communities are not patterning according to any continuous north–south trajectory. Finally, note that the overall rates of AUX contraction, even in northern climes, are actually quite modest. Auxiliaries are typically full forms.

However, NEG/AUX contraction may differ across the different auxiliaries *be*, *have* and *will*, which may help to explain the irregularity of these overall proportions. The next set of figures shows the distribution of each auxiliary separately by community. Figure 5.10 shows the overall distribution of AUX contraction with *be* by community, with separate proportions for *'s* and *'re*. It shows that the frequency of AUX contraction for *is/are* is very high. In Wheatley Hill, Cumnock, Cullybackey and Buckie it is categorical or near categorical. Henfield has proportions somewhat lower. In Maryport, York and Tiverton there is robust variation. AUX contraction occurs, but it is highly variable with NEG contraction. Alternation within the same speaker is common, as in (50).

(50)   a. The driver*'s nae* gan naewhere. (BCK/d)
        b. Och, that land*'s no* so great, Andy. (CLB/p)
        c. She*'s no* fond of the farm work. (CMK/u)
        d. You*'re not* fit to ga home. (MPT/k)

This result clearly pinpoints *variation* in NEG/AUX to three communities, York, Tiverton and Henfield. It also confirms Selkirk's (1981: 114) observation that auxiliary *be* is unique with respect to NEG/AUX contraction more generally.

Figure 5.11 shows the overall distribution of AUX contraction with *have* across communities.

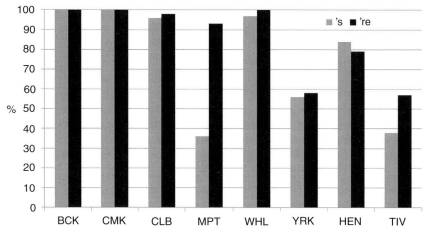

Figure 5.10 Distribution of AUX contraction with *be* by community

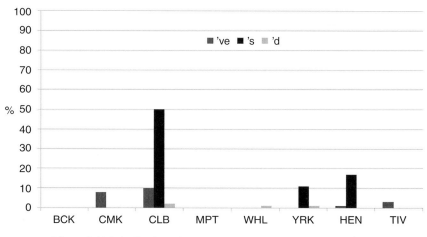

Figure 5.11 Distribution of AUX contraction with *have* by community

A stark contrast to Figure 5.10, Figure 5.11 reveals very little or no AUX contraction with *have* in any community. North and south are parallel – full auxiliary forms prevail, as in (51).

(51)   a. I *have na* seen him for a while now. (BCK/@)
       b. I *have nae* the patience to put it on. (CMK/n)
       c. She *hasn't* lost her sense of humour. (MPT/%)
       d. The crops *hadn't* been cut, you see. (CLB/d)

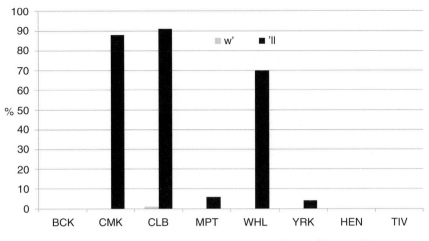

Figure 5.12 Distribution of AUX contraction with *would* and *will* by community

It is curious that these examples do not display very much AUX contraction with *have* since this has been reported as a northern feature (Hughes and Trudgill, 1979: 189; Wales, 2006: 189). In fact, the only variant of *have* that has AUX contraction to any degree is *has* which contracts to *'s*.

Figure 5.12 shows the distribution of AUX contraction for the two forms *will* and *would*. It exposes yet another pattern. In this case, full form auxiliaries prevail with *would*, either with contracted *n't* or *nae/na,* as in (52).

(52) a. She *wouldn't* let me over the doorstep. (CLB/n)
      b. We *wouldn't* know whether it was true or not. (MPT/n)
      c. The old thing *would nae* go. (CMK/f)
      d. She *would na* ging with nobody else. (BCK/e)

In contrast, variation between contracted and full auxiliaries with *will* splits the communities dramatically. AUX contraction is near categorical in Cullybackey (91%) and Cumnock (88%), making the examples in (53) the norm. Note that in Wheatley Hill the 70% represents only seven out of ten tokens.

(53) a. That kind of language*'ll no* get money for you. (CLB/f)
      b. But there'll be a lot you*'ll no* understand either. (CMK/u)
      c. It*'ll not* be our Peter's area. (WHL/d)
      d. I*'ll not* say why. (MPT/u)

In sum, AUX contraction is highly dependent on the auxiliary itself. Contraction of *have* or *would* is rare. AUX contraction of *will* is obviously an Irish feature, but it is unclear how much it is a 'northern' feature. Despite

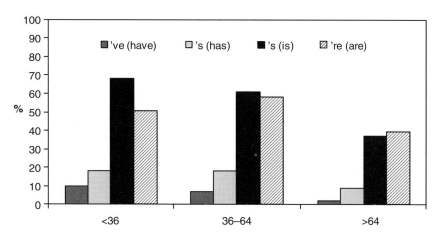

Figure 5.13 Distribution of AUX contraction with *have* and *be* in apparent time in York

considerable contexts in the data where AUX contraction *could* be used, the elderly northerners in Maryport, York and Buckie do not use AUX contraction very much at all. The only context where there is robust use of AUX contraction is with auxiliary *be*, and here too the regional distribution is bounded. In fact, it appears to be a feature of southern British dialects and/or those closer to the mainstream (York) (see Figure 5.10). It may be the case that AUX contraction among northerners is a recent development and so does not appear among these elderly individuals. We can consider this possibility by tracking the generational differences in the York English Corpus. Figure 5.13 displays the proportion of use of AUX contraction across three age cohorts for *have* and *be*, the two auxiliaries where AUX contraction is present. It reveals that there is a consistent difference between *have* and *be* across generations. Further, notice the increasing use of contraction among the younger generations. All forms advance across generations except for *are* which has a downturn towards more use of *aren't* in the youngest generations. The increasing use of AUX contraction is particularly pronounced with auxiliary *is* which advances incrementally in each generation. This corroborates the idea that AUX contraction, generally, is strengthening in northern English.

Don the door

So they say that Joe decided to don on his door. And he run forward to the door. [004] D'you know what he means by 'don'? Don on the door? …[008] He run for to kick the door. (Kate Devoy, 62, 004, Jim Baird, 66, 008, PVG)[15]

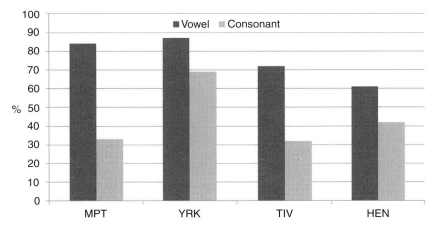

Figure 5.14 Effect of preceding phonological environment on AUX contraction with *be* across communities with variable NEG/AUX contraction

Grammatical patterns

Two constraints are known to operate on NEG/AUX contraction – preceding phonological environment and verb status (Tagliamonte and Smith, 2002). Figure 5.14 shows the effect of preceding phonological environment on the contraction of *be* in Maryport, York, Henfield and Tiverton, the four locales where NEG/AUX contraction is variable. It reveals that the preceding phonological environment exerts a strong effect on the choice of AUX contraction. Vowels have a greater proportion of AUX contraction over consonants across the board. Thus, in all the varieties the choice between NEG or AUX contraction is phonological, and this effect is parallel across communities.

Cumbria

Cumbria's very hard to understand. There's a feller there and he's in budgies. He was along wi Rodney and them. And he comes on the phone here, 'hand the phone to somebody else, I can nae understand a word you're talking about!' (Michael Adair, 74, PVG, 008)[14]

What does the use of contraction tell us about dialects?

Let us return to the original hypothesis that spurred the analysis of NEG/AUX contraction: *the further north one goes in Britain, the more AUX contraction one gets.* This observation seemed to present an ideal test for distinguishing varieties in Britain, particularly on a north–south dimension. If this were true, then the two extremes of north and south should have exhibited divergent patterns. However, the results reveal not only that this is not the case, but also that the regional pattern of NEG/AUX contraction in British dialects exhibits a finely demarcated picture.

The differences between communities are not due to a north–south distinction. The extreme of north and south on some counts are identical. There is virtually no AUX contraction outside of *be* in Tiverton (south-west) and in Buckie (far north). Nor is it Scots vs English. Neither can the differences be explained by the peripheral vs mainstream status of the locales. York is an urban centre and a major tourist destination, whereas Maryport, Henfield and Tiverton are small, geographically removed locales. Yet York patterns along with all of these with relatively low rates of AUX contraction with *be*. Indeed, what is remarkable from the graphic picture is the favoured status of AUX contraction with *be*, i.e. *isn't/aren't*, across *all* communities. The only regionally distinct pattern is the highly circumscribed use of AUX contraction with *will*. The hypothesized Scottish ranking frequency of *be* first followed by *will* and then *have* (Miller, 1993) is visible only in Cumnock (Scotland) and Culleybackey (Ireland). The fact that Buckie (Scotland) does not share this constraint ranking provides a good exemplar of the extreme differences among Scots dialects. In this case, the geographically relevant finding is the use of AUX contraction of *will* in Lowland Scotland and Northern Ireland. Thus NEG/AUX contraction is not a good litmus test for north vs south, east vs west or Scots vs English. It is an Ulster-Scots feature.

However, the comparative cross-variety approach provides a number of different lines of evidence that can be used for testing parallels and contrasts across varieties. Perhaps most importantly, we have discovered that there is a dramatic difference between *be* and the other auxiliaries that is consistent across all the communities. In every location *be* has AUX contraction, and in each case it has higher rates of AUX contraction than *will* or *have*. In this all the communities appear to be following the same pattern, not just the Scots communities and not just northern varieties, not even just the Ulster-Scots communities. Given this perspective, it is interesting to note that *be* is the primary location for NEG/AUX variability in American English (Yaeger-Dror, Hall-Lew and Deckert, 2002; Yaeger-Dror, Hall-Lew and Deckert, in press) and for early African American Vernacular English (Walker, 2001). Thus, in the grammatical environment where regional British dialects exhibit the most variation overall, so too does North American English. It is true, however, that all the Scots varieties have categorical AUX contraction with *be*, just as they would be expected to do historically. However, in contrast to what might also be expected, there is a marked contrast across the same varieties with *will* (NEG contraction in Buckie, AUX contraction in Cumnock and Culleybackey). In this case it appears that each of the Scots communities has selected one variant or the other, not a single variant across the region or variability. Finally, we have been able to pinpoint the grammatical environment (*be*) and the locales where there is variation between NEG and AUX contraction (Tiverton, Henfield, York and Maryport). In these cases, the choice of form can be explained by the influence of the preceding phonological environment.

Dialect puzzle 5.1

The discerning reader will be able to answer the following questions by carefully reading the examples and dialect excerpts in Chapter 5.

Questions

a. Find an unusual intensifying adverb.
b. Identify a particularly prominent adjective.
c. How many supertokens can you find in the examples?
d. The opposite of an intensifier is a downtoner. Find one.
e. Spot a zero plural.
f. Find an expression for having something on the stove or a task in progress.
g. Find an intensifier that modifies an adverb.
h. Find a bare habitual verb.
i. Spot an expletive.
j. Find a unique variant of 'go'.
k. Identify an instance of double negation.

Answers

a. *'Tis jolly nice, really.*
b. *Lovely*. It occurs six times in the examples in Chapter 5!
c. N = 3: *folk was/folk were*; *dry irons was/steam-irons were*; *the ones that was in the farms were there same.*
d. *Aye, I could've passed it quite easily; I could've had a job quite easy.*
e. *Five mileØ inland.*
f. *I had a pot of jam on.*
g. *I very near burnt my hand.*
h. *You Ø get a real good battering.*
i. *Haen't seen a bloody tulip yet!*
j. *She would na ging.*
k. *The driver's nae gan naewhere.*

---

6 Joining sentences

There's a good wheen of young 'uns does nae know our language.
(Molly Ellis, 89, CLB, 017)

In this chapter I examine a number of features that involve ways that words are organized in sentences and how sentences are joined together. The study of the organization of words is referred to as syntax. Syntactic variation in language is another way that dialects distinguish themselves. Variation among different word orders is a common feature that distinguishes languages of the world, but it is not typically a feature that distinguishes dialects. Nevertheless, the specific markers of linking words can often differ from one community to the next. English has many ways of joining sentences together and dialects often use different strategies from mainstream English. Moreover, the forms linking sentences together have changed considerably in the history of English.

Relative clauses

One of the most frequent ways of joining sentences together is by attaching a subordinate clause to a main clause. When the subordinate clause adds information about what is being talked about in the main clause, it is typically headed by a relative pronoun. In contemporary English the standard relative pronouns are *who*, *which*, *whose* and *whom*, as in (1), the so-called WH- forms.[1] However, at least two other forms exist: *that*, as in (2), and no marker at all, the 'zero' relative pronoun, as in (3).

(1) a. And the miner *who* was stripping this coal had nine-and-a-half pence. (CMK/037)
     b. You used to know people *who* lived opposite you. (MPT/w)
     c. We used the old nets *which* we would call strabbles. (PVG/c)

(2) a. He was the man *that* first set off the oil industry. (CMK/c)
     b. They were good herring *that* we got. (PVG/g)

(3) a. Oh the stories Ø he used to tell us about it. (CMK/H)
     b. And there's nowt Ø has t'same taste. (MPT/h)

Relative pronouns refer back to a subject or object in the main clause and have the capacity to indicate the animacy of that referent. The relative pronoun *who* is used for human or animate subjects and *which* or *that* is used for non-animates (Quirk, 1957: 97–8). However, sociolinguists have noticed that this often does not accurately describe what is going on in dialect data. Some commentators have claimed that *who* and *which* are written forms and are not actually used in spoken language (Romaine, 1982: 212). This is supported by investigations of language corpora, for example the British National Corpus (Tottie, 1997) where there is a 'paucity of WH-forms'.[2] In contrast, others researchers say that 'the WH-strategy has affected not only standard English English and American English, but nonstandard varieties as well' (Ball, 1996: 261). Such claims suggest that synchronic data from nonstandard dialects in Britain will provide an important position for understanding linguistic change in this area of grammar. The Roots Archive and the British Dialects Archive offer a unique perspective.

Bool

And what you call a bool. Maybe you do nae know a bool. That's where they kept the pipe. The old men kept the pipe in the bool. And they reached into the bool and the firelighters in the, what you called the bool, a wee hole in the fire. (Michael Adair, 74, PVG, 008)[3]

Historical perspective

English has not always had the WH- forms as relative pronouns. The original relative pronoun in English was *that*, which developed from a demonstrative pronoun (Romaine, 1982: 58; Wardale, 1937: 95). Earlier in the development of English there was also a perfectly acceptable zero variant, which was found both as object and commonly as subject of the relative clause (Fischer, 1992: 306).

The WH- forms came into English as a change from above (Nevalainen and Raumolin-Brunberg, 2002; Romaine, 1980; Tottie, 1997: 465). When they were first used as relative pronouns, they were confined to formal use, and there was 'a clear lag between the more literary texts and spoken usage' (Ball, 1996).[4] The form *who* was the last to develop (Romaine, 1980: 223) with early examples reported in 1426 (Rydén, 1983: 127). Gradually, *who* became more and more frequent for human subjects and *that* was relegated to non-human subjects. According to Ball (1996: 246–7), 'these two changes – the replacement of *which* by *who* and the assignment of *that* to nonpersonal antecedents' laid the foundation for the modern dominance of *who* for personal subject restrictive relatives. By the late nineteenth century Fowler and Fowler (1931: 80) write that there was 'formerly a tendency to use "that" for everything: the tendency now is to use "who" and "which" for everything'. According to this general trajectory, one might hypothesize that the WH- forms have taken over the system in contemporary varieties of English, even peripheral ones such as the Roots Archive.

However, there is another perspective in the literature. According to Romaine's study of Middle Scots (1982: 212), 'the infiltration of WH into the relative system can be seen as completed in the modern written language … but it has not really affected the spoken language'. Similarly, in a study of the British National Corpus, Tottie (1997: 470–1) reports that there is a 'paucity of WH-forms'. Part of the reason for the contradictory claims may be the type of data under analysis: a survey of current research reveals that most studies are based on written materials, formal and/or educated speech or standard varieties. Yet, in one of the strongest statements regarding the use of relatives in nonstandard varieties, Ball (1996: 243) claims that 'there is no vernacular norm for either British or North American English with respect to the distribution of relative markers'. Instead, she reports 'a wide range of variation both in the relative paradigm and in relative frequencies within a given regional paradigm' (Ball, 1996: 243).

In this scenario the literature presents highly contrastive claims. This makes relative markers an interesting case to explore in dialect data. Further information from the Roots Archive and the British Dialects Archive will offer a unique perspective on community-based regional norms and help to tease apart the difference between standard, written norms and vernacular, spoken data. I now turn to discovering whether or not the standard WH- forms have penetrated these dialects and, if so, how.

Ceilidh

That's right you had a ceilidh in the house. And all the light you had then maybe was a one wee oil-lamp hanging again the wall. And mind you that did nae show much light. And you gaad in round the neighbourhood and one song, somebody told a story and somebody played a bit of music. And then you had a wee bit of dancing. And whiles it was that tight in the kitchen you were kicking the peats out of the- out of the fire onto the floor. (Michael Adair, 74, PVG, 008)[5]

Methodology

The English relative pronoun system presents a diverse set of problems that must be addressed in order to analyse this feature accountably. The biggest hurdle is that English relative pronouns distribute quite differently in the two types of relative clauses – restrictive and non-restrictive. In the contemporary language, non-restrictive relative clauses are nearly always marked by *which* and *who*. In contrast, restrictives can be marked with one of the WH- forms or *that* and zero. This means that if non-restrictive clauses were to be mixed in with restrictive relative clauses it might appear to be the case that WH- forms are used a great deal. Instead, we want to focus on variation within restrictive relative clauses only.

In order to confine the analysis to restrictive relative clauses, I followed a consistent procedure based on methods adapted and honed from earlier research. All non-restrictive clauses were excluded. These include tokens where an entire sentence served as antecedent as in (4), antecedents which were a full NP, as in (5), and for which the relative clause added ancillary and/or additional information, as in (6):[6]

(4)   The whole sentence is the antecedent
       a. He had to stay wherever he – sleep wherever he worked, which meant then the wages was nae so big. (CLB/p/016)
       b. We had a doctor last week, um basic doctor from Aspatria, which was very, very interesting. (MPT/x/024)

(5)   Antecedent is a proper noun
       a. And *John-Docherty* who died fishing was there. (PVG/h/008)
       b. Wir M-P- here for many years was the late *Emrys-Hughes* who was a son-in-law of Keir Hardy. (CMK/o/015)

(6)   Additional information
       a. Look at how dramatically the accent changes say, from the north of Ireland … to the south of Ireland, which is only about, what, about four-hundred miles. (PVG/c/003)
       b. I went for mi pay, and I got twenty five bob, which is one pound twenty five today. (MPT/a/001)
       c. She had three sisters, who were all married and away. (CMK/q/017)

Following these procedures, 1,922 restrictive relative clauses were extracted from the data. Then each context was coded for a series of factors known to influence the choice of relative marker in English, including the function of the relative clause, animacy, type of subject, etc. In the following analyses, the data from Portavogie and Cullybackey are combined as the number of tokens was modest, and separate analyses showed that their patterns of use for relative markers were the same (for further discussion, see Tagliamonte et al., 2005).

Dog

The wee feller went to Belfast. And he's standing – they were standing looking at a shop window. And he turned round and he says to his ma, 'that's a nice wee dug'. So there's folk standing there, she says 'that's not a wee "dug", that's a wee "dog"'. So he says 'Well, it's terrible like a wee dug!' [004] If you go to Portaferry it'll be a 'dowg'. The Ballymena folk would talk about a 'dowg'. (Kate Devoy, 62, PVG, 004)[7]

Distributional analysis

In the Roots Archive and British Dialects Archive variation amongst relative pronouns, as in (7), is extensive.

(7)   a. So the thing *that* the local people started to do was the worse thing *that* they could possibly have done. (CMK/b)

    b. Or a Cockney git *which* is someone from – like a Scouse git. It's someone *who*'s from there. (YRK/%)

    c. There's a certain amount of people *what* just stay but generations ago … And then there's people *who*'s out for like the Bank Holiday. (TIV/b)

However, given the conflicting claims in the literature, the progress of grammatical change must be assessed. It is possible that the synchronic dialects will put the grammatical history of the WH- forms in perspective.

At the outset, it is critical to partition the data according to whether the antecedent of the relative pronoun is the subject of the subordinate clause, as in (8), or the object or direct object of the subordinate clauses, (9).

(8)   a. There were a bunch of *men* [Ø came yin day]. (CMK/d)

    b. I was the only *yan* [*who* put up with them]. (MPT/^)

    c. One o' the strongest *fellers* [*that* ever I've seen working and fit was Kevin Bell.] (PVG/h)

(9)   a. It was a *bottle* [Ø she'd made for t'vicar]. (MPT/x)

    b. The *money* [*that* they got] has made money. (CMK/d)

    c. And he sung, you know, them *songs* [*that* you would never hear now]. (CLB/l)

These two types of relative clauses have consistently been reported to pattern differently with respect to their relative pronouns due to the different propensities for human/animate nouns. Subject relatives tend to be human/animate while object and direct object relatives tend to be inanimate, as is visible in (8) and (9) (e.g. Alford, 1864: 90; Curme, 1947: 166; Denison, 1998: 278; Swan, 1995: 473).

Table 6.1 shows the distribution of relative markers in subject relative clauses categorized according to the critical semantic distinction of animacy of the antecedent NP. It shows that *that* is used more often as the relative pronoun for subject antecedents that are inanimate objects (80%). Animals pattern along with them (78%), as in (10). This shows that the constraint is human vs non-human:

(10)   a. In fact these fish here, you see these two fish *that*'s up that over there? (PVG/h)

    b. And that rats *that* were dripping out of that river was unbelievable. (CMK/A)

However, the human–thing contrast is not nearly as polarized as we might have expected it to be. In the most favoured place for the relative pronoun *who*, subject function human antecedents, as in (11), it appears only 31% of the time. When the human antecedent is the noun *people*, as in (12), there is a slightly higher frequency, 39%.

Table 6.1 *Distribution of relative markers by animacy in SUBJECT relatives*

	that		who		which		what		Ø		
	%	N	%	N	%	N	%	N	%	N	**TOTAL**
Human	**52**	408	**31**	244	**1**	6	**1**	10	**14**	112	780
People	**49**	56	**39**	45	—	0	**2**	2	**10**	11	114
Collectives (Human)	**78**	25	13	4	**3**	1	—	0	**6**	2	32
Animals	**78**	18	—	0	**4**	1	—	0	**17**	4	23
Things	**80**	343	**1**	0.2	**9**	38	**1**	4	**10**	41	427
total		850		294		46		16		170	1376

(11) a. The miner *who* was stripping this coal had nine-and-a-half pence. (CMK/K)
      b. And there was army captain *who* was boss. (PVG/r)
      c. I was only yan *who* put up with them. (MPT/^)

(12) a. The people *who* go up there I would say, maybe don't get downtown. (PVG/£)
      b. Most people *who* never heard of it you know just would hardly believe it. (CMK/K)

Unexpectedly, given prescriptive grammars, human subjects are marked with *that* the majority of the time (52%), as in (13).

(13) a. See thon wee woman *that* was his wife (CMK/K)
      b. And where would you get a woman *that* could milk the cow? (CLB/a)
      c. I had an auntie *that* was a dressmaker. (MPT/t)

I now consider whether this pattern is true of every community in the archive. Figure 6.1 shows the distribution of *who* in human subject relative clauses, this time separating each of the communities in the archive individually.

It is evident that *that* dominates the system across communities. The WH-form *who* is infrequent. Even in this restricted place in the grammar (subject relative clauses – the context where *who* is prescribed by contemporary grammar books), it never reaches 50% of the data. Notice the dramatic cross-variety distribution. Two locations – York and Wheatley Hill – exhibit an obvious difference in frequency from the others. Recall now that *who* came into English grammar as a change associated with formal language and written styles. A striking difference that contrasts York and Wheatley Hill from the other locations is their urban orientation. York is a small city. Wheatley Hill, on the other hand, is within easy reach of Durham, a small city, as well as being not far from the large urban centre of Newcastle upon Tyne.

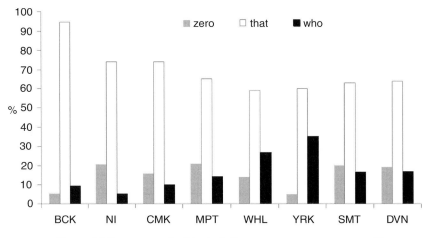

Figure 6.1 Frequency of subject relative pronouns across communities

Walking to Durham

[013] I've walked them roads when it's been snow and you know when it's turned to slush and it's frozen, the roads have been bumpy. I've walked them everyday. I wouldn't stay in. And then of course when I come up here, it never bothered me. I used to walk to Durham you know a lot. (Ellie Beck, 72, WHL, 013)[8]

The use of *who* in these communities can be put into further perspective by comparing the frequency of *who* in other studies in England. Table 6.2 summarizes the available information on the frequency of *who* in subject relative clauses in other British communities.[9]

Table 6.2 demonstrates that the relevant correlation for use of *who* is the type of data. Every sample comprising educated, urban varieties in England has heightened rates of *who*. It is quite clear that there is no overarching north–south divide because the southern, but *non-urban*, rural communities of Suffolk and Dorset have no *who*. They pattern precisely as the British Dialects Archive data for Tiverton (Devon) and Wincanton (Somerset). These results starkly highlight the correlation of *who* with the standard language.

Let us now consider the other less-common subject relative pronoun, zero, which appears as a low frequency variant in all communities, except York. This form has long been attested in English, but is considered nonstandard by contemporary grammars. Many researchers have noted that subject zero relatives tend to be found in certain types of sentence constructions. Existentials in particular, as in (14), are often attested as favouring zero, as are clefts, whether with *it*, as in (15), or *that* as in (16). The same is true of sentences with possessive *have* or *got*, as in (17).

Table 6.2 *Overall frequency of* who *in subject relatives in England and Scotland*

Variety under investigation	Type of data	% *who*
Standard British English (Quirk, 1957)	Educated spoken	91
Standard British English (Tottie, 1997: 467)	London-Lund Corpus	91
Standard British English (Sanders, 2002)	Standard spoken, does not include existentials or clefts	72
Reading (SW England) (Cheshire, 1982: 73)	Conversational data from urban working-class adolescents	57
Tyneside (NE England) (Beal and Corrigan, 2002: 127–8)	Conversational data from different socio-economic classes and age groups, 1960s and 1994	52
Ayr (Macaulay, 1991)	Conversational data with lower- and middle-class Scots	48
Ulster (Geisler, 2002: 137)	NITC corpus; combines different ages, sex, occupation and location	29
Suffolk (Peitsara, 2002:174)	Conversational data from old, rural, working-class speakers in early 1970s	15
Dorset (van den Eynden Morpeth and Hogeschool, 2002: 182)	Conversational data from old, rural, working-class speakers, 1985–1987	9
Ayr, south-west Scotland (Macaulay, 1991)	Conversational data lower-class Scots	1.6

(14)   Existentials
 a. There was a woman Ø lived at the end of the row, and she was as good to us as a friend. (CLB/l)
 b. There was a body Ø I was just talking to t'other day. (MPT/h)
 c. Aye, there's still a odd yin of them Ø goes on yet. (CLB/t)

Cleft sentences
(15)   a. But in them days it was two fiddles Ø supplied the music to the dance. (CLB/h)
 b. No, it was Sonia Ø fainted before. (PVG/i)
 c. I thought Willy was bad you know … you know it was nae everybody Ø knowed it you know. (CLB/i)

(16)   a. That was whole trailer Ø used to run for mayor for Siddick. (MPT/r)
 b. And that's the same people Ø has been here since. (CLB/m)

(17)   Possessives (with *have, got*)
 a. I had an aunt Ø lived down the street. (MPT/s)
 b. I've a niece Ø stays in Aberdeen too. (CMK/d)
 c. We had a man Ø led that strike. (CMK/p)

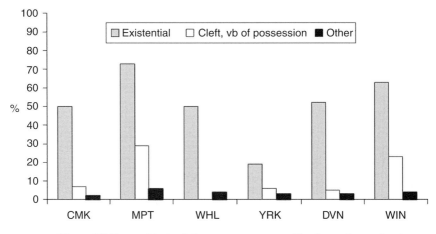

Figure 6.2 Zero subject relatives across communities by sentence structure

Figure 6.2 shows the distribution of zero subject relatives across communities according to sentence structure and exposes a remarkably consistent pattern. Each variety, whether north, south, peripheral or mainstream, shares the same underlying constraint: more zero relatives in existential constructions followed by clefts and fewer with possessive constructions. Although the use of zero relative pronouns is infrequent in some locales (e.g. York), all the varieties share the same underlying constraints on their distribution.

Let us turn now to the other side of the relative pronoun system, the non-subject relatives. Table 6.3 shows the distribution of relative pronouns in non-subject relative clauses categorized according to animacy of the antecedent NP.

Notice that inanimates (things) make up the majority of forms in this part of the system (711/869, 82%). Unlike the subject relatives, type of subject does not have any effect on non-subject relatives. The percentages of *that* use across subject types hovers between 40% and 55%. The same is true of the zero form. The difference between the two most numerous categories – human subjects, (18), and 'things', (19) – is only between 47% and 55%.

(18) a. So we picked out *the yins that* we thought would make a go of it. (CMK/B)
      b. He was *the smartest fella* Ø I've ever seen. (MPT/%)
      c. There's *animals* there *that* we would never see if there was nae a zoo. (AYR/x)
      d. We had *the best neighbours* Ø ever anybody could have. (CLB/l)

(19) a. Those are the wee *things that* you learn. (CMK/l)
      b. This *fiddle that* he had, it hung up there. (CLB/l)
      c. I suppose I done *anything* Ø I was told to do, like. (CLB/t)

Table 6.3 *Distribution of NON-SUBJECT relative markers by animacy of the antecedent NP*

	that		who		which		what		Ø		
	%	N	%	N	%	N	%	N	%	N	TOTAL
Human	**47**	56	**6**	7	**0**	0	**0**	0	47	56	119
People	**40**	6	**7**	1	**0**	0	**0**	0	53	8	15
Collectives (Human)	**55**	6	**0**	0	**0**	0	**0**	0	45	5	11
Animals	**46**	6	**0**	0	**8**	1	**8**	1	38	5	13
Things	**40**	284	**0**	0	**3**	22	**2**	14	55	391	711
total		358		8		23		15		465	869

Comparative cross-variety analysis can offer another dimension to these issues. Romaine argued that Scots in particular had lagged behind Standard English in implementing the use of the WH- relatives (Romaine, 1982: 222). While these results reported here confirm that this is true, they also reveal that the distinction between Scots and English dialects is not absolute. In fact, the differences are a matter of degree. Nowhere is this more obvious than in the comparison between Cumnock in Scotland and Maryport in England. These two varieties consistently pattern together, and this too is marked in history and present commentary:

The closeness of Lowland Scots with Northumbrian English … has remained until the present-day… (Wales, 2006: 50)

Even more striking, is the comparison between these two varieties and the south-west varieties – Somerset and Devon. This comparison reveals that it is not even the case that these northern dialects are so different from the southern dialects with respect to this feature. Cumnock, Maryport, Tiverton and Wincanton actually share many of the relevant patterns: all of them use *that* more than the more mainstream (and standard) variety spoken in York, and all of them use zero relatives more. Moreover, the ranking of the major constraints that operate on these markers is parallel across them. The real difference is between York and Wheatley Hill and everywhere else, whether north or south. Thus, instead of a Scots–English split, or a north–south split, these results reveal that it is the relative proximity of the dialects to mainstream norms that matters. Moreover, just as Romaine argues for placement of the different styles/registers of Scots at different points along the continuum of change (Romaine, 1982: 241), I suggest that the same may be done for the different dialects of British English studied here. Each one of them may be placed at a different point along the continuum of change based on their relative degree of participation in ongoing changes in English (Tagliamonte and Smith, 2000). From this perspective, the WH- words are a long way from taking over the relative marker system in the vernacular language, if in fact they ever will.

In sum, the trajectory of linguistic change in the (written) historical record (e.g. Ball, 1996) made it *appear* that the WH- forms were the favoured forms in English and would eventually become the dominant relative markers. However, the results presented here show that the spoken language (in this case vernacular dialects – in the Roots Archive and the British Dialects Archive) steadfastly resist that trajectory. The vernacular maintains *that* and zero for restrictive relative clauses, while *who* and *which* are relegated to other uses, such as non-restrictive relative clauses, as in (20).

(20) a. He took one wheel and I took another one and let the wheels down, you know what I mean, like, *which* is not a nice thing to do. (CLB/018)
       b. [028] You're holidaying and stuff as well, *which* is great. (CMK/028)

Fettle

I was of bad fettle I'll tell you. Sick, poorly, and of course I couldn't see and everything was – but talk about getting looked-after! If I fancied an apple, they would grate it up so that I hadn't to chew it, Cos eh, they were marvellous, weren't they? (Brian Marshman 72, MPT, 032)

I was of bad fettle … And my manager said, 'Get yourself away yam' … I got up pit, went in t'bath, got washed, changed, come yam … Surgery was in where t'vet's is now … 'Twas young Doctor Rafferty I seen. He says, 'Take them' he says, 'I think they'll fettle you up.' (Keith Price, 89, MPT. 018)[10]

What does the use of a relative pronoun tell us about dialects?

Let us return to the conflicting claims in the literature introduced earlier. We would like to know how far the encroachment of the WH- words into the English relative pronoun system has gone. These results provide confirmation of Romaine's claim that it 'has not really affected the spoken language' (1982: 12). These findings, coupled with Tottie's (1997) research on the British National Corpus demonstrate that the use of WH- forms in British English has not entirely permeated the standard spoken language either, not simply in Scots, but in every community we have examined. If so, then perhaps the spoken vernacular has been lagging behind the written standard for quite a long time.

The scarcity of WH- forms in the dialect data is almost certainly the product of general 'distance' from changes taking place in mainstream varieties. As Romaine (1982: 151) suggests, WH- entered the language in syntactically complex structures such as oblique and genitive. At the outset, this suggests a correlation with learned writing and this is confirmed in the findings of historical data (e.g. Hope, 1994; Nevalainen and Raumolin-Brunberg, 2002;

Rissanen, 1984; Tottie and Harvie, 2000). In the communities studied here, WH- forms are an overlay from outside the vernacular grammar, and they are essentially foreigners. In other words, the scant number of WH- forms in the dialect did not result from language-internal processes, but are impositions from above. They may never be adopted wholesale into the vernacular in these locales. Indeed, given these findings, it may well be the case that *that* never shifted away from personal subjects in these varieties in the first place. Instead, it is still holding its own as the universal relative marker (Baugh, 1935: 296).

Finally, these findings provide support for an important distinction in linguistic change – those changes that are imposed from the outside (like the WH- relative markers) and those that arise from within (like the *that* and zero relative markers) proceed very differently in mainstream vs peripheral varieties. The relative marker system provides a particularly good example of this. Indeed, these findings demonstrate how resistant the vernacular can be in the face of 'extraneous' (Dekeyser, 1984: 76) standard norms.

Thimbles

[004] What's your wee birds? [008] Eh? [004] What's your wee birds? Is it birds? [008] No, them's thimbles. (Kate Devoy, 62 and Jim Baird, 66, PVG)[11]

Complement clauses

Another common construction involving the link between two sentences is a complement clause, which begins with a function word called a complementizer or subordinating conjunction. In English the most common complementizer is *that*. However, in contemporary English *that* is not required. In fact, most of the time it does not occur. In some cases, *that* alternates with a zero variant, Ø, as in (21).

(21)   a. Somebody *told me* here lately Ø the trees is all cut down at the back …
          Somebody *told me that* the Macneils was up again for sale. (CLB/q)
       b. *I wish that* forty or fifty years ago I'd as much confidence. *I wish* Ø I'd had it then. (MPT/@)

Synchronic perspective

This phenomenon has been studied in written as well as spoken materials. Rates of zero are overwhelmingly high for spoken data. For example, Thompson and Mulac (1991a) found zero in up to 90% of the speech of North American university students,[12] and Walker and Cacoullos (2003) found zero in over 90% of instances of Canadian English (Poplack and Walker, 2002, 2003).[13] Research on written data, on the other hand, reports considerably lower rates of zero, and thus high rates of *that*. In a study of written American English (c. 1961), Elsness

(1984) reports a little over 1% occurrences of zero in some cases.[14] Learned science writing has 1.3%; however, in letters and biography, this rises to 14.6%, and there is another substantial rise with newspaper articles and fiction – 52.1% and 58.1% respectively. These regular increments according to level of formality of the written genre show that this linguistic feature – like the WH- relative pronouns – is highly sensitive to the nature of the language material.

Contemporary studies have two explanations for the zero variant: (1) It is the result of grammaticalization of collocations such as *I think*, *you know*, *I mean* into adverbial expressions where no complementizer is required, and (2) It is the result of complexity such that *that* only appears when the sentence structure has an increased cognitive load. According to the first hypothesis, the subject-matrix verb collocations produced by omitting the complementizer, e.g. *I think Ø I can*, gradually evolved into a phrase, e.g. *I think*, which is used for a different meaning (Thompson and Mulac, 1991a, 1991b). Phrases such as *I think*, *you know* or *I mean* come to be used as 'parenthetical expressions' that mark a speaker's judgements about the possibility that something is or is not the case, as in (22). In essence they have become verbs expressing belief (Fischer, 2007).

(22) a. *I think Ø* it was just the threat of it … (MPT/x)
      b. *You know Ø* John Thompson'll preach the gospel to you a lot and all the rest but never listen. (CLB/f)

According to the second hypothesis, the overriding factor conditioning the appearance of *that* is the complexity of the surrounding linguistic context (Rohdenburg, 1998). The overt complementizer is preferred in contexts with past tense or modals, as in (23a), with a noun phrase subject rather than a pronoun, as in (23b), or both (23c), with negation, as in (23d), and when there are intervening adverbials or other material between the subject and verb, as in (23e–f).

(23) a. He *said that* he was a boot and shoe repairer. (MPT/b)
      b. My Uncle Willy *says that* Willie McClemence was one o' the cleverest men ever he sailed with. (PVG/c)
      c. Mi father *said that* in the night time I started with a crow like a rooster. (CLB/l)
      d. I did nae *realize that* you booked your bed. (CMK/o)
      e. I *telt* you [a while ago] *that* they shut the shop too. (CMK/d)
      f. I still *say* [till this day] *that* people are too clean. (MPT/h)

The key difference between these two explanations is their underlying assumptions. The first assumes a diachronic development in which parenthetical expressions developed out of matrix-verb collocations in complement clauses. The second assumes no developmental trajectory, but rests solely on the nature of the context. The next step is to turn to the historical record for insight.

Definition

Grammaticalization is a process that changes lexical words into functional parts of the grammar (e.g. Hopper and Traugott, 1993), in this case a change from a matrix subject + complement clause, *I think that you are nice*, into an adverbial expression, *You're nice, I think; you are, I think, nice*, which expresses the speaker's point of view.

Varnish

I've tried a lot of different types of varnishes. Different types of stains. You have to stain the wood too like. You can stain it till a dark or lighter colour like. I like the lightness like you know. Seemed to be better. (Alec Murray, 88, CLB, 018)[15]

Historical perspective

Use of complementizer *that* has changed radically from Old English to the present day (Palander-Collin, 1997; Rissanen, 1991; Warner, 1982). In Old English, *that* is almost categorical (Mitchell, 1985: 1,976ff.). In the Wycliffe Sermons (c. 1382) 98% of the complement clauses are marked with *that* (Warner, 1982). However, by Late Middle English, there is robust variation with the zero variant and by Early Modern English zero is common (Palander-Collin, 1997; Rissanen, 1991).

A critical backdrop for the diachronic trajectory of this change comes from the Helsinki Corpus (Kytö, 1993a). Two major studies of this feature (Palander-Collin, 1997; Rissanen, 1991) reveal that four high-frequency verbs, *know*, *think*, *say* and *tell*, all increased in tandem between Late Middle English (1350) and Early Modern English (1710). However, examination of Middle English reveals that the most frequently occurring parentheticals at that time, e.g. *gesse*, *level*, *undertake* 'guess, believe, undertake', do not occur most frequently with zero (Brinton, 1996). This reveals that the tendency towards zero in parenthetical expressions may differ from one point in history to another. Moreover, parenthetical expressions of earlier centuries are unlikely to be entirely the same as those in the early 2000s. It is not even clear that we have sufficient knowledge of what earlier expressions of this type would have been like in the spoken vernacular. Nevertheless, Rissanen (1991: 283–4) shows that 'speech related text types' such as trial records and comedies show higher rates of zero when compared to more formal writing genres such as scientific and educational treatises. This means that the effect of register has been around for a long time and is not a recent development.

In sum, the combined findings from studies of complement clauses, both written and spoken data, contemporary and historical, offer the following perspectives on the use of zero: First, there is a noteworthy increase in use of zero over time. Second, in historical and contemporary data alike there is evidence of considerable variation by genre. In contemporary studies, where both written and spoken English can be studied, the frequency of zero is much higher in spoken data. Third, lexical verbs involved in parenthetical expressions appear to differ from one time to another and may be sensitive to register as well. It is not certain that we have comprehensive knowledge of the colloquial parenthetical expressions from times past.

Hymns

[032] I love all hymns. [033] Aye, I do, tha knows. Old hymns, anyway. I love them all. I really div. Now that's summat else. (Violet Marshman, 71, and Brian Marshman 72 MPT, 032, 033)[16]

Given the findings from the Roots Archive, we can expect that the communities will reflect an earlier stage in the history of English. If complement clauses are gradually evolving towards more uses of zero based on the grammatical development of parenthetical expressions, then there should be evidence to support this in the data. If complement clauses are marked under conditions of complexity, then the communities should pattern in tandem.

Methodology

From the archive materials, we extracted all matrix + complement constructions which appeared to be complement clauses. Such tokens are indicated as 'included' in (24). A typical facet of spoken language, however, is how to distinguish the parenthetical expressions from the matrix subject + verb collocations of a complement clause. We know from previous research that verbs such as *think*, *say* and *know* are typical contemporary parentheticals (Thompson and Mulac, 1991a, 1991b). Because they function as adverbials (Thompson and Mulac, 1991a: 239–40), they can appear in numerous different locations in a sentence. When we found these verbs in contexts other than the usual complement clause contexts, we excluded them, indicated as 'not included' in (24) (Thompson and Mulac, 1991a: 241). These types never occurred with a complementizer, obviously, since they are no longer functioning as matrix subject + verb collocations.

(24) a. [021] I *think* [included] he met me, actually, yeah. [Interviewer] Right. How did you come across one another? [021] Well, I was sitting in the – I would be about twenty-five, *I think*, [not included] and I was sitting in the Empire Theatre in Maryport, on my own, watching the picture. (CMK/021)

  b. [019] I *think* [included] she won the Waterloo Cup of some big, prestigious thing. I hae nae much an idea about greyhound-racing, but – We called the old boat Silver Anna. She was an old [included], *I think* [not included]. She stood about two birds clear of the water. (MPT/019)

Table 6.4 *Low frequency (<15%)* that *constructions by verb*

Verb	%	N	Total N
mean	1.6	1	450
suppose	3.0	2	67
think	3.1	45	1,450
know	4.9	36	736
mind 'remember'	5.6	3	54
sure	7.0	4	57
remember	7.1	5	70
wish	8.8	3	34
All 'believe' type verbs	3.6	105	2,918
say	14.5	95	653
All other verbs	31.8	169	532

c. [002] Sure, even the people in the south o' this island *I think* [not included] really, if they were getting without being intimidated and all, they would hae went in under the Commonwealth. You know. I *think* [included] they would. (PVG/002)

In all, this procedure provided over 4,102 tokens of matrix subject + verb collocations in canonical complement clause contexts. Each token was then coded for various predictors implicated in the variable presence of *that* in the literature.

Reapers
Very seldom people had reapers, you know … We were lifting thon sheafs yet high and gathering them up high. (Patrick Kelly, 84, CLB, 009)[17]

Distributional analysis

Even with this stringent practice for discarding parenthetical expressions outside of the canonical subject + verb cases, we discovered that subject + verb combinations in complement clause contexts were nearly entirely zero. Table 6.4 shows the verbs with less than 15% occurrences of *that* ordered according to increasing frequency of the complementizer. The bottom of the table shows the subtotal of all these verbs, then the frequent verb *say*, and then all other verbs in the sample for comparison.

Table 6.4 illustrates the dearth of constructions that have an overt complementizer – the overall rate of *that* is only 9%. This means that 91% of the data is zero, precisely the same proportion reported in North American studies (Thompson and Mulac, 1991a; Torres-Cacoullos and Walker, 2009b). This is the first indication that there is no change over time, at least not recently.

It is obvious, however, that there are very different rates of zero according to lexical verb. So-called 'believe type' verbs in this data include *mean, suppose, mind* and *remember*, as in (25). These are overwhelmingly zero and all exhibit the predicted function of expressing the speaker's belief or attitude.

(25)   a. Made your own fun, aye. I *mean* there were nae television. (CMK/E)
       b. I *suppose* they hae to stay with him all night too? (CLB/q)
       c. I *think* you got them with tea-coupons at ya time. (MPT/d)
       d. So you *know* there's cleaning up to do. (MPT/n)
       e. I *mind* I catched them up in the kitchen and took them in the room. (CLB/a)
       f. 'Are you *sure* you want to go?' Oh I says 'aye'. (CMK/O)
       g. I can *remember* she used to sing them. (MPT/t)
       h. You *wish* now you'd listened more. (CLB/v)

In contrast, the frequent verb *say* has moderate rates of *that* (14.5%) and retains its lexical meaning of reported events, as in (26).

(26)   a. They *say that* these ancient folk lived on small burns and the burns were teeming with fish. (CMK/A)
       b. I *said that* I would have a go. (CLB/f)

The remaining verbs have substantially more occurrences of *that*, 31.8%, as in (27). Here too the lexical meaning of each matrix verb endures.

(27)   a. He *was surprised that* Bob Cahoon had sent this down and it would nae work. (CMK/A)
       b. I *forget that* I's old. (MPT/k)
       c. Well I says I'll *vie that* it'll come. (CLB/f)

The next step is to view how these verb types pattern across communities. This is shown in Figure 6.3, which shows that the pattern of use of *that* by verb type is exactly parallel across communities. 'Believe' type verbs rarely occur with *that*. The verb *say* has modest rates, while the large group of 'other' verbs show the highest frequency. Note the heightened frequency of *that* in York. Table 6.5 probes this community a little deeper by examining the use of the three verb types by speaker sex – typically a good litmus test for formality/style distinctions. Women, on average, tend to use more formal language and more standard forms than men (Labov, 2001).

Table 6.5 reveals that neither 'believe' type verbs nor the verb *say* are affected by the sex of the speaker. However, with other verbs there is a conspicuous distinction: females are much more likely to use *that*. Given the sociolinguistic principle that females tend to use more prestige features than males (Labov, 2001: 266), this pattern provides another bit of evidence to suggest that the use of *that* is triggered not only by complexity, but also by formality. However, in 'believe' type verbs and the verb *say* there are different factors involved.

Table 6.5 *Distribution of* that *by verb type and speaker sex in York*

	'believe' type verbs		*say*		Other verbs	
	%	N	%	N	%	N
Female	10	755	26	140	65	227
Male	8	500	26	111	41	267

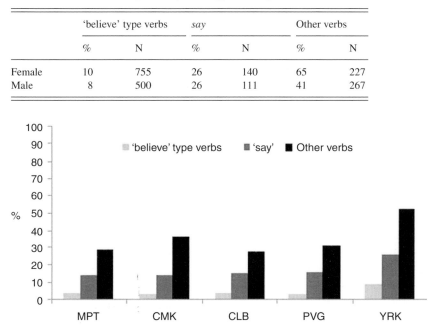

Figure 6.3 Proportion of *that* by verb type across communities

I now consider whether the 'believe' type verbs, which we might construe as the quintessential parenthetical, have increased over time. One way to test this possibility is to examine whether their frequency shifts across communities. Figure 6.4 shows the total number of 'believe' type collocations in each community. If it was the development of these constructions that spearheaded the development of zero generally, then there should be evidence of this in the geographic distribution.

Figure 6.4 makes plain that the proportion of parentheticals does not vary from one locale to the other just as the proportion of zero overall did not vary. From the most remote fishing villages in Northern Ireland to the urban centre of York the proportion of zero is the same.

What does the use of a complementizer tell us about dialects?

Unlike the other features investigated so far, the frequency and use of complementizer *that* is the same across the communities. This result is particularly telling in light of the fact that in most cases the Roots communities have shown dramatic differences and these have been interpretable as the more insular

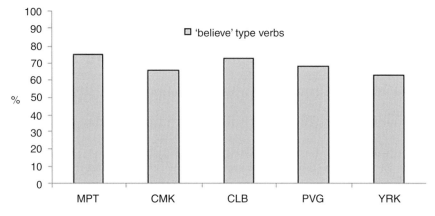

Figure 6.4 Proportion of 'believe' type verbs across communities

varieties retaining older forms and constructions. Given the startling surge towards zero over the past several hundred years, we might have expected these conservative dialects to retain greater use of *that*, but they do not. It is also possible that the comparison itself is flawed. All the historical studies are, of course, based on written data, while the synchronic dialect data is spoken and highly vernacular. Thus, the diachronic and synchronic data may not be comparable at all, but represent highly divergent types of language.

What the dialect data clearly does demonstrate is that there is a consistent frequency and a regular pattern for the zero complementizer according to the nature of the verb. The relatively rare instances of *that* occur in contexts where the subject, the verb phrase and the syntactic structure are complex. This provides evidence to suggest that the so-called parenthetical expressions are not the same, but represent independent developments. Further, it may be the case that the historical development tracked in written data was a change in the nature of these registers over time rather than a change in the system of the language.

Slippy

[020] When I was working in Ballymoney in the wintertime it was too far. I rid the bike different times to Ballymoney and that's about fourteen miles for Clough. [3] For your work? [020] Aye. to mi work. But then went to Glarryford Station in the wintertime went down and whiles you got it and whiles you did nae because the roads was slippy. You're oftener on the ground than what you were on the bike. (Jack Nesbitt, 78, CLB, 020) [18]

Clauses of purpose, reason and result

English uses clauses headed by adverbs in order to express purpose, reason and result. Purpose clauses are used to explain the purpose of an action. The most common type of purpose clause is marked by a *to*, which is called the infinitive. In formal writing other adverbs may occur such as *in order to* or *so as to*. Reason clauses are used to answer the question 'Why?' These are introduced by the conjunctions *because*, *as* or *since*. Result clauses are used to explain the result of an action or situation. Result clauses are introduced by conjunctions such as *so*, *so that*, or *such that*. The adverbs that signal these meanings are also called connectors because they link sentences (clauses) together. The adverbs that are used to make these connections may differ from one variety of English to another, and dialectal variation is often found.

In order to express purpose, contemporary Standard English uses the adverbs *because*, *since*, *as*, *as long as*. Notice that these words are all more or less synonyms of 'because', which originally meant 'by cause'. An interesting feature of the Roots Archive is that *for* is often used for this meaning as well, as in (28).

(28)   a. I had to stack his bed yesterday morning and change it *for* he was soaking. (PVG/x)
       b. We're maybe no as bad as Glasgow and some of the cities, but er – *for* I think everything in moderation. (CMK/y)
       c. Well, says I, 'you'll have to marry, Willie, *for* you can't stay with me all your life because you need your life to live'. (CLB/x)

Synchronic perspective

In twenty-first-century English usage, use of *for* to mean 'because' is considered formal and literary (Quirk and Greenbaum, 1973: 294). Indeed grammarians argue whether it is still part of the standard language or not. Among the commentators who accept *for* as a causal connector, the rules of usage dictate that it cannot be used in first position, and must only come last in the ordering of clauses.

Historical perspective

The causal conjunctive use of *for* is actually a very old variant for marking causal clauses. It can be traced back to the earliest stages of English. According to Rissanen (1983, 1998b), it may have emerged in northern varieties due to the close contact between Scotland and France in the fifteenth century. From the eighteenth century onwards *because* increases in frequency while the variant *for* recedes (Rissanen, 1983: 399).[19] Indeed, use of its usurper, *because*, is considered 'the most dramatic innovation' in the marking of causal clauses in Middle English.

Fadge

[008] But in them days you know ... there were plenty of spuds. That's one thing that wasn't rationed, you could've got them. Mi mother used to bake the fadge. And whiles

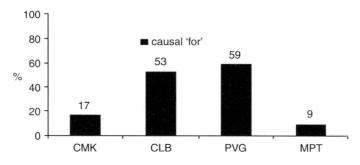

Figure 6.5 Frequency of causal connector *for* across communities

there she would've got oatmeal and she'd've baked the oatmeal bread and the peat fire there she would've set the peat in front of the fire and set the wee farls out oaten-bread to dry them. (Rob Paisley, 78, CLB, 008)[20]

Mammy went out with a big – fresh bran was white – and she went out and filled her big basin full of that white bran and she baked that bran bread. And the next thing then was ordinary soda-bread and the next thing was pancakes and she baked any potatoes that was left of the dinner, the fadge. She would bake fadge for that. So that's what we were bred on. (Martin Gonne, 86, CLB, 015)

Methodology

In order to analyse the use of *for* as a causal connector in the Roots Archive, all the instances of *because* and *for* – the two markers of cause and effect in the data – were extracted. This amounted to 1,090 tokens, which, not surprisingly, were overwhelmingly marked with *because* (69.3%). Nevertheless, the *for* variant represents just over 30% of the data, 335 tokens.

Distributional analysis

Figure 6.5 shows the proportion of causal connector *for* out of all the contexts in which either *for* or *because* was possible. The frequency of *for* in Cullybacky and Portavogie is considerable, over 50% of all the causal clauses. In Maryport and Cumnock, however, the use of the older form has substantially retreated, with Cumnock retaining almost twice as many as Maryport.

   The next task is to test whether the use of *for* patterns in accordance with prescriptive discussions, namely that *for* can only be used in non-initial position in the clause structure. Figure 6.6 partitions the clauses according to type, whether initial, as in (29a), middle, as in (29b), or last, as in (29c). If the

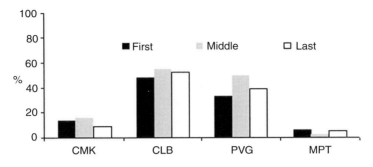

Figure 6.6 Distribution of *for* according to location in sentence

descriptions in contemporary grammars are correct, *for* should be preferred in last position and rarely, if it occurs at all, in initial position.

(29)   a. I says 'And the rats is in legions at back o' the wall,' I says 'and thank God for them. *For* they were nae there, there'd be a plague,' I says '*For* they help to get up all the old offal and all that's dumped.' (PVG/g)
       b. I decided to pack it up, which was a very big – probably the biggest decision of my life *for* I was in love with it. It was a love story, like.
       c. Aye, you'd better watch yourself on the roads Margaret *for* they're so danger-ous. (CLB/e)

Figure 6.6 reveals that there is no pattern to the use of *for* according to the nature of the clause order. It is nearly as likely to occur in first position as any other.

Kye

I was nae just fourteen. I was milking cows night and day ken. Aye, you'd learn to milk kye, ken. Aye, and er, this is afore they got a milk machine in. (Kirsty Campbell, 69, CMK, 005)[21]

What does the use of a conjunction tell us about dialects?

In this case, the distributional results clearly pinpoint the Northern Ireland communities as being the locus of retention undistinguished by location. Cumnock and Maryport have far less, indicating that these varieties have moved further towards the now standard form *because*; however, there is a difference in that Cumnock retains more of the conservative variant than Maryport. Taken in conjunction with the frequency of verbal –*s* (Figures 5.1, 5.2. and 5.3), we can interpret the distributional pattern Northern Ireland → Cumnock → Maryport as a straightforward proximity to mainstream usage trajectory. This result coupled with the historical trajectory described by Rissanen (1983, 1998b) suggests that the use of conjunctive *for* in the Roots Archive is a straightforward retention of an older form.

For to infinitive

In order to express purpose, contemporary Standard English uses the adverbs *to*, *in order to*, *so as to*. An interesting feature of the Roots Archive is that *for to*, as in (30), and even *for* is used for this meaning as well, as in (31).

(30) a. I need to have a bike *for to* get the job. (CMK/O)
      b. And I washed nine baskets of prittas every day and them was boilt *for to* feed everything. (CLB/a)
      c. They got in the cage *for to* come up the mine. (MPT/¢)

(31) Oh, you had two days in the week for that. *For* learn to sew and learn to knit, you did. (CLB/e)

Synchronic perspective

The use of *for to* as an infinitival marker is fairly widely reported in Scots and Irish dialects, where it is considered a preservation of a historical complement structure (e.g. Beal, 1993; Edwards and Weltens, 1985; Henry, 1995; Macafee, 1983; Macaulay, 1991).

Examination of the British Dialects Archive uncovered a few tokens of *for to*, outside of these core areas, in both northern and southern England, as in (32)–(33). This suggests it is a lingering form across regions.

(32) a. He'd light a furnace *for to* wash the clothes. (TIV/a)
      b. Jobs took five times as long but you had the labour *to* do it. (TIV/I)

(33) a. I was called up *for to* go and get a medical. (WHL/c)
      b. They've got the money *to* pay the debts. (WHL/k)

This feature is also mentioned in the inventories provided by Schneider (2004) and Hickey (2004), though not as a diagnostic. Patterns of *for to* use distinguish contemporary dialects. Henry (1995) categorizes varieties by type based on usage patterns of *for to* – weak and strong. In weak *for to* dialects, *for to* is used in purpose clauses only, with the sense of *in order to*, *so as to*. She claims that these dialects are more widespread and common, and most individuals who use *for to* use it with purpose meaning, e.g. Glasgow, as in (34) (Finlay, 1988; Macafee, 1983: 51).

(34) You don't need to faw ten thoosand feet *for to* to get killt. (Macaulay, 1991: 106, 239)

In strong *for to* dialects, on the other hand, *for to* is used as an alternative to *to* in a wider range of infinitival clauses. Henry, for example, notes that in Belfast it has an extremely wide range of uses, including exclamations, e.g. *for to tell her like that!*, subject position, *for to pay the mortgage is difficult*, and in various other contexts (Henry, 1995: 83). As is typical, variation is

the norm. People who use *for to* will typically use the standard construction as well (Henry, 1995: 85). However, the fact that it only occurs among
the lower class in places where it is used at all (Macaulay, 1991: 106) suggests that certain sectors of the population are more likely to retain older
features.

In for it

And if you were outside you done something wrong and somebody says 'I'll tell thee
father' … 'Cos er you thought, 'oh if he gas yam and tells my father I's in for it' you
know. (Jack Dobson, 66, MPT, 025)[22]

Historical perspective

Variable use of adverbs of purpose (i.e. *for to* and *for*) has been a longitudinal
feature of English and, according to Warner (1982: 166), had strong contextual
conditioning. *For to* is 'selected especially in adjuncts, in other particular constructions and by certain verbs'. The favoured verbs include *caste, conforte,
constreyen, desire, flee, longe, marke, shame, stire* and *take* (Warner, 1982:
166). Although there is a historically attested correlation of *for to* with purpose
adjuncts, Warner suggests that this is due to the fact that purpose adjuncts are
very frequent in general (Warner, 1982: 126). Thus, it is important to take into
account that *for to* can be used in non-purpose clauses as well. This is particularly true of earlier stages of English, as non-purpose uses can be easily found
in literary works, as in (35)

(35)   By all their influences you may as well / Forbid the sea *for to* obey the moon.
       (Shakespeare, *Winter's Tale*, I, 2.551)

Distributional analysis

In the British Dialects Archive this form was very rare. In Tiverton, there were
only three tokens, in Wheatley Hill eight. Everywhere else, *for to* is non-existent. In the Roots Archive several communities had substantially more tokens
(N = 90) – Maryport, Cullybackey and Cumnock. Table 6.6 shows the use of
for to out of all *to* infinitive clauses in these communities. The table reveals
that *for to*, despite numerous examples across communities, is fading away.
It becomes interesting to ask about the vitality of a form that has receded
into this advanced stage of obsolescence. We do not know if a linguistic
feature dies out one person at a time or in all people equally. Further, we
do not know if a linguistic feature dies out in one context at a time or in all
contexts equally. In some cases obsolescent features have been shown to
retain linguistic conditioning (e.g. Jones and Tagliamonte, 2004), in others
the constraints have deteriorated (Wolfram and Schilling-Estes, 1995). A first

Table 6.6 *Distribution of* for to *infinitive across varieties*

MPT		CLB		CMK	
%	N	%	N	%	N
2	49/2,773	1	12/1,440	1	23/2,423

Table 6.7 *Diffusion of* for to *in each community.*

MPT		CLB		CMK	
%	N	%	N	%	N
46	18/39	41	7/17	15	6/40

step is to check the distribution by individuals in the community. Table 6.7 shows the number of individuals in each community who actually use the form.

In Maryport and Cullybackey it is widely diffused to close to half the individuals, but relatively few individuals use it in Cullybackey. This suggests that a concomitant of obsolescence is a dwindling use of the form across the population.

A second step is to conduct a distributional analysis that will expose contextual patterning. Recall that descriptions of the *for to* infinitive point to a distinction between purpose vs non-purpose contexts. Figure 6.7 tests this pattern in the data.

The frequency of use is extremely small. Nevertheless, this exercise reveals that *for to* is retained precisely in the contexts where it has long been attested – purpose clauses. The only community that retains uses other than purpose clauses is Maryport although the numbers were very small indeed (N = 25), as in (36).

(36)   a. Joyce made the decision *for to* have this one. (MPT/¢)
       b. It was just a case of walking round and checking that lads had permit *for to* fish. (MPT/h)
       c. They picked three choirs out *for to* sing out at night. (MPT/u)

What does the use of an infinitive marker tell us about dialects?

The extreme rarity of the form makes it difficult to determine whether the (small) intercommunity differences are the result of actual dialect differences or simply the lingering use of a dying form.

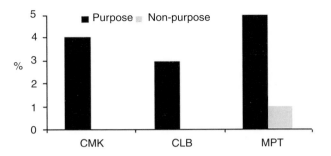

Figure 6.7 Descriptions of the *for to* infinitive in purpose and non-purpose contexts

Dialect death

It was a sad thing because the dialect was dying out, as they say … and you would carry on talking that way, because the dialect was dying out. You know you were calling your mother-in-law then you'd say yan, you dinnae say 'twa', that's no 'echt', you know, it's no 'seeven'. You know, this is when you were counting. Although the 'yan' would be used more here than er the 'twa', but it was 'yan, twa, three, far', you know, four. 'Five, six, seeven and echt.' (Dan James, 64, PVG)[23]

Dialect puzzle 6.1

The discerning reader will be able to find the following items by carefully reading the examples and dialect excerpts in Chapter 6.

Questions

a. Find a sentence with double intensification.
b. Find a sentence with two different intensifiers.
c. How many supertokens can you find?
d. Provide three terms for male individual(s).
e. Find an unusual adverb placement for *ever*.
f. List three nonstandard verb forms.
g. Find a cleft.
h. Find a sentence-final *like*.
i. Identify a dialect word for *nothing*.
j. Spot an indefinite pronoun with the ending *–one*.

Answers

a. *… which was very very interesting.*
b. *I think if it's terribly bright, awful bright sun, it's no so good.* (CMK/i)
c. Supertokens N = 2: (1) *git which; someone who;* (2) *people what … people who*
d. *feller, chap, men*
e. *one o' the cleverest men ever he sailed with …*

f. *catched, boilt, knowed*
g. *For to learn to sew and learn to knit, you did.*
h. *It was a love story, like.*
i. *Nowt, And there's nowt Ø has t'same taste.*
j. *Someone. It's someone who's from there.*

7   Time, necessity and possession

> I suppose everybody else has their own dialect so we've got our own little
> dialect so.
>
> (Barry Brandon, DUR, 010)[1]

In this chapter I examine a number of features that involve the way people talk about time (i.e. tense), modality (i.e. ability, permission and obligation) and aspect (i.e. the manner of an action). The tense/modal/aspect system of English has changed dramatically over the past several hundred years. I will focus on three areas. Each one has been involved in extensive variation and change. The first involves changes in the future temporal reference system as the older forms *shall* and *will* give way to a newer construction with *going to*. The second involves reorganization of the modal system, in particular the expression of obligation/necessity. In this case an old modal, *must*, is fading away as two other forms, i.e. *have to* and *have got to*, compete for this meaning. The third involves transformations in the forms used to express stative possession, i.e. ownership and personal attributes. Where once *have* was the only variant, over the past several hundred years *have got* has encroached on its territory. Examination of these systems of grammar in the Roots Archive may reveal earlier stages in the development of these areas of grammar. In turn, this may provide a window on how grammars evolve.

The future

The future is an ideal choice for cross-community analysis in the context of ongoing change. Its major variants, *going to* and *will* (often *'ll*), as in (1), are widely used and shared by most, if not all, varieties of English. Although people sometimes think there is a meaning difference between these forms, in running conversation they are often interchangeable, as in the examples in (1).

(1)   a. 'How you *gonna* do that?' 'Oh,' said I, 'I*'ll* soon do it.' (CMK/m)
      b. I says, 'It*'ll* only be six month.' Didn't know it *were gan* be six year. (MPT/r)
      c. And it *won't* get any better, it*'ll* get worse. (CMK/t)

> d. But I just seen the Daily Mail, they're *going to* do away with that gollywog. (CMK/r)
> e. If I don't get out t'eat afore long I's *ganna* die. (PVG/a)

This area of English grammar has not changed recently or quickly. Instead, it has been changing slowly over a long period of time. The oldest form is *shall*, which is now considered formal. While it is considered passé in many places, it is still reported to be in widespread use in southern England. More generally, the standard form is *will*. The newest layer in the system, *going to* came into the future temporal reference system about the middle of the fifteenth century – and is thought to be increasing in frequency ever since, so 500 years or more of ongoing change.

Brogue
Everybody has a brogue o' their ain, haen't they? (Robin Mawhinney, 55, PVG)[2]

Synchronic perspective

Contemporary grammar books are relatively consistent in their description of the future temporal reference system. Most conclude that *shall* is no longer in productive use, at least in North American varieties. It has retreated to formulaic utterances and expressions, e.g. *Shall we go?* The long-standing controversy over the meanings and functions of *shall* and *will* (Visser, 1963–73) are also receding. Much of that literature was founded in how the choice between *shall* and *will* is 'coloured' by different modal or attitudinal nuances, such as relative degree of volition, certainty, intentionality, point of view and judgement. However, because this is dependent on *shall* and *will* being robust alternates, the arguments are by the turn of the twenty-first century mostly moot. An early systematic study of the alternation between the two in British and American drama showed that *will* ousted *shall* in declarative sentences (Fries, 1925, 1927). However, this displacement is now virtually complete, as the major variants in the late twentieth and early twenty-first centuries are overwhelmingly *will* (mostly *'ll*) and *going to*. *Will* is often considered the default option and is the form most frequently attested. *Going to*, however, has been claimed to encode many different meanings, including 'current orientation', 'intention' (Nicolle, 1997: 375; Royster and Steadman, 1923/1968), 'future fulfillment of the present' (Fleischman, 1982; Leech, 1971; Quirk et al., 1985; Vet, 1984), a sense of determination or inevitability (Nicolle, 1997: 375; Palmer, 1987; Royster and Steadman, 1923/1968), immediate or impending future (e.g. Poutsma, 1926; Sweet, 1898) and an association with colloquial or informal speech styles (Quirk et al., 1985: 214). Interestingly, despite the debate over form–meaning correspondences, most researchers admit that these two forms exhibit 'no demonstrable difference' between them (e.g. Danchev and Kytö, 1994: 384; Palmer, 1974: 163; Quirk et al., 1985: 218).

The innumerable hypotheses, postulations and claims about which variant is used under which conditions are finally being tested in quantitative and corpus-based analyses (Close, 1977; Nesselhauf, 2006, 2007, 2010; Tagliamonte, in press; Torres-Cacoullos and Walker, 2009a). These empirical studies consistently report a highly variable system split between *will* (including the contracted form *'ll* and the negative form *won't*) and *be going to* (and its phonological variants) along with modest use of the present and present progressive. I now turn to consider how the future temporal reference system became like this.

Quoits

[037] Another thing that was very keen amongst the miners er socially was quoiting. [1] What's quoiting? [037] Oh, they play it up at Stonehaven. It's like a kind of disc with a hole in the middle of it and they threw these, you see. The Americans play with horseshoes. The same principle. (William Burns, 82, CMK, 037)

Historical perspective

The variant forms used for future meaning all have their origins in lexical verbs. *Shall* was originally a verb of obligation and *will* was a verb of volition or desire. These origins undoubtedly caused the hundreds of years of debate concerning the rules of their usage (Belcher, 1813; F., 1838; Hulbert, 1947; Molloy, 1897). *Going to* also originated as a verb, in this case the progressive aspect of the lexical verb *go*, meaning movement towards a goal. This early meaning of movement towards a goal can be found in Shakespeare, as in (2a), alongside *shall* and *will*, as in (2b–c) from the *Sonnets* (c. 1609).

(2) a. Hark! The kings and the princes, our kindred, *are going to* see the Queen's picture. (*Winter's Tale*, V, 2.3278)
     b. My love *shall* in my verse ever live young (*Sonnet* 19, 266)
     c. Time *will* come and take my love away. (*Sonnet* 64, 894)

Gradually *going to* became prevalent for a more general sense of prediction (Royster and Steadman, 1923/1968: 402) and connotations of intention and/or purpose increased, as in (3).

(3) a. He is a kind friend to you, for he *is going* to give you lodging. (Dickens, *Bleak House*, c. 1852–1853)
     b. Miss Lydia *is going* to be married; and you shall all have a bowl of punch to make merry at her wedding. (Austen, *Pride and Prejudice*, c. 1813)

By the seventeenth century *going to* had become frequent and is reported with a wide array of lexical verbs while still retaining strong associations with its literal meaning of 'intention' and 'movement' (Danchev and Kytö, 1994). Eventually *be going to* started occurring with inanimate subjects and stative verbs.

The prevailing view in the literature suggests that *going to* has been steadily gaining ground (e.g. Mair, 1997b; Poplack and Tagliamonte, 1999; Tagliamonte, 2002a). Due to this gradual development, it is not surprising that different varieties are positioned at different points on the trajectory of change; for example, *going to* is said to be more frequent in North America (Berglund, 1997; Szmrecsanyi, 2003; Tagliamonte, 2002a; Wekker, 1976). Further, North American English also has more use of *going to* in contexts that represent a later stage in its development. Consider the examples in (4) from the American author Mark Twain in the late nineteenth century, where examples of *going to* are frequent and those with inanimate subjects are easy to find.

(4)   a. That party *is going to* succeed, it*'s going to* elect the next president.
      b. I now learn with regret that it *is going to* be set to music.
         (Both from Mark Twain, *Innocents Abroad*, c. 1869)

More generally, this distinctiveness of two major varieties of English offers the analyst a unique opportunity to examine how grammaticalization proceeds, since it is evident that these two major varieties are at two different points in the trajectory of change. Given these observations about the development of *going to*, we might anticipate that the dialect data would retain an earlier stage in this development (Tagliamonte, Durham and Smith, 2011), and if so, a greater use of *will* and/or *shall* reflecting a stage in which *going to* had not yet made inroads into the future temporal reference system. Furthermore, due to the fact that the reported acceleration of *going to* is relatively recent, we may be able to track advances on the trajectory of change in comparative analysis of the Roots Archive and the British Dialects Archive.

Blether
   And then Bert's dad, Old John-Raffle, would say 'Right', he says 'We'll go in and have wir supper now, boys.' Now, all that he wanted you in for your supper for was a blether. He liked a blether. And that was you 'til midnight. And then you had to walk back over that hill and get to your bed and get up and at your work at seven o'clock in the morning again. (Willy Lang, 75 CMK, 027)[3]

Methodology

All the future temporal reference constructions in the data were extracted and coded according to procedures developed in earlier quantitative studies (Poplack and Tagliamonte, 1999; Tagliamonte, 2002a; Torres-Cacoullos and Walker, 2009a). In this area of grammar, however, the same form can be used for a range of different meanings, and there are many idiosyncratic forms that can be used for future meaning. All expressions that were clearly temporal and made reference to future time were included. In order to focus on the main components of future temporal reference, we excluded future readings of the simple present and present progressive. Not only are these constructions infrequently used for future temporal reference, they are highly circumscribed to scheduled events, as in (5) (Biber et al., 1999; Torres-Cacoullos and Walker, 2009a).

(5)   a. She goes to Carlisle *in September*. (MPT/041)
       b. And we've a fish van *comes tomorrow morning* at half-past-nine. (CMK/032)

Some studies of future temporal reference have sometimes included future in the past contexts, as in (6) (Poplack and Tagliamonte, 1999: 334). These contexts are nearly categorically rendered with *going to*.[4] However, scholars have argued that future-in-the-past contexts are substantially different from standard future temporal reference in terms of frequency of forms (predominance of *be going to*), patterns of use (antithetic constraints) (Torres-Cacoullos and Walker, 2009a: 327) and having a highly restricted set of contexts where there is interchangeability of future forms.[5] Therefore these contexts were excluded from the analysis.

(6)   a. He thought they never *was gonna* get out of it. (CLB/007)
       b. I was terrified he *was gonna* tell the whole class that I'd cried. (MPT/%)

Shall is well known to be rare to non-existent in Ireland and Scotland (e.g. Crystal, 1986). Indeed, most examples in the British Dialects Archive were in the York English Corpus, and these were used almost entirely by women and in formulaic questions, as in (7)

(7)   a. What *shall* I do? (YRK/m)
       b. *Shall* I put this back on? (YRK/R)
       c. How *shall* I put it? (YRK/y)

Thus, it appears that *shall* may never have been part of these dialects. In fact, of the three tokens in the Roots Archive, two are in quotes from the Bible, as in (8), suggesting a prescriptive overlay, rather than systemic usage.

(8)   I says 'You know what it says in the Bible, the first *shall* be last and the last *shall* be first.' (PVG/d)

In addition tag questions (all *will*) and a few *about to* constructions (N = 4) were recorded, but not included. This left 2,946 tokens of variable future temporal reference contexts.

Distributional analysis

Variants of *will* represent the vast majority of the future temporal reference system in all these communities. The bulk of the system is represented by

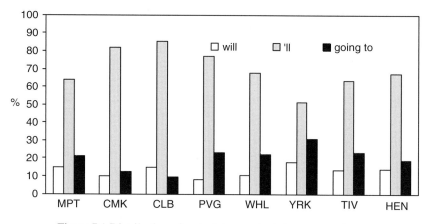

Figure 7.1 Distribution of main future variants by community

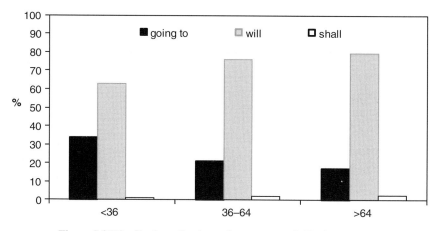

Figure 7.2 Distribution of *going to* by age group in York

contracted *'ll* while the full form *will* is relatively infrequent. This is likely a product of the informality of this spoken language material where contraction is paramount. Notice that *going to* – the black bars – hovers between 10% and 20% in most locales. Only in York is there a slightly higher rate of *going to*. We may wonder why this is the case. In fact, there has been an increase of *going to* across generations in the community mirroring its progression into the future temporal reference system (Tagliamonte, 2002a). We can illustrate this by plotting the frequency of *going to* in apparent time, i.e. by performing a distributional analysis of *going to* by speaker age group, as in Figure 7.2. This shows that *will* is the most frequent variant in all age groups, but it is declining. *Shall* is rare but still gradually fading away. In contrast, *going to* increases as the individuals get younger with the greatest shift between the middle-aged and younger group – the individuals born between 1943 and 1980. This is consistent with Nesselhauf's research on the British portion of the Archer corpus (c. 1650–1999)[6] where *going* to increases most dramatically in the twentieth century. Thus, we have confirmation that *going to* is on the rise in spoken British English at the turn of the twenty-first century (Tagliamonte, 2002a). Notice that the proportion of *going to* is modest in the oldest generation, 17%, which aligns this generation with all the other elderly individuals in Figure 7.2. Thus, the dialect data provides a perspective on the status of *going to* as it is just beginning to infiltrate the future temporal reference system. Notice how these findings highlight how important it is to carefully circumscribe corpus data so as to be comparable across data sets. Features undergoing change may differ markedly from one generation to another. In this case, it is critical for the analysis of *going to* to ensure that the individuals being compared were born at approximately the same time.

There have been extensive studies of this area of the grammar. Indeed, the development of *going to* is a quintessential example of grammatical change (Bybee and Pagliuca, 1987; Hopper and Traugott, 1993). In the vast literature on this subject several grammatical contexts stand out as explaining the competition between *will* and *going to*. *Going to* is thought to have originated in subordinate clauses, to be strongly correlated with 2nd/3rd (i.e. non-1st) person and has a long history of being associated with imminent future readings. *Will* in contrast is correlated with 1st person and far future readings. With this information, we can examine the dialects to see whether these patterns are remnants of the original lexical meanings of these forms or later developments in the process of grammatical change.

Figure 7.3 tests the effect of the type of clause in order to determine if *going to* is more prevalent in main or subordinate clauses. It shows that Cumnock and the two Northern Ireland communities (combined here due to small Ns in PVG as 'NI') show no distinction between main and subordinate clauses. In contrast, all the other communities have a strong and parallel tendency towards the use of *going to* in subordinate clauses.

Figure 7.4 tests the effect of grammatical person in order to determine if *going to* is more prevalent in 2nd and 3rd person contexts leaving *will* for 1st person singular. It shows that here too Cumnock and Northern Ireland have little or no difference across grammatical persons. *Going to* is used rarely, regardless of clause type. In contrast, all the other communities have a strong and parallel tendency towards greater use of *going to* with 2nd and 3rd person subjects. This shows how *going to* is beginning to penetrate the grammatical system

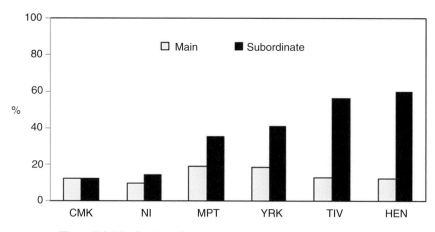

Figure 7.3 Distribution of *going to* by type of clause

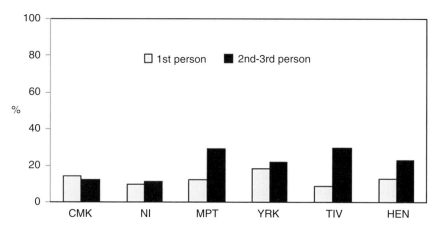

Figure 7.4 Distribution of *going to* according to grammatical person

by extending into particular subject types. Note, once again, the mitigated constraint ranking in York.

Figure 7.5 tests the effect of temporal reference in order to test whether *going to* is more prevalent in imminent or 'near' future contexts. It shows a mixed situation. The effect of temporal reference is regular and consistent in Cumnock, Northern Ireland, Maryport and Henfield. In each case, *going to* is more frequent in contexts where there is no reference, whereas near and far futures are rarely marked with *going to*. In contrast, York reflects a levelled system, suggesting that *going to* has expanded into all temporal reference domains. In Tiverton (where there are relatively few tokens), we might

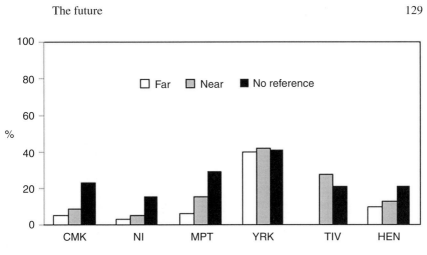

Figure 7.5 Distribution of *going to* according to temporal reference across communities

reasonably interpret the lack of *going to* in far future contexts as being comparable to the other peripheral locations.

Finally, Figure 7.6 tests the effect of affirmative vs negative contexts. This also shows a mixed situation. The effect of negation is visible in only two communities, Tiverton and Henfield. In each case, *going to* is more frequent in negative contexts. Everywhere else the effect is relatively modest or inconsistent.

Three contextual trends appear to be consistent across the southern communities (Tiverton, Henfield) but absent in the Roots Archive (Cumnock and Northern Ireland): the correlation of *will* (*'ll*) (1) with 1st person, (2) with subordinate clauses and (3) with negation. On the assumption that the Roots communities (Cumnock, Maryport, Cullybackey and Portavogie) represent an early stage in the evolution of English, this suggests that these constraints developed over time. One correlation stands out as being present in the Roots Archive, but erratic elsewhere, namely, the effect of temporal reference. In communities where *going to* is least frequent overall, it appears most often in contexts that have no particular temporal reference, as in (9).

(9)   a. Maybe he'*s gonna* keep quiet. (CLB/b)
       b. Well, what are *you goina* do wi all this? (PVG/d)
       c. I don't know what she'*s going to* do, hen. (CMK/u)

An additional insight that is provided by the comparative analysis of the various contextual patterns is that Maryport stands out as further along the pathway of change than the other Roots Archive communities. (Note: This is not the first time we have seen this pattern.) This community patterns with

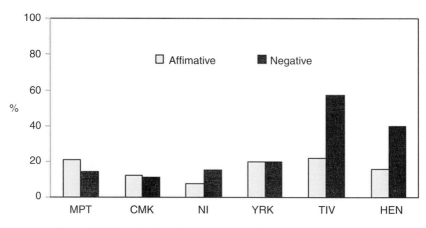

Figure 7.6 Distribution of *going to* according to type of sentence

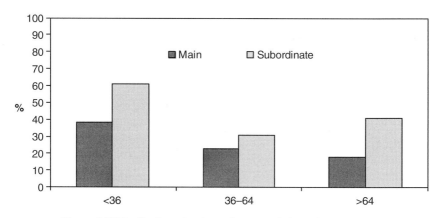

Figure 7.7 Distribution of *going to* by type of clause in York

Cumnock and the Northern Ireland communities with respect to no effect of negation and that *going to* is more likely in unmarked temporal contexts; however, Maryport patterns along with the more advanced communities in the correlation of *going to* with subordinates and the heightened use of *will* (*'ll*) for 1st person.

The York data offers the possibility to corroborate these cross-community trends by examining whether they are operational in the same way in apparent time. Figures 7.7–7.10 show the distribution of *going to* by age group for each of the contextual constraints.

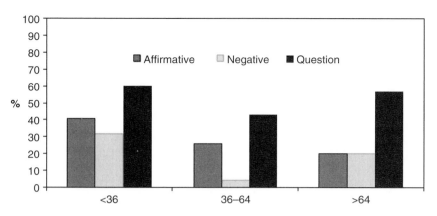

Figure 7.8 Distribution of *going to* by type of sentence in York

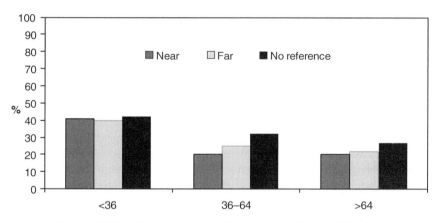

Figure 7.9 Distribution of *going to* by temporal reference in York

Figure 7.7 shows that from the oldest to the youngest individuals in York, subordinate clauses consistently have more *going to* than main clauses. This pattern is stable across the community.

Figure 7.8 shows that questions are more frequently rendered with *going to* across the age groups. This pattern is stable across the community.

Figure 7.9 shows that there is a qualitative change from oldest to youngest individuals in the pattern of use. In the older generations, *going to* is more likely with no reference contexts, but in the youngest generation, where *going to* is more frequent, there is no difference. This pattern exposes levelling across the community.

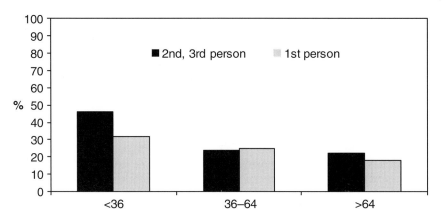

Figure 7.10 Distribution of *going to* by grammatical person in York

Figure 7.10 tests for the effect of grammatical person across generations in York. It shows another qualitative change from oldest to youngest individuals. In this case, grammatical persons were once parallel with respect to use of *going to* but by the youngest generation there is an obvious effect such that *going to* is more frequent in non-1st persons. Thus, the change is a development towards specialization of *going to* for 2nd and 3rd person. Correspondingly, *will/'ll* becomes more frequent in the 1st person. This pattern exposes the development of a constraint across the community, in this case specialization of *will* for 1st person as a result of the frequent collocation *I'll*.

In summary, the trends visible across communities – stability in some cases, levelling and specialization in others – are reflected across age groups in a single community. These two independent lines of evidence confirm that the results reflect bona fide developments in the future temporal reference system.

Tarn

D'you know what a tarn is? [Interviewer] Er, now, isn't that like a little lake? [004] it's a mountain lake, not an ordinary lake, it's a mountain lake up in the middle o' the mountains you get a wee lake, well a tarn and a lake. (Kate Devoy, 62, PVG)[7]

What does the use of going to *tell us about dialects?*

The study of *going to* has provided an enriched perspective on linguistic change. By using not only frequency as a measure, but also patterns of use as reflected in a number of key constraints attested in the literature, incremental steps in the progression of change can be inferred. From the overall distribution of *going to* in the Roots Archive compared to the British Dialects

Archive, we can see that *going to* is making slow progress in the most peripheral dialects of the Roots Archive. In some cases, it represents only about 10%
of the system. Put in perspective, it is not surprising that among the features
Mencken (1963: 160–2) noted for Irish influence on American English was
the preference for *will* over *shall*. Even today, these Irish dialects still do not
use much of anything else.

Yet the use of *going to* has not advanced nearly as much as might have been
expected even in the more mainstream communities. Where it is used most –
among the youngest generation in York – it is present only 40% of the time.
Even in the locations with the lowest frequency of use, some constraints are
present that are still socially entrenched in the most advanced North American
situations, e.g. *going to* is used most in contexts where there is no clear temporal reference. Other patterns attested in the contemporary literature must
have developed, as *going to* infiltrated the temporal reference system and jock-
eyed for position with *will*. In these cases, we find *going to* used more often in
subordinate clauses and with 2nd and 3rd person subjects while *will/'ll* is used
more often in 1st person main clauses.

When these results are taken together, they offer a new perspective on
grammatical change. They demonstrate that some constraints stay stable over
time, supporting the Constant Rate Effect (Kroch, 1989). Yet other constraints
evolve, e.g. temporal reference and grammatical person. This means that the
Constant Rate Effect may not be operational in all changes or it may only
be reflected in certain types of constraints. When a grammaticalizing feature
undergoes extension, e.g. across temporal reference, or specialization, e.g. the
frequent collocation *I'll*, the visible consequence is levelling across categories
rather than maintenance of contrasts.

In sum, the perspective gained from the Roots Archive enables us to
peek into the early days of the development of the *go* future in English.
Contemporary research on the future temporal reference system will do well
to track the development of *going to* not only in these northern varieties, but
also across dialects of English elsewhere. This will enable analysts to determine whether *going to* is on schedule to take over the future temporal reference system. Alternatively, it may be the case that the division of labour has
become divided between *will* and *going to* and that the future temporal reference system is, in fact, stable.

Thrang

I thought I knew broad Cumberland dialect, like. Not long after we were married, I were
pottering about in back-yard, doing – I don't know what I was doing, I was doing summat. And she come out and she says till us 'What's the thrang with it?' I said 'what's her
saying?' 'What's the thrang with it' I says thou's got to be Dearham lass, I don't know
what thou's on about! (Andrew Meyer, 63, MPT)[8]

Necessity and obligation

The forms *must*, *have/'ve got to*, *got to* and *have to* are used interchangeably to express obligation, requirement or necessity, as in (10).

(10)   Certain sprays *have to* be done, and it's *necessary* to do it. (TIV/h)

These variants represent the full range of old and new forms in the deontic modality system, from the older modal *must*, as in (11), variants with *have + got*, as in (12)–(13), to the newest layer, *got to*, as in (14).

(11)   a. You *must* do something, you see, for the war effort. (CMK/i)
     b. And they'd lie maybe for an hour and that the sun shining, and that's nae use. You *must* get them out. (CLB/j)

(12)   a. He's *got to* do what he's telt, oh aye. (CMK/G)
     b. Oh, it's Davey-Johnson. Come on in Davey, thou's *to* hear this. (CLB/f)

(13)   a. This *has to be* polished – this wee cabinet what's sitting beside you *has to* be polished. (CLB/q)
     b. The doors is locked and you *have to* watch who comes in. (CLB/e)

(14)   a. He can't operate the plough hisself, he *got to* tell somebody what to do. (TIV/h)
     b. You *got to* watch them, ken, you *got to* watch them. (CMK/d)

Because these forms entered the language at specific points, which have been documented in time, their distribution across dialects may shed light on the stages of development of this grammatical system and thus the nature of linguistic change in this area of English grammar.

According to Bolinger (1980), the modal auxiliary system of English is undergoing 'wholesale reorganization'. Indeed, Krug (1998) observes that *have got to* for the expression of necessity and/or obligation is one of the biggest success stories in English grammar of the last century. Such claims suggest that synchronic data spanning several generations in apparent time may provide insight into the mechanisms underlying ongoing grammatical change in this area of grammar.

Change with the times

It'll always change, and it'll go on changing. And I think you'll find it must go on changing if a community's going to live. If you stand still, you go backwards. 'Cos everyone else is going on past you! So um you've got to move with the times. (Richard Drake, 77 HEN, 007)[9]

The Roots Archive and the British Dialects Archive exhibit robust variation, even alternating from one sentence to the next, as in (15).

(15)   a. She's *got to* be on the move. *Got to* be doing something, this is it. (CMK/u)

b. All my brothers is the same. All *got* wee totty feet. Oh they all – it's a trait in our family they've all *got* wee totty feet. (CMK/028)

c. He's two big cabins in Ottawa. And he's *got* another cabin in Ottawa. (CMK/011)

Such variability in the grammar can be interpreted as layering, where different forms reflect grammatical change (Hopper, 1991: 23, 124). On the other hand, variation of this type may simply be the result of functional distinctions, where different forms reflect unique functions. In other words, the distribution and patterning of these forms in contemporary dialects may provide us with the ability to assess whether innovation, obsolescence or stability best explain the facts.

Top of the pump

And the young boy – the eldest yin stole the lid of my pump. And he confessed till it. There another woman lost the top of hers (laughs). And she come in to me one night and I was in the bath. She says 'Molly I've seen a man asking for you.' I says, 'Did you?' 'Aye' she says, 'I did.' Says I 'who was it?' She says, 'it was Mr. – Crawford the auctioneer'. You see it was him that was the auctioneer. She says er he had knowed she was working in Braefield. And she says, 'I was in the day for there was somebody stole the top of my pump.' (Laughs). 'And I was into see he whiles had the tops.' He whiles had second-hand stuff. And er she says 'I went into see if I could get the top of for my pump. And that's when he asked me.' She says 'asked if you were' – he knowed I was in Braefield. And he said er to tell me he was asking for us (laughs).[10] (Molly Ellis, 89, CLB)

Historical perspective

The historical trajectory of changes in the deontic modality system can help explain this variability. *Must* was the Old English means to express permission and possibility (Warner, 1993: 160–1), but by the Middle English period a wider range of meanings had developed, including both deontic readings, as in (16), as well as epistemic readings, as in (17), which developed from the late fourteenth century (Warner, 1993: 180). Deontic meanings relate to obligation and necessity, while epistemic readings relate to implied certainty.

(16) Deontic
   a. You *must* go to church on Sunday whether you liked it or no. (CMK/G)
   b. If I go to Scotland he says it *must* be for six months. (CMK/J)

(17) Epistemic
   a. 'By god' I says, 'They *must* think I'm good.' (PVG/r)
   b. Some were a lot cleverer than me when I think about it. *Must* be the way of the world, that! (MPT/Σ)

According to the OED the use of *have to* in the sense of 'obligation' is first attested in 1579, although it may have been even earlier (Crowell, 1955). From this time onwards, variation with *have to* and *must* is reported. The construction *have got to* or with *got* by itself entered the English language much later – not until the nineteenth century (Visser, 1963–73: 479). Both Visser (1963–73) and the OED label the forms with *got* as colloquial, even vulgar. In fact, prescriptive grammars have long regarded it as somewhat stigmatized, and present-day English grammars usually consider it informal.

However, in a large-scale analysis of the British National Corpus of English, *have got to* and *gotta* were found to be 1.5 times as frequent as the older forms *must* or *have to* (Krug, 2000) in British English of the 1990s. According to this general trajectory, it would seem that the construction with *got* is taking over as the marker of deontic modality in English.

What is deontic modality?

Deontic modality encompasses a range of meanings including obligation, permission and necessity (Coates, 1983: 32). However, there is actually a 'cline' ranging from readings that might translate as 'it is imperative or important that …' to those that mean something more like 'it is necessary or a requirement that …' (Coates, 1983: 32). Most commentators argue along the lines that each form encodes one of these different meanings. Use of *must* is thought to be 'directly applied and irresistible', whereas *have to* is 'resistible' under certain circumstances (quoted in Hopper and Traugott, 1993: 79; Sweetster, 1988: 54). This makes *must* 'strong obligation', since the consequences of not doing it are most severe. In contrast, with 'weak obligation' if the obligation is not fulfilled, 'the consequences are not too serious' (Bybee et al., 1994: 186). Thus discussions of the deontic system typically associate one form or another to a particular reading. Most accounts group *have to* and *have got to* together, as toned down choices in contrast to *must*, distinguishing neither subtle meaning differences nor contrastive strength to the choice between them (Huddleston and Pullum, 2002: 183).

This presents several problems for the analyst. First, in conversational data, the distinction between strong and weak is difficult to tease apart. For example, the actions in (18) seem relatively 'strong' in their consequences. In contrast, the actions in (19) appear more trivial. Yet both cases are variable.

(18) a. We *must* have those who are fit to help those who are not so fit. (CMK/q)
      b. She's working till late 'cos she *has to* bide and count up all the money and all the rest of it. (BCK/g)

(19) a. Every time you come to mine, I'*ve to* make you coffee. (BCK/g)
      b. When you've got a man suddenly plunged into your life you'*ve gotta* feed him, haven't you! (HEN/d)
      c. Next time Papa's down we *must* get him an ice cream. (CMK/M)

A strong–weak distinction, either as contrastive or as a continuum, is thus virtually impossible to categorize impartially. To do so inevitably leads to circularity from the imposition of the analyst's own subjective interpretations. The main point of relevance here is that there is a cline of meanings and a range of intensities encompassed by deontic modality. But without consistent study it is impossible to determine how or if the forms match the interpretations. Moreover, as we shall see, the variants of *have to* and *have got to* represent the vast majority of uses in the dialect data. This demonstrates that there is something more going on than meaning contrast between the forms.

This scenario of long-term evolution of forms for the same function, their contrasting morphosyntactic classifications alongside a documented cycle of loss and renewal, presents an interesting case study. First, because the major variants (*must* → *have to* → *have got to* → *got to*) entered the language at different points in time, their distribution across dialects of the language may shed light on the stages of development of the deontic modality system. At the same time, the forms used to express deontic modality have varying degrees of auxiliary-hood ranging from *must* as a full-fledged modal to the other contenders, each with varying degrees of this status. Tracking the synchronic status of this system – form and function – across dialects should add to the existing knowledge base on this system. This, in turn, should inform us of the nature of this area of English grammar as well as its status in the larger history of its development (Bybee et al., 1994).

The nicest dialect's in Mornes. Kilkeel. He says it's far softer than – our's is more harsh. (Michael Adair, 74, PVG, 008)[11]

Synchronic perspective

The newer layer of forms used for deontic modality, i.e. *have got to* and *got to*, have long been infused with social meaning. Krug (2000) argues that *have got to* originated in nonstandard speech. Both Visser and the OED label it as colloquial, along with *got to*, while *gotta* has the added characterization of being 'vulgar'. Present-day English grammars consider *have got to* and *got to* 'informal', equating them primarily with spoken data (Biber et al., 1999:487–9; Palmer, 1979). In contrast, *must* is associated with formal registers and written exposition (Biber et al., 1999).

Contemporary analysts also report that there are distinct regional associations for the forms: *have got to* is said to be the most common form in spoken British English (Coates, 1983), while in American English *got to* and *gotta* are typical (Denison, 1998: 173). *Have got to* and *got to* have been found to be increasing dramatically in frequency in contemporary British and American

English, so much so in fact that Krug (2000: 63) regards the change towards *have got* as a riveting success story.[12] Because the forms have their own sociolinguistic interpretations as well as a distinct regional diffusion, their distribution may shed light on social influences in language change.

With the diachronic and synchronic picture in perspective and the structural and sociolinguistic aspects in mind, let us turn to the dialect data.

The Birthday Present

But anyway, I was gonna have a treat for mi birthday, but I didn't know what it was, you see. Well, it was put off, once or twice, 'oh, er you're gonna have it next week, Auntie'. And when next week came and I thought, 'Well, when's this surprise coming up? Didn't know a thing about it, mind. So anyway, got word on the Friday, 'It's on for tomorrow, Auntie, be ready at eight o'clock' or whatever time I'd to be ready. Course it was a drizzly old morning, and Mary went out on front with old mac on and umbrella up, shaking mi head and making a face, and they took mi photograph, looking like that, d'you know! And I thought, 'Oh, this is gonna be an awful day, wherever we're going.' Anyway, we got away to Carlisle, and then we turned onto t'airfield. And he says, 'You not know yet what you're doing?' 'No!' So I was introduced to the pilot, nice young man that works with Ron. Er coming out, 'You won't be frightened now?' 'Frightened?' they said 'Oh, she's frightened of nothing!' I said 'I'll sit on t'wing if you like!' As long as I could look down on that coastline. So we had a good run round, we were up there for an hour. And I said to t'pilot, 'By-gum, aren't these planes slow!' And he says 'We're only doing a hundred and ten-mile an hour!' But you see, you've no concept of how fast you're going when you're – you don't see things passing same as on the road, do you? (Mary Pulleyn, 77, MPT)[13]

Methodology

The corpora were searched for every instance of *must*, *have to*, *have got to*, *got to* that encoded the meaning 'it is imperative/necessary for ...' (Coates, 1983). An issue that arises is that these same forms are used for other meanings. These must be removed so as to focus on the deontic modal system. Epistemic modality, as in (20), encodes inferred certainty (rather than obligation or necessity). This is a later development, which has become almost totally encoded with *must* in contemporary English (Coates, 1983: 48; Palmer, 1979: 53; Tagliamonte, 2004).

(20) a. Working in the shoe factory and I thought 'there *must* be more to life than this'. (MPT/m)
      b. Oh aye, I thought it bit peculiar, mind, *must be* Irish I think, ken aye. (CMK/a)

Contexts involving past or future tense were excluded. Consistent with descriptions of the English modal system, these were categorically encoded with *have to* (Palmer, 1979: 114; Tagliamonte, 2004), as in (21).

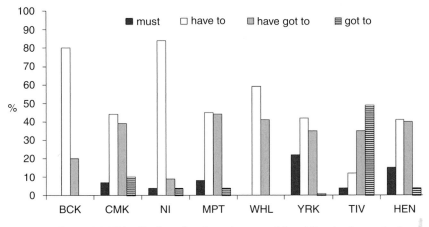

Figure 7.11 Distribution of main variants used for obligation/necessity by community

(21) a. So, I says, I'll *have to* look for a job. (MPT/a)
      b. You'll *have to* go to Shoreham. (TIV/b)

Expressions such as in (22) were also excluded as they tended to occur with *must* (71%, N = 31).

(22) a. *I must admit*, I enjoy it. (MPT/%)
      b. I mean, *I must admit* we had quite a good life in Trieste, you know. (CMK/C)
      c. *I must say*, I like Eric's egg. (CLB/003)

I also removed infrequent tokens of negation and questions for the simple reason that they were rare (N = 19, N = 12).[14]

   These procedures ensure that, when we examine the deontic modality forms, we are restricting the analysis to the contexts that encode the same meaning. This is a highly circumscribed area of the grammar – affirmative declarative contexts that express 'it is imperative/necessary that'. In total, there were 602 contexts.

Distributional analysis

Figure 7.11 shows the frequency of each of the main variants used for obligation or necessity across communities. It reveals the rarity of *must* (the dark columns) in all the communities, with slightly elevated proportions in Henfield, where it is used 15% of the time (14/95) and York, at 22% (22/100). Note the unique distribution of forms in Tiverton, where the variant *got to* is the most frequent variant used 49% of the time (33/68). Two varieties distinguish themselves with an overwhelming preference for the variant *have to* (the white columns) – Buckie (80%, 20/25) and the Northern Irish communities (84%, 47/56). Robust variation between *have to* and *have got to* (the grey columns) is found in Henfield, Maryport, York, Wheatley Hill and Cumnock.

As discussed earlier, linguistic features can often be predicted to exhibit a north–south divide in Britain (Trudgill, 1990; Wales, 2006). Absence of deontic *must* is a well-known characteristic of Northern Ireland and Scotland (Macafee, 1992a).[15] Indeed, these findings concur with Corrigan's research, which shows clearly that *have to* is the most frequent marker of modality in Northern Ireland (2000: 37). It is not surprising that elderly speakers in conservative varieties do not use *have got to*, since it is newer in the system and currently on the rise in present-day varieties of British English (Krug, 1998, 2000). In England, prevailing descriptions in the literature would lead us to expect substantial use of *have got to* (e.g. Biber et al., 1999: 489; Krug, 2000). However, these communities reveal unexpectedly high rates of *have to*, even in the most southern communities, Tiverton and Henfield. Given that *have to* is older than *have got to* by centuries, the high rate of *have to* may be interpreted as a reflection of ongoing retention of an older layer in the development of forms in somewhat peripheral locales.

Given this interpretation, the contrast between Tiverton and Henfield – both small villages in the south – becomes an interesting quandary. This could be the product of the relative isolation of the communities from outside norms, the higher level of education among individuals in the community, or other factors. Research on the south-west more generally has demonstrated considerable retention of conservative features (Jones and Tagliamonte, 2004; Klemola, 1996; van den Eynden, 1993). Indeed, Tiverton retains many features from earlier stages in the history of English (Godfrey and Tagliamonte, 1999). Thus, while frequency of *have to* might be expected, the high rates of *got to* seem contradictory. However, this variant is widely attested across south-west dialects, Essex and Wales (Krug, 2000: 112, map 3.1). Interestingly, Henfield, positioned within the Home Counties, is the single geographic area in the south that is reported to have scant use of *got to* according to Krug's analysis. Thus, the use of *got to* in Tiverton and *have got to* in Henfield may simply be a reflection of regional dialects in the south. However, an alternative scenario is that the favoured form in the evolving layers of deontic modality (i.e. *have got to* or *got to*) is selected at the same point in the progression of development rather than consecutively, as previously thought, as the frequent use of *got to* amongst these elderly speakers in Devon suggests. Supporting this hypothesis is the historical record: both *have got to* and *got to* are attested around the same time period, suggesting that they are equally old. Thus, while some research assumes that *got to* is newer than *have got to* and currently increasing

(Krug, 1998, 2000), in Tiverton, at least, it appears to have been selected as the favoured variant of the *have got to* layer from its inception.

Summary The results from the distributional analysis reveal a wealth of information that gains a heightened focus from the cross-community perspective. The dialects lay out a reflection of the history of the deontic modality system in geographic relief. This information may be interpreted with a view to the history and development of the deontic modality system. The broad historical context documents a progressing cline from *must* to *have to* to *have got to*. On one hand, the cross-community variation provides an indication of the state of development of the grammatical system. Where *have to* is more frequent, it can be taken as evidence that the variety is more conservative. Indeed, the two most remote communities exhibit the most instances of *have to* – Northern Ireland and Buckie. In contrast, where *have got to* is more frequent, it can be taken as evidence that the new layer has made inroads into the system. Interestingly, variation between these two variants is found across dialects spanning Scotland (Cumnock), north-east England (Maryport, York, Wheatley Hill) and south-east England (Henfield).

An important next step for the analysis is to uncover the underlying mechanism(s) that may be guiding this development. The communities may be operating on their own accord, reflecting independent developments, parametric variation or dialectal divergence. It may also be possible that an overarching drift within the system can be identified. Supra-local patterns may be visible and, if so, it will be relevant to know how diffused they are and over what territory.

Words from the wise

It is now actually possible, in the case of recently formed colonial Englishes, not only to deduce but actually to confirm that drift occurs; to produce contemporary illustrations of how drift operates; and to demonstrate in more detail how it happens. (Trudgill 2004: 132)

Definition

'Drift' is a concept originally coined by Sapir: 'language moves down time in a current of its own making. It has a drift' (Sapir, 1921: 150). Drift refers to the inherited tendencies in languages or language families that lead to parallel developments

---

Welsh

[008] Welsh accent's hard to listen. [003] Aye, aye, and the farther you go south in after like Dublin, it gets hard to – you have to – you don't enjoy a conversation, I think, for

you have to listen. It could be embarrassing if you miss something and you have to ask them to repeat theirselves. So you have to listen. [008] I have to do that onyway wi mi hearing! (Pete Dennet, 69 and Michael Adair, 74, PVG, 008 and 003)[16]

Constraints analysis

Despite the semantic, pragmatic and stylistic facets of *must* that are emphasized in most treatments of deontic modality, the variability observed in the data hardly involves this form. Instead, there is vigorous competition between *have to* and *have got to*. Given that the current Standard English system evolved from an earlier one in which *must* is assumed to have been the majority form, at least two hypotheses can be put forward to explain the current competitors: (1) they may have inherited the semantic and pragmatic functions of the earlier system or (2) they may be differentiating the system along a new functional divide. Either way, we may be able to view a contrast between *have to* and *have got to* with respect to whatever ongoing reorganization (restructuring) is underway.

Subjective vs objective The different forms within the English deontic modality system are widely held to differentiate the nature of the obligation or necessity under discussion. Huddleston and Pullum (2002: 183) distinguish two types: subjective vs objective obligation. Subjective obligation is considered prototypical deontic modality (Coates, 1983: 32). The speaker imposes authority on his- or herself or on others, as in (23).

(23) a. I'*ve got to* force myself to get up in the morning. (CMK/C)
          [speaker imposes authority on themselves]
       b. I was lying in corridor or keeping my head down, quite comfortable. Somebody come, 'Brian, you'*ve got to* come up on the bridge' he says 'do guard' he said. So, I went up on the bridge. (MPT/n)
          [speaker imposes authority on another]

Objective contexts, on the other hand, arise when the authority comes from some other source, not the speaker. This type of obligation is apparent in reports of rules, regulations and standard practice, as in (24).

(24) a. You'*ve to* go out the back door if you want a cigarette. (CMK/A)
       b. 'Cos of course Ron *has to* sit in front like t'co-pilot, you know. (MPT/s)

It also occurs very often in generic statements of necessity, as in (25).

(25) a. You *have to* have eyes in t'back of your head. (MPT/Σ)
       b. If you want to get on you *have to* do a certain amount of work. (CMK/d)

Figure 7.12 tests the distribution of *have to* according to the contrast between subjective and objective obligation in the data across communities.[17] It reveals

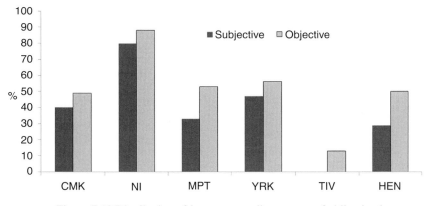

Figure 7.12 Distribution of *have to* according to type of obligation by community

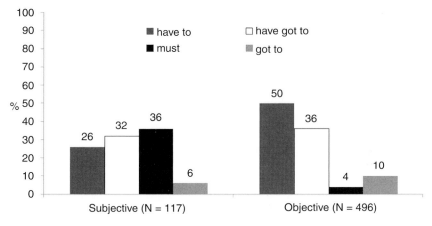

Figure 7.13 Distribution of forms for deontic modality according to type of obligation, all communities combined

that *have to* is more frequent for objective readings and this is consistent in each community. By contrast, *have got to* is more frequent in subjective readings. The findings in Figure 7.12 will be more revealing of the contrast between subjective and objective readings if we combine the communities and examine the distribution of all forms in each context, as in Figure 7.13. This figure reveals that subjective contexts are quite evenly spread among three forms. While *must* is the most frequent form as predicted, the somewhat surprising result is that both *have to* (26%) and *have got to* (32%) are used nearly as much. Indeed, the extent of variation in an area of the system that is widely agreed to be the core context for using *must* is striking. In contrast, objective contexts are dominated by *have to*, representing 50% of all forms. *Got to* is a minor variant in both contexts.

In sum, by dividing the data according to the nature of the obligation (subjective vs objective), it becomes apparent that *have to* retains a niche in the objective contexts in all locales. Although *must* is circumscribed to subjective readings, *have got to* and *have to* can be used as well. This means that although *must* once held the role of marking strong subjective obligation (at least in southern varieties), e.g. *you must look after Amy* (PVG/h), other forms are encroaching. Notice too that this split in the grammar of deontic modality does not differ from community to community. The system is the same in each locale. This means that, although the communities differ in their choice of form, the nature of the grammatical system remains the same. It encodes a distinction between whether the speaker is compelling the hearer to do something (subjective) vs a more generic sense of obligation (objective).

What does variation in the deontic modality system tell us about dialects?

The layering of *must, have to* and *have got to* offers insights into the status of the grammar at a particular point in time as well as an indication of how changes have been taking place in the language. The contrast between proportion of older and newer forms by geographic location provides a particularly interesting mirror of the pathways of change, in this case the putative transition from *must* to *have to* to *have got to*.

The spoken dialect data reveals that deontic *must* is used in contexts where it is prescribed by the standard language, i.e. in contexts of subjective obligation with definite subjects, but not very often. In fact, it does not look as though *must* will ever become firmly established in some regions. It is interesting to speculate why deontic *must* does not thrive in contemporary spoken English. Some researchers argue that it may be the loss of the particular stylistic register associated with *must* (e.g. Biber et al., 1999), which has sometimes been attributed to 'an anti-authoritarian development' (Conradie, 1987: 179). Such developments may originate in changes external to the system, likely in distinctions of style, genre or register (see Facchinetti, Krug and Palmer, 2003). Perhaps it is the more general trend in English towards 'colloquialization' (Leech, 2003: 236–7; Mair, 1997a; see also Mair and Hundt, 1997). Supportive to this idea is the general decline in auxiliaries expressing speaker's attitude or evaluation generally (Warner, 1993). It is not the case that the dialects do not use *must* overall. Indeed, it is used robustly for epistemic modality and in specialized formulaic utterances, *I must admit*, *I must say*. Elsewhere, it appears in contexts with an overlay of formality, as in (26a), where *must* is used for rules and regulations, for orders from a superior officer (26b) and for self-imposed obligation (26c).

(26) a. [005] They didn't seem to put so much emphasis on danger with children in those days. I mean, they aren't allowed to be adventurous now, the same. I think that's why there's more vandalism. Because there aren't the exciting things to do because you're banned from this and banned from that. *Mustn't* ride your bike on the pavement, and you *mustn't* do this and you *mustn't* do that. But we had the freedom to roam. (HEN/005)

   b. 'You *must* not open that door until we come tomorrow morning. Seven o-clock to pick you up.' And he said 'If anybody is you know gives you any trouble' he says 'get onto that phone straight away, give us the number to ring.' (YRK/10)

   c. I *must* write and thank her. I think she's lovely. (YRK/o)

Definition

Colloquialization refers to the tendency for written language to become more like spoken language as writers seek to produce a more accessible, informal style (Biber et al., 1999). The prime time for this was between the seventeenth and twentieth centuries. Indicators of colloquialization include more use of the progressive, contractions and zero relative clauses (e.g. Mair, 2006: 189).

Thus, spoken synchronic dialects show us that when people are expressing obligation/necessity in discourse, they opt to use a range of forms, including, but not limited to, *must*. Indeed, the variation in this area of grammar is robust and highly varied, offering particularly nuanced insights into the evolving grammar. The literature predicts ongoing change towards *have got to* and *gotta*; however, the dialects in Northern Ireland, Scotland and northern England are holding on to *have to*. As with other features, it will be interesting to see how these developments play out in the next generations.

Possession

English expresses stative possession by various means.[18] William Burns, aged 82 (speaker 'K') in Cumnock, provides a good illustration of the different forms *'ve got*, *have*, and *'ve*, as in (27).

(27) a. I *'ve got* eight nephews. (CMK/K)
   b. I *have* a book. (CMK/K)
   c. I *'ve* no experience. (CMK/K)

This type of alternation can be found in adjacent sentences uttered by the same individual, as in (28).

(28) a. I've *got* a cousin that *has* it and she gets it every month. (CMK/I)
      b. They *got* a lovely family Bible ... Thomas *has* it. (CLB/q)
      c. We always *have* an advance-party, each troop *has* about three or four ... It's *got* its advantages, that. (MPT/n)
      d. I've *got* two granddaughters ... Joyce and I just *have* the one daughter. (PVG/¢)

Such robust variation diagnoses an actively changing system in the grammar of these communities. In fact, this system is highly variable in many varieties of English. Alternation of forms can often be found in adverts, signs, magazines and newspapers. This feature is also widely held to differentiate varieties of English (see Trudgill et al., 2002). Thus, it presents a prime site for measuring community differences as well as tapping into change in progress. Because we are able to catch this change while it is still happening, it can provide valuable evidence for understanding diachronic processes. First, let us consider how this situation of vigorous variability arose.

Historical perspective

Variation among these forms is the result of longitudinal layering. The oldest variant is the use of the main verb *have*, attested from the late tenth century onwards. In fact, *have* was the only form available for encoding stative possessive meaning for many centuries. In the late sixteenth century *got* was added, producing *have got*. The earliest attestation of *have got* in the OED is from Shakespeare, as in (29) and is dated just prior to the turn of the sixteenth century. Note the supertoken.

(29) What a beard *hast* thou *got*; thou *hast got* more haire on they chin, then Dobbin my philhorse *has* on his taile. (1596, Shakespeare, *Merchant of Venice*, II, 2.659)

At some point in time *have* began to be contracted, leading to *'ve/'s got*. Then, by the Early Modern period, the contractions sometimes elided leaving *got* alone (Crowell, 1959: 280; Jespersen, 1961b: 47–54; Visser, 1963–73: 1,475, 2,202–4). This part of the story is British.

In contrast, by the late 1800s, American grammarians condemned *have got* as 'vulgar' (Rice, 1932: 291), 'not very beautiful' (cited in Rice, 1932: 291). The form *got* was even considered a 'bogie word', a source of fear, perplexity or harassment (cited in Rice, 1932:292). This overt stigmatization is observable in the following quotes from the mid-nineteenth and early twentieth century (cited in Rice, 1932: 291), as in (30).

(30) a. This form of speech should never be used to express possession. (c. 1855, Gwynne, 1855)
      b. use of the word got ... [for 'have' is] not only wrong, but if right, superfluous. (c. 1870, White, 1927)

c. Wrong: *Have* you *got* a knife with you? Right: *Have* you a knife with you? (c. 1907, Wooley, 1907)

Despite the condemnation of the use of *have got* by early nineteenth-century American writers, as we have just seen, British writers had been using *have got* for at least a hundred years or more. For example, Shakespeare, Lewis Carroll, Dickens and Malory all used the construction and so did grammarians like Lindley Murray (1795/1968) and William Cobbett (1818/1983). However, in Britain this form must not have garnered the same negative effect because use of the *have got* variants had more than doubled in frequency from 1900 to 1935 (Kroch, 1989)

Roots

She's got no roots and – and it worries me, does that. Mind you I suppose this is typical parents, really. Um but it worries me that she's got no roots. She's got nowhere she really belongs to. (Derek Burns, 60, YRK, speaking about his daughter)[19]

Synchronic perspective

In contemporary descriptions, the forms used for stative possession are said to be both socially and regionally delimited (e.g. Trudgill et al., 2002). The main distinction reported in the literature is between British and American usage. Huddleston and Pullam (2002) report that *have got* is British and informal and more frequent than *have* (Biber et al., 1999: 466). In contrast, *have* is 'stylistically neutral', and in American English it is more frequent than *have got*. *Got* has generally been considered American (Jespersen, 1961a: 53). In contrast, in twentieth-century American play data (Jankowski, 2005: table 4), which can be taken to provide a cautious representation of contemporary spoken American English, *got* occurs much more frequently (20%) than it does in spoken Canadian English (6%) (Tagliamonte, D'Arcy and Jankowski, 2010).

Explanations for change

Three possible explanations for the change from *have* to *have got* have been proposed in the literature. The first is syntactic: Variation between *have* and *have got* is rooted in the longitudinal change towards *do* periphrasis more generally, from which the verb *have* remains a long term holdout (Kroch, 1989: 218 n. 241). Under this explanation, *have got* persists due to its resistance to *do* support, e.g. *Have you got?*; *I haven't got*, etc. At the same time, there is a general view in the literature that the verb *have* is changing from an auxiliary verb to a lexical verb. In North America, where this change has progressed further, greater use of *do* is present, e.g. *Do you have?*; *I don't have* (Trudgill et al., 2002). A second explanation is prosodic. This explanation rests on the hypothesis that the *got* forms arose through weakening and subsequent insertion. *Have* reduced to *'ve/'s* then needed more phonetic substance for clarity so *got* was inserted. Then with the reinforcement of *got*, the contraction was no longer necessary and could be elided, i.e. *have → 've/'s → 've/'s got → got*. A third explanation involves grammaticalization. In this case, it is thought that the past tense form of the active verb 'acquire' (i.e. *got*) was reanalysed as a marker of possession. This would have happened according to a grammaticalization pathway of extension from one stage of development to another. If any (or all) of these hypotheses are correct, contextual factors related to each explanation will provide evidence of the relevant patterns. Thus, an important question to ask is what are the grammatical determinants of this linguistic change and can these be confirmed in contemporary dialect data?

Note

Periphrasis refers to the use of words instead of inflections. *Do* periphrasis refers to the use of the verb 'do' in negative sentences, e.g. *I do not know*, and questions, *Do you know?* This is also referred to as *do* support because 'do' supports the tense morphology of the sentence.

Methodology

Research has shown that variation among the forms used for stative possession is restricted to present tense (LeSourd, 1976; Quinn, 2004, 2009; Tagliamonte, 2003). Thus, every token of *have*, including the morphological variants *has* and *'ve/'s got*, *(have) got* and *got*, were extracted from the Roots Archive and the British Dialects Archive. This provided 3,715 tokens. Each token was then coded for a series of factors implicated in the trajectory of development of the forms, including (e.g. pronoun or noun phrase), the presence of contraction and the nature of the complement (e.g. abstract or concrete).

The old wireless

Aye, but och there were nothing had the character of them old Bakelite wireless that whistled and cracked and got on. And then everybody seemed to want to hear boxing matches. And I don't know where they were but this thing aie whistled and chirped and got on. And there maybe two or three old neighbours come up to hear this you know. Which must tell you now that no everybody even had a wireless … Aye, there were a lump of old boys come to listen to that boxing and we were feared to open our mouth. We were whiles banished altogether to the back of the house or down the road. And you were sort of fascinated with this whistling and crackling and chirruping and going on at this thing. And then everybody was an expert and they would prod at her and turn her a bit. You know, but then there were a lump of copper-wire that got throwed out the window. You know … it done it nae good but some of the old boys thought it done it good. (Sandy Milroy, 60, CLB, 019)[20]

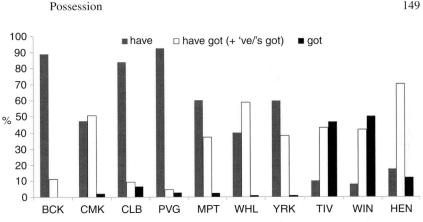

Figure 7.14 Proportion of stative possession forms by community

Distributional analysis

The first step in the analysis of stative possession is to determine the overall distribution of forms across communities. Figure 7.14 shows the comparative cross-variety perspective.

The Roots Archive communities are split. The two Northern Ireland communities Cullybackey and Portavogie, along with Buckie, on the far north shore of Scotland, stand out at the far lefthand side of Figure 7.14. In these communities, by far the majority form is *have/has*, suggesting that in these varieties *have got* and *got* are still at a very early phase in their development. In contrast, Cumnock, Maryport, York and Wheatley Hill have robust variability between the old and new forms. Henfield in Sussex has the most *have got*. Recall that this community is mostly middle class, suggesting that use of *have got* has prestige. Finally, the two south-west communities, Wincanton in Somerset and Tiverton in Devon, have near equal use of *have got* and *got*, the newest layer in this system. In essence, the communities mirror the diachronic development in this system. They reflect three stages in the development of *have got*: early, mid-range and near completion. A further step is to inquire how this is happening.

The data from some of these communities (York, Buckie and Wheatley Hill) spans the age spectrum from youngest to oldest individuals. This means that I can use the apparent time construct to corroborate this interpretation.

Figure 7.15 reveals that in each community the oldest generation uses the most *have* and there is a shift in apparent time towards more *have got*. The individuals under thirty-five show the highest rates of use in Buckie and York and close to the highest rates in Wheatley Hill. In contrast the oldest individuals (those over sixty-five) have the lowest rates.

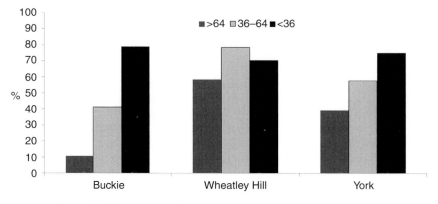

Figure 7.15 Proportion of *have got* across age groups by community

In sum, not only are the communities arrayed from north to south, from peripheral to urban, from conservative to mainstream with regard to increasing use of *have got*, but this trajectory is also reflected in generational differences in each individual community.

Muckel

A muckel. He said he had a muckel o' beasts. He says 'Come on,' he says 'I'll show you it's only a muckel o' beasts up here.' And Samuel looked at me, and I knew then a muckel, I know that it's 'a few'. (Kate Devoy, 62, PVG, 004)[21]

Constraints analysis

As we saw earlier, frequency is only part of the evidence that can be used to examine change in progress. Let us now consider the constraints underlying the three explanations that have been put forward to explain the change from *have* to *have got*: syntax, contraction and grammaticalization.

Syntax As is well known, the verb *have* in English is undergoing change (Trudgill et al., 2002). Much of this flux is visible in the way lexical *have* behaves in *do*-support contexts, a difference that is considered one of 'the best known transatlantic distinctions in syntax' (Denison, 1998: 202). The use of *do* support with lexical *have* (e.g. *don't have*) is said to have evolved first in North America and only later spread to Britain. However, recent research reports that there is 'a very wide range of options' across varieties of English worldwide for negating *have* (Nelson, 2004: 300), to some a 'bewildering' set, as in (31) (Biber et al., 1999: 160).

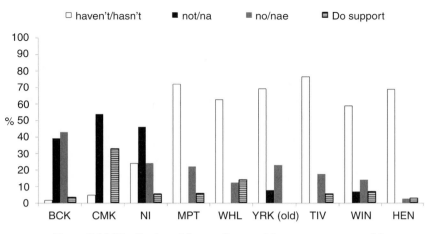

Figure 7.16 Distribution of forms of negated *have* across communities

(31)   a. Pattern 1: I *don't have* (any) money.
      b. Pattern 2: I *haven't* any money.
      c. Pattern 3: I *haven't got* any money.
      d. Pattern 4: I *have no* money.
      e. Pattern 5: I'*ve got* no money.
        (all from Biber et al., 1999: 300)
      f. Pattern 6: I *ain't got no* money.

Figure 7.16 reveals a range of different negation patterns. You can see why the many options for negating lexical *have* could be called bewildering. However, let us put the patterns into geographic perspective. First, Buckie stands out. The system is dominated by negatives that are marked with *na* 'not' or *nae* 'no', as in (32).

(32)   a. I *have na got* a trade
      b. They'*ve nae* family

The remaining communities have patterns of negation that are quite regular. From Maryport to Henfield *haven't/hasn't* dominates as the favoured way of negating *have*. This contrasts with Nelson's (2004) findings for the ICE-GB corpus where there was 41% *do* support for lexical *have*. Here there is only a smattering of *do* support, except in Cumnock, where it appears 33% of the time, as in (33). Elsewhere it appears to be a low frequency option, as is *no* negation.

(33)   a. I *don't have* him the day but I have him three days a week. (CMK/e)
      b. I know when I *don't have* any sweeties in the house. (CMK/u)

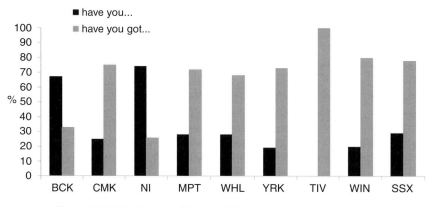

Figure 7.17 Distribution of forms of *have* in questions across communities

The next step is to consider questions, another context in which we can tease out the behaviour of *have*. Figure 7.17 shows different types of constructions used for questions across dialects.

Use of *have* predominates in Northern Ireland and in the far north of Scotland (Buckie), as (34) and (35), but everywhere else the most frequently used form is *have got*, even in Cumnock (16/21), as in (36).

(34)   Northern Ireland
     a. *Have* you an orchard probably, *have* you? (CLB/n)
     b. Well how *have* you such nice skin? (PVG/d)b.

(35)   Scotland
     a. *Has* she a brooch and all? (BCK/9)
     b. *Have* you any kept out for the cat? (BCK/6)

(36)   Cumnock
     a. *Have* you aie *got* visitors? I says, 'aye'. (CMK/G)
     b. *Has* anybody *got* a match? (CMK/d)

The results from the examination of negatives and questions shows us that in contemporary British dialects there is a spectacular divide between northern varieties where *have* is still the major form and more southerly locations where *have got* has made significant inroads in the grammar.

However, negatives and questions are infrequent in this data (less than 400 negatives and only 130 questions out of nearly 4,000 tokens), so despite the dramatic differences by sentence type across communities, much of the variation between *have* and *have got* must be accounted for elsewhere.

Lassies

Well Fiona Kerr gave me this wee crochet thing that her mother did. And it's a right wee lassie's thing. It's lacy, ken, with the wee ribbons. She says my mother's been doing that

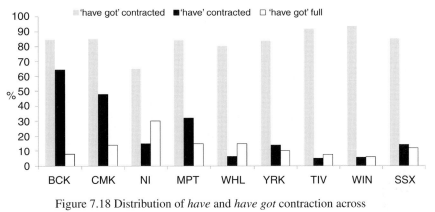

Figure 7.18 Distribution of *have* and *have got* contraction across
communities

pattern fae she was a lassie. Whenever somebody had a baby she would crochet this wee
matinee jacket. (OM, CMK, 007)[22]

Contraction Another explanation for the transition from *have* to *have
got* is that *have got* developed as the result of weakening (Crowell, 1959). The
original form was *have* in its various morphological forms; however, it was
always a single-syllable word with stress. By the sixteenth century, contraction
developed, making it possible for *have* to be reduced to a single element preceding pronouns, as in (37).

(37)   a. She*'s* only one daughter and her two grandsons. (CMK/m)
       b. He*'s* a beautiful head of hair. (CMK/v)
       c. He*'s* a lot of customers. (CMK/n)
       d. He*'s* a farm. (PVG/g)

The reduction of *have* to a single sound [v] or [z] paved the way for the insertion of *got* as in (38), as speakers responded to a need to mark the subject–verb
relationship more overtly (Crowell, 1959: 283).

(38)   a. He*'s got* three daughters and a son. (CMK/h)
       b. We*'ve got* a church. (CMK/d)
       c. I*'ve got* this car. (PVG/h)
       d. You*'ve got* Scotch blood in you. (PVG/@)

This hypothesis predicts that there should be a correlation between the contraction of *have* and the use of the *got* constructions. Figure 7.18 tests this
possibility by examining the distribution of contraction across communities. It exposes the contraction of *have* in the dark bars. It represents a substantial proportion of the system in Buckie, Cumnock and to a lesser extent
in Maryport. Everywhere else contraction of *have* is a minor variant in the

system. This isolates contraction to a specific set of communities and suggests a regional differentiation. More importantly, there is no uniform relationship between the contraction of *have* and either full or contracted forms of *have got*. Instead the contracted forms of *have got* predominate everywhere – the light bars – (except in Northern Ireland where, as you recall, *have got* is rare). The full forms of *have got* occur most often in Northern Ireland too. This may be explained as an early developmental situation where weakening of *have* has not yet occurred. Everywhere else this form is infrequent and hovers around 10% of the system. It may be the case that Scots dialects preserve an earlier stage in this change that has since been lost in more mainstream varieties.

There may be a way to go back to this earlier phase. Recall that there is another nuance to this development. Contraction of *have* supposedly began in pronominal contexts. If so, then the use of *got* should be sensitive to the type of subject. In other words, we may be able to use this correlate to track the development of this system in another way. First, all contexts of stative possession were marked by *have*. Then contraction of *have* took place, leading to use of *got* in contexts with pronouns. The last stage would be when *got* is used with noun phrases. This hypothetical development is summarized in (39):

(39)   • All contexts take *have*.
      • Contraction of *have* (*'s*/*'ve*).
      • *Got* is inserted to 'reinforce' the contexts with contracted *have*, e.g. *I've*, producing *I've got*.
      • *Got* extends to noun phrase contexts, e.g. *The queen's got*.

In other words, if contraction of *have* led to *got*, then *got* would have been initially favoured with pronouns and later spread to noun phrases. More frequent use of contraction with pronouns would be a remnant of this history. Pronoun subjects such as *I*, *you*, *they* may continue to favour the incoming *have got* constructions in their contracted form, as in (40), while *have* may be retained for noun phrase subjects, e.g. *a lot of folk*, *every area* and proper names, etc. as in (41), at least in a community where the system is still in flux.

(40)   Pronoun subjects
      a. I*'ve got* a phone number. (CMK/!)
      b. You*'ve got* Scotch blood in you. (MPT/@)
      c. Be better than that bloody great big angel they*'ve got* at Newcastle. (MPT/f)

(41)   Noun phrase subjects
      a. *A lot of folk have* more time to study. (CMK/l)
      b. *Raynor Fletcher has* his house down on the quayside. (MPT/s)
      c. *Every area has* different words for things. (PVG/d)

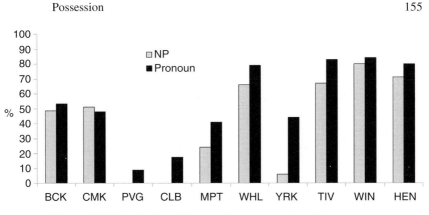

Figure 7.19 Distribution of forms of contraction by subject type across communities

Figure 7.19 shows that in the Northern Irish communities *have got* only occurs with pronouns (and there very infrequently). This is consistent with the idea that the earliest entry point for *have got* was in pronominal contexts. In the three communities in England (Maryport, Wheatley Hill and York) where *have got* has made considerable in-roads to the system, the predicted constraint is visible: more instances of *have got* with pronouns. In the south, however, where *have got* has taken over the system, the constraint is visible, but minimal. In essence, Figure 7.19 shows a logical trajectory of change corresponding to the relative degree of isolation of the communities. However, its presence is minimal in the Scots communities – Buckie and Cumnock. There is hardly a difference in frequency between noun phrases and pronouns here. This is unexpected and requires explanation.

The reason is that both *have* and *have got* get contracted before pronouns in this locale. Further evidence comes from how this constraint patterns in apparent time in York in Figure 7.20. This shows that the effect of type of subject is only operational among the oldest individuals in York where *have got* is just entering the system. By the younger generation the effect has levelled out. This shows that the change was driven by contraction.

There is another explanation that may play into the evolution of this change.

Grammaticalization Jespersen (1961a: 47) observed that *have got* probably entered the stative possessive system for use with physical, concrete things that could be acquired. In this way, *have got* retained the essence of the original form *got*, which was the past tense form of the verb 'get' meaning 'to acquire', as in (42).

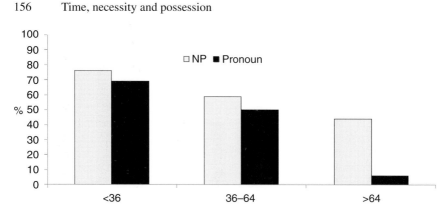

Figure 7.20 Distribution of *have got* by subject type by age in York

(42) a. That's how the street *got* its name, Tower Street, called after that tower. (CMK/017)
      b. He *got* a letter from the King with a commendation. But he never *got* a medal. (MPT/020)

According to this hypothesis, the form 'have got' would first be used with stative possessive meaning in the case of physical concrete things that could both be acquired and possessed, e.g. *a car*, as in (43).

(43) Ken, if you'*ve got a car* – if you'*ve got wheels*, that makes it all the easier. Ken, well my daughter Morag down in Kilmarnock, she'*s got a car*. (CMK/033)

At a later stage in this development, *have got* presumably generalizes to other types of complements that are not concrete, but can be acquired and possessed (at least figuratively), including abstract ideas and concepts, qualities, relationships, etc. as in (44).

(44) a. But mother *has got a spirit* of her own and always had. (MPT/034)
      b. I'*ve got* all the *time* in the world. (CMK/1)
      c. You'*ve got* the inside *knowledge*. (MPT/d)

In the Roots Archive, these two meanings co-exist, as in (45):

(45) a. And I *got an x-ray* … You'*ve got osteoporosis*. (CMK/028)
      b. *Got a letter* in there. Just *got it* the other day. (YRK/058)

Inevitably, there are contexts that are ambiguous. The example in (46) describes a situation in which the subject could have acquired (earned) the 'certificates' or could simply possess them.

(46) [033] He'*s got all these certificates* ken. He went to college up at er – he come fae Ayr up to Netherthird. And he went up here for years and he'*s got all this certificates* and he'*s got* a lot, ken, he can go nae further. (CMK/033)

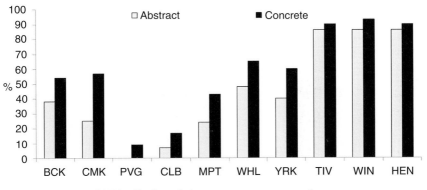

Figure 7.21 Distribution of abstract vs concrete complements across communities

The grammaticalization hypothesis predicts that there should be a correlation between the use of *have got* and the contrast between concrete and abstract complements. Older layers in the system should show a preponderance of *have got* in concrete contexts, but as *have got* penetrates the stative possessive system and undergoes extension, abstract complements should increasingly take *have got*. Indeed, when this effect was tested in British play data, the type of complement effect was visible across three time periods spanning 1750–1935 – *have got* was favoured (and significantly so) for concrete complements rather than abstract ones (Noble, 1985). Moreover, this result was one of the key pieces of evidence that Kroch (1989) used to substantiate the Constant Rate Effect – the idea that change progresses at the same rate across contexts. Figure 7.21 tests this possibility by examining the distribution of abstract vs concrete complements across communities. It shows a constant effect across communities. Despite the (considerable) differences in the frequency of stative possessive forms, *have got* consistently occurs more with concrete complements. A closer look at the nuances across communities reveals, once again, the trajectory of change. In Portavogie *have got* has barely made inroads. In this case *have got* is only used for concrete complements. In Cullybackey, where the rate of *have got* is slightly more elevated, we find the first uses with abstract complements. The effect is pronounced in Buckie, Cumnock, Maryport, Wheatley Hill and York; however, among the three southern communities (Tiverton, Wincanton and Henfield) the effect has levelled, an indication of increasing development of *have got* across all complements.

Further evidence for the constancy of this contextual effect comes from the generational distributions. Figure 7.22 reveals that the type of complement effect is present for each generation. Thus, the type of complement effect is

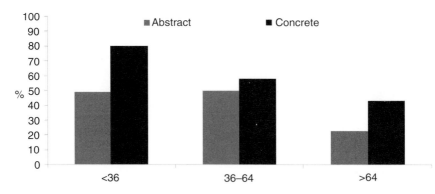

Figure 7.22 Distribution of *have got* by complement type by age in York

remarkably constant, not only across every single community, but also across generations in the same community. Moreover, this is the same whether the community has only limited or near categorical use of *have got*. This semantic contrast pervades the system from communities where *have got* is just beginning to be used for possession to those where it represents the lion's share of the system.

What does variation in stative possession tell us about dialects?

The study of stative possession has provided an enriched perspective on this linguistic change. As with the use of future *going to* and deontic *have to*, both frequency and patterns of use combine to show the steps in the progression of change. The overall distribution of *have got* in the Roots Archive compared to the British Dialects Archive reveals that *have got* is making incremental progress across the geography of the British Isles. In the northern communities, it represents only about 10% of the system. In the southern communities, its frequency is on par with *have*.

Examination of several key explanations for the development of *have got* offered insights into the development of this change. Some constraints are incredibly constant over time (*have got* is favoured with concrete complements). This is true regardless of whether *have got* is just beginning to penetrate the community grammar (as in Northern Ireland), whether the variability between *have got* and *have* is robust, or whether *have got* has nearly taken over the whole system (the younger generation in York). Other constraints are clearly regionally delimited (contraction with *have*) at least in the synchronic data. However, the dialects reveal that contraction of *have* must have paved the way for the insertion of *got*, just as Crowell suggested.

When these results are taken together, they offer a new perspective into grammatical change. They demonstrate that some constraints stay stable over time, clearly supporting the Constant Rate Effect (Kroch, 1989). At the same time, it is apparent that different constraints at varying points in the history of a grammaticalizing system may shift and change over time. As grammaticalization proceeds, a constraint may show gradual levelling as a new form extends to all contexts in the latter stages of development. For example, there are no constraints operating on the use of verbal –*s* in 3rd person singular anymore, at least not in the standard language. The perspective of early onset effects, such as the correlation of concrete complements with *have got*, may differ across communities. Other effects, such as the effect of contraction, may reflect dialect-specific differences (e.g., Scots vs English) or – especially when the same constraint differs in apparent time – highlight a particular stage in a stepwise process. An example is the nonsignificance of the type of subject constraint in southern England. In other words, contextual constraints propel change forward in different ways at different phases in the evolution of a system. In this way, vernacular dialects are particularly useful because they expose the underlying mechanism of a linguistic change and how its operation may differ from one stage to the next. Further, we gain information about aspects of the system that are independent vs those that are local.

Dialect puzzle 7.1

The discerning reader will be able to answer the following questions by carefully reading the examples and dialect excerpts in Chapter 7.

Questions

a. Find an example of subject drop, i.e. a sentence without a subject.
b. Find a zero plural.
c. Identify two instances of nonstandard agreement in 1st person singular.
d. Find a nonstandard term of endearment.
e. Search for an adjective meaning 'unusual'.
f. Find a token of definite article reduction.
g. Provide a single-word cleft.
h. Find a dialect word for 'stay' or 'continue in the same condition'.
i. Can a discourse marker occur in sentence-medial position? Find one.
j. Find dialect variants for *go* in the progressive.

Answers

a. *Didn't know it were gan be six year.*
b. *Six year Ø.*
c. *I's ganna* die. *I were* pottering about
d. *Hen.*

e. *Peculiar.*
f. *t'co-pilot*
g. *It's got its advantages, that.*
h. *she has to bide and count up…*
i. *You must do something, you see, for the war effort.*
j. *I's ganna; it were gan*

8   Expressions

Shall I tell you that broad Yorkshire farmer's expression? It's not rude. It's an old Yorkshire farmer's expression. 'If a fella met a fella in a fella's field could he tell a fella what a fella means?' Have you heard of that one? It's a conundrum, isn't it.

(Daisy Smith, 69, YRK)[1]

In this chapter I examine features that involve adverbs. An adverb is any word that modifies other words, including verbs, adjectives, clauses, sentences and even other adverbs (but not nouns).[2] An interesting fact about adverbs is that they are not always realized as a single word, but also include phrases and clauses. Adverbs, adverbial phrases and clauses are identifiable by the fact that they often answer questions such as 'how?', 'in what way?', 'when?', 'where?' and 'to what extent?' This is why they are often called 'expressions'.

Adverbs and adverbial expressions are perhaps the most popular features of language because they are the most obvious in running discourse between people. Expressions can encompass 'proverbs' or 'sayings', a term used to describe any habitual expression of wisdom or truth, as in the proverb recounted above, and in the sayings in (1).

(1)   a. I mind that's a saying she had, you know, well '*You'll take it before it takes you.*' (CLB/005)
       b. There's a saying that you used to hear quite often – if somebody's maybe at work and somebody says to them '*Your jacket's on a shoogly nail.*' (CMK/015)

Expressions often retain words that have since gone out of productive use in the language, as in (2).

(2)   Then there used to be another habit they used to get. The wall between the boys and the infant school, we used to climb up there on top of there. And we were stood there one day and the master come round. 'I got you this time,' he said, and grabbed all six of us. And 'twas only two of them that was doing it. The other four weren't having nothing to do with it! We had hundred lines! '*Thou shalt* not climb no walls!' (WIN/017)[3]

However, any words or phrases can be considered expressions when they occur frequently and/or are imbued with meaning that goes beyond their standard uses. There are even metalinguistic ways of referring to these types of constructions, including 'a turn of phrase', 'formulaic utterance', among many others. Consider the examples in (3) which illustrate some of the most frequent adverbial expressions in the Roots Archive.

(3) a. She always churned you know and I remember *many a time* I churned. *Many a time*. (CLB/013)
     b. That was where we met and then er and *of course, as I say* we'd been to school together. (MPT/034)

Variation among certain classes of adverbs and adverbial expressions is ubiquitous and pervasive. They often identify people and places and inevitably differ from one generation to the next, from one community to the next and from one variety of English to the next. Some of the unique expressions in the Roots Archive occur only once or twice, as in (4).

(4) a. They say *as cute as a fox* and I think they're dead right too. (CLB/013)
     b. I was standing, full o' drink, full o' rum, *as full as a coot* as the saying is. (PVG/002)

Despite tremendous variation in adverbial expressions across dialects, this is one of the most understudied areas of language variation (but see Waters, 2011). This is perhaps due to the fact that adverbial expressions that function as discourse markers have traditionally been thought to be empty fillers, words that have no meaning or function in the grammar. On the assumption that they have no referential meaning, they are assumed to be used unsystematically, according to speaker whim. Yet due to the fact that adverbial expressions are so colourful and interesting, they are often thought to be uniquely representative of personalities and/or locales where they appear most frequently. This is often a misconception. In many cases, expressions that seem novel, either to a particular person or place, can actually be traced back to an earlier antecedent in the history of the language. I will explore several discourse phenomena that started out innocuously as adverbs, but have been evolving to become a very different type of feature in the grammar, namely discourse markers and particles.

Speak properly
You know you're told you've got to speak properly. You're not allowed to say 'eh?' or 'what?' You're supposed to say 'pardon'. But they say no, that that is actually the dialect way of saying 'pardon'. (Dan James, 64, PVG, 001)[4]

The study of expressions is often subsumed under the catch-all term 'discourse-pragmatics'. Many adverbial constructions are called 'discourse markers' because, instead of functioning as adverbs proper, they are used to regulate the flow of conversation. Typical discourse markers are *oh, well, now, then, you know, you see, I mean* (Schiffrin, 1987). Other discourse markers involve connectives such as *so, because, and, but* and *or*. However, canonical adverbs such as *actually, basically, frankly* can also function as discourse markers. Adverbial expressions such as *as a matter of fact, on the other hand* can also be considered discourse markers. In order to be a discourse marker, the word or construction must have some discourse level function. The linguistic features typically referred to as discourse markers (see, e.g., Schiffrin, 1987) can be differentiated on syntactic and pragmatic grounds. Some of them are 'markers' and others are 'particles'.

The bus accident

I was on a bus – I was on a bus yin day er, coming home fae Curluick. And it was – it was hard frosty weather, icy roads. And the bus was coming down through the Straven moor. That's fae Straven down to Muirkirk. And we're just about – we're just about a mile off the cemetery when the bus went over the banking. Aye, and it went over onto its – went over onto its top. And it was like a concertina, ken. Aye, like a concertina. [Interviewer] Oh was anybody hurt? [004] Aye, well, there was a boy lost an eye. Er, I was sitting aback of the driver but kind of – you just seen the bus, ken. It was pitch black of course, but the lights was on, ken. You just seen the bus sliding and went out through this fence and then it couped. It slid down this banking and it was yin of the old type of bus, ken. No like the modern type, ken. (Hugh Keane, 84, CLB, 004)[5]

Definition

The word 'ken' is simply the verb 'to know' in Scots and Scottish English and is frequently used as a discourse particle. Notice that it occurs five times in the *Bus accident* story above.

Discourse markers occur in clause-initial position. Linguistically, they are defined as adverbs that are structurally attached to the leftmost edge of the initial clause of a sentence (Traugott, 1997 [1995]). Their function is to link parts of a conversation together by signalling the relationship between utterances or stretches of discourse (Schiffrin, 1987: 31; Swan, 1995). Markers will typically be employed to exemplify, clarify or elaborate. Consider the conversations in (5) and (6). Notice how the turn initial markers aid in the flow of conversation from one interlocutor to the next. Nearly every utterance has an overt signal at the beginning, e.g. *aye, oh well, och,* etc. In this way, discourse markers act as 'interactional signposts' (e.g. D'Arcy, 2008: 6).

(5)   a.   [3] *Aye.* They used to be far more work in the spuds for they holed them and then molded them up and …
      b.   [013] *Oh, well* I think so. And if they're too we – weedy you'd ne – had to weed them by hand,
      c.   [3] That's right.
      d.   [013] *Aye. Och* I spent all mi time at them things. I knew all about.
      e.   [3] They didn't do – they don't do that now.
      f.   [013] *Not at all.* Making up pats *and whatnot.*

(6) a. [015] *Oh aye. Oh dear a dear.* That was a yarn. That was a laugh.
    b. [3] That was a laugh.
    c. [015] *Aye,* yes that was, *aye.*
    d. [3] That was something.
    e. [015] *Aye,* And they were a nice family too. Jolly. (CLB/105)

In contrast, discourse particles mark focus or epistemic stance, such as expressing understanding or checking comprehension. Note that the end of the snippet of conversation in (5f) closes with *and whatnot*, apparently a comment made by the speaker that the interviewer shares in the world knowledge of what 'making up pats' in planting potatoes is all about. In this way discourse particles generate a positive stance on the relationship between interlocutors, such as rapport or shared identity (Schiffrin, 1987; Schourup, 1985, 1999). Notice, however, that so-called discourse markers may not always appear in sentence-final position, e.g. (6c). A full exploration of sentence-initial vs sentence-final uses of these markers and particles would be a worthwhile undertaking. It is not clear whether the pragmatic functions and syntactic positions are isomorphic. Some additional examples are shown in (7). Note the alternation of sentence-initial and sentence-final uses. Indeed, it is often impossible from textual data alone, and without further analysis of context and pattern, to determine which is which!

(7) a. He's yin of them boys that when he's out with his wife, *you know*, he could nae stand up straight and talk to you. He – he puts his chin on her shoulder and hides you see. And looks in by the side of her neck *you know*. He hides his face. *You know* a kind of shy boy. (CLB/011)
    b. I've never known yet why I went in nursing. Because *you see* the two of us, a friend of mine that lives in Nottingham, she was always gonna be a nurse and I was gonna be a teacher. And my mother only allowed me to go into nursing on conditions that if I didn't like it I would come back and er I would go to college. *You see* I was still young enough. (MPT/043)
    c. There's a lady she was right friendly with. And er, she took er, multiple-sclerosis, *ken*. And er eventually she was er, really quite crippled, *ken*. And Kirsty went up every morning for a number of years and did her housework. And gave her a bath, *ken*. And er, gave her a bath *and that* and attended to her needs, *ken*. And er they *kind of things*, *ken* for years. And the woman died eventually. (CMK/004)

Discourse particles are thought to be a good measure of the intimacy of conversation, so much so that when they are not present, the interactions tend to be perceived as 'unnatural, awkward, dogmatic or even unfriendly' (Brinton, 1996: 35; cited in D'Arcy, 2008: 6). Consider the examples in (8); notice how the discourse particles are meant to create rapport with the interlocutor. As readers/outsiders, it is difficult to actually understand what is being said in (8a), and unless one happens to know about weaving, the full semantic content of (8b) is quite obscure.

(8) a. And one of her friends was on about this lad who she'd been seeing who works
        at the stables. She goes down *like* mucks out stuff like this. This lad who –
        who she'd been seeing and saying er *like* how old he was *and that you know*
        and *like* bragging about. Well, you would at that age *you know what I mean*?
        (WHL/015)
     b. Well there's good weavers and there's bad weavers. But, *you know what I mean
        like* you get perhaps – get a half a dozen women there and you could pick
        out one that maybe couldn't tie a knot, *you know what I mean*. And you'd get
        another one that's very adept with her hands fingers and can tie the weaver's
        knot *you know what I mean like*. And there's a lot of work in it too *like you
        know what I mean like*. (CMK/018)

Discourse markers and particles are said to be very frequent in mainstream
varieties of English. However, most of those attested in contemporary varieties,
i.e. *well, you know, I mean, eh*, etc., can be found in the Roots dialects, as in
(9). This lends support to the idea that discourse markers and particles have
always been present in the vernacular.

(9) a. *Well* I was in hospital sixteen week. (MPT/042)
     b. Oh she'd a funny name too, but I have nae mind of it. Amazing *eh*?
        (CMK/036)
     c. It's lovely like in music and all that *you know* – a Scotch accent. (PVG/008)
     d. I used to buy in all the stuff for the camp other than food. You know whisky,
        cigarettes, *things like that*. (MPT/073)
     e. No was hard, *I mean,* you were working in the main works in them places for
        washers. (CLB/003)

Exploring these types of expressions used in the Roots Archive and the British
Dialects Archive will provide a much-needed backdrop for contemporary
studies.

Clipping sheep

Oh aye, I loved clipping with hand-shears but the – they've got to be out of touch now.
It used to be about here … The whole thing's all changed. Used to be I would have clip
your sheep, you know, I would have went to you a day to clip and you'd have come a
day to me. And it would ended up there were five or six boys, you know. You clipped
yours the day and yours the morra. It's all bit of crack too, and maybe a wheen of
Guinness and you know, it was a – just a day's fun. (Mike O'Leary, 53, CLB)[6]

Like

Perhaps the most infamous expression in the English-speaking world in the
late twentieth and early twenty-first centuries is *like*. *Like* can be used as a lexical verb, an adjective, or a conjunction and in various other contexts where it is
considered nonstandard. These usages have attracted a great deal of attention.
A large number of studies have focused on 'quotative *like*'. In this case *like* is
used to introduce dialogue that is recounted in conversation, as in (10).

(10) a. We'*re like*, 'How was it?'
      b. And they'*re like*, 'Oh, it was different.'
      c. We'*re like*, '"Good" different?'
      d. They'*re like*, 'You'll see, you'll see.' (TOR/26)

Quotative *like* is a North American innovation that is associated with young people. Not surprisingly, there is not a single instance of quotative *like* to be found in the entire Roots Archive. Nor does it figure in the British Dialects Archive; the rare examples come from the youngest individuals in the corpora, as in (11)

(11)   She *was like* 'You're not supposed to take it with milk, na na na.' Being awful, I'*m like* 'Look, I can hardly take it.' (Sophie Ball, 23, YRK/049)

The fact that there is no such usage among the elderly generation across the British Isles corroborates the idea that there is no historical antecedent for this function of *like*.

However, there are many other uses of *like*, often referred to as 'discourse' *like*, which occur consistently across the Roots Archive and other communities. By this I mean *like* when it is used as a discourse marker or discourse particle (D'Arcy, 2008: 3). Many of these uses are considered typical of North American dialects, as in (12) from contemporary North American English.

(12) a. 'Cause we made *like* a video.
      b. Now *like* my plan is to go *like* with one friend to the movies and stuff like that.
      c. *Like* I know when *like* wherever I start *like* going – buying my own clothes or whatever.
      d. I can read *like*, a whole day and *like*, 'Hmm.'
      e. She'd always wear *like* those tight *like* leather or *like* really tight clothes.
         (all from Toronto English, Canada, c. 2003–2004)

The source and direction of this linguistic change is still not clearly understood. The first step in exploring these uses of *like* is to consider their history.

A bit of fun

I thought I was going bravely down the new road into Carrowdore. That's where he passed me, like. (noise) Shot out of a gun, like. But see … had them boys on the bends, like. You could hae passed them on the bends, like. But see once they had the straight, them big Yamahas, they just left you like that, like. We were only in it for the fun, like. Bit of fun. (Sean Cully 57, PVG)[7]

Historical perspective

At the outset, it is important to point out that use of *like* as a preposition, conjunction and suffix are long established (Romaine and Lange, 1991: 244). Even adverbial uses of *like* have been documented for well over two centuries.

Attestations in the OED date back to the late eighteenth and early nineteenth centuries, as in (13).

(13)   a. Father grew quite uneasy, *like*, for fear of his Lordship's taking offence.
           (c. 1778 F. Burney Evelina II. Xxiii. 222)
       b. In an ordinary way, *like*.
           (c. 1826 J. Wilson Noct. Ambr. Wks. 1855 I. 179)
       c. 'Why *like*, it's gaily nigh like to four mile *like*.'
           (c. 1840–1 De Quincy Style ii. Wks. 1862 X. 224)
       d. He hasn't passed his examinations *like* … He has that Mr. Karkeek to cover him, *like*.
           (c. 1911 A. Bennett Hilda Lessways I. vi. 49)

By the mid-twentieth century, use of *like* was condemned as 'colloquial and vulgar'. Jesperson (1961a: 417–18) reports that *like* is used 'to modify the whole of one's statement, a word or phrase modestly indicating that one's choice of words was not, perhaps, quite felicitous', as nicely exemplified in (14).

(14)   *Like* well I was nae really telling a lie *like* it was a sort of 'tween the lie and the truth. (Pete Dennet, 69, PVG, 003f)

Jespersen goes on to say that *like* 'is generally used by inferiors addressing superiors'. What we can glean from this is that discourse *like* was in use and could modify various different parts of a sentence. It also apparently had some kind of interactional or pragmatic function.

Feared

[Local Interviewer] You can't leave your door unlocked anymore. [005] You cannot. [Local Interviewer] In them days the door was never locked. [005] Never locked at all. You could've kept them open at night and nobody ever come in to bother you. No-one never lifted a thing … The doors is locked and you have to watch who comes in. And you're feared when anybody comes to the door, you're feared to open it if you don't know who they are. They could come in like and startle you and sure what can you do? What could I do with anybody that come in? Sure I could do nothing. [Local Interviewer] Er like er times have changed terribly. (Kate McBride, 88, CLB, 005)[8]

Synchronic perspective

The word *like* has attracted considerable attention in North America beginning in the early 1990s and continuing to the present day (D'Arcy, 2006, 2007, 2008; Dailey-O'Cain, 2000; Meehan, 1991; Miller and Weinert, 1995; Romaine and Lange, 1991; Siegel, 2002; Underhill, 1988).

From what can be synthesized from contemporary studies, quotative use of *like* arose in North America in the early 1980s (Tagliamonte and D'Arcy, 2007; Tagliamonte and Hudson, 1999). However, it is often assumed that the other nonstandard uses of *like* have their roots in North America too. Consider the uses of *like* as a discourse marker, as in (15a) from a young woman in North America (D'Arcy, 2005b, 2006, 2007). Compare it to (15b) from a young woman in York, England.

(15) a. But then this year it's gonna be actual more *like* ground-breaking 'cause I'm learning so many more skills. And *like* I'll actually be able to re-wrap some *like* dressings and wounds and I'll actually see wounds for *like* the first time besides paper cuts and my own scratches and stuff.
(Toronto, Canada, female, aged 19, c. 2005)

    b. One time he came and he was *like*, really *like*, sort-of, you know, n – not nasty but sort-of, sort-of slightly 'Er, er,' digging kind of comments. I said 'Oh'. And then he was *like* being really really nice, and then I'm *like* 'Look, *like* you know, I don't want either of this. I don't want it, you know,' kind of thing, and so that was just a bit funny.
(York, England, female aged 23, c. 1997)

Compare these with the examples in (16), which come from Toronto and York as well, but from older women.

(16) a. Well you just cut out *like* a girl figure and a boy figure and then you'd cut out *like* a dress or a skirt or a coat, and *like* you'd colour it. (TOR, Isabelle Atherly, 75)

    b. It was just *like* a black cotton stuff, but you used to have to back your curtains with it, so that um, it was just *like* a lining, I suppose. (YRK, Millie Larkin, 70)

To date, there is no independent validation of *like*'s 'new' status in North American English. Nor has it been determined that the function of discourse marker *like* is comparable across varieties of English. Few studies have considered the origins of this so-called 'innovation'. The Roots Archive and the British Dialects Archive offer an unprecedented opportunity to track an earlier stage in the development of *like* and thus a further understanding of the origins of this feature.

The examples in (17) show the use of discourse *like* in the Roots Archive. If it were not for the dialect features that co-occur with *like*, e.g. *nowt*, *t'*, *nae*, *ken*, etc. the examples would be indistinguishable from uses of *like* in the North American examples. Recall that these individuals are all over sixty in 2001–2003.

(17) a. I was only *like* forty – forty-one or forty-two or something, aye. (CMK/J)
    b. We were doing *like* a nature study. (PVG/d)
    c. All for nowt *like* just for t'pleasure of it. (MPT/z)
    d. I couldn't stand it *like* I just couldn't. (MPT/a)
    e. Northeast there was always a little bit of road *like* it was my thinking bit of road. (MPT/#)
    f. That was *like* the visitors and we says we would nae mind, ken. (CMK/G)
    g. They were just *like* sitting waiting to die. (CMK/c)

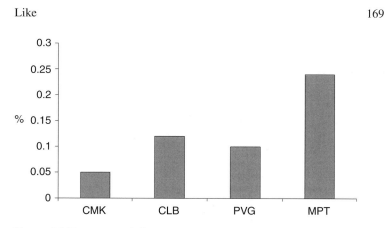

Figure 8.1 Frequency of discourse *like* out of the total number of words by community

h. In those days *like* there was very little traffic. (CLB/r)
i. We were *like* walking along that Agohill Road. (CLB/l)
j. We were doing *like* a nature study. (PVG/d)
k. All builders is the same now, *like*. That Barmwith *like* he's the same. It's always over the time, five or six weeks *like*. (PVG/f)

A first approximation of the use and function of *like* is to determine how frequent it is. In North America, use of discourse *like* is remarkably vigorous, so much so that it is subject to overt commentary by virtually everyone. Among teenagers, it is among the top five most frequent words used and can represent up to 4% of the total number of words used by an individual. In the Roots Archive, nothing near this frequency is found. In total there were only 845 tokens of discourse *like* in Cumnock, Maryport, Portavogie and Cullybackey.

Figure 8.1 shows that the proportion of discourse *like* is extremely low; the maximum on the *x* axis is only 0.3%. In North America, the frequency of *like* overall is ten times this rate (see Tagliamonte, 2005).[9] Nevertheless, no-one would have expected these senior citizens in rural south-east Scotland, northwest England and Northern Ireland to have it at all.

Because *like* is so infrequent in this data, it could simply be the result of idiosyncratic usage or individual style. To check this possibility, we can examine this use of *like* across the population in the Roots Archive. The results are shown in Figure 8.2, which shows that, while certain individuals use considerably more discourse *like* than others, the feature is spread across all communities and most individuals. Thus, we cannot discount it as an idiolectal anomaly. Instead, it represents an infrequent, but pervasive, phenomenon.

Another interesting question is that if *like* is a case of change in progress, then the uses of *like* in this dialect data should provide a glimmer of its earlier antecedents.

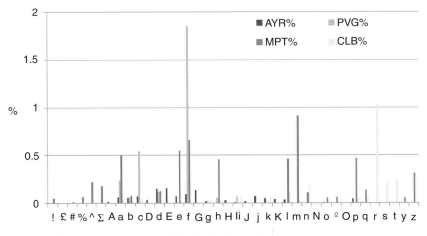

Figure 8.2 Frequency of *like* by individual speaker by community

Dearham

We had a good laugh eh, because we talked Dearham eh, and it suited Isobel's mum. They were never telt to talk rough like, but it suited her like. And er we had a good time eh and a laugh and that. (Elsie Williams, 86, MPT)

Recent research has shown that discourse *like* has been entering the grammar of English in a regular and predictable way one functional head at a time, and this has been going on for at least since the early twentieth century (D'Arcy, 2005a, 2008). In other words, discourse *like* has a patterned trajectory as it grammaticalizes in English. According to D'Arcy's research, the left periphery of the sentence is the most hospitable context for *like*, i.e. in structural terms, the CP and DP positions. These are the syntactic entry points for discourse *like*. Given these results, it could be hypothesized that discourse *like* is at an early stage of grammaticalization in these dialects. If so, we might expect to find it more often in DP and CP positions.

Definition

In the study of language certain structures are referred to by the nature of the phrase. The DP is the determiner phrase, e.g. *the man*, while the CP is a complementizer phrase, which is typically the beginning of a sentence.

In order to take the first step towards answering this question, each token of discourse *like* was coded for where it occurred in the syntactic structure. Clause-final position is the traditional location for *like* according to reports for

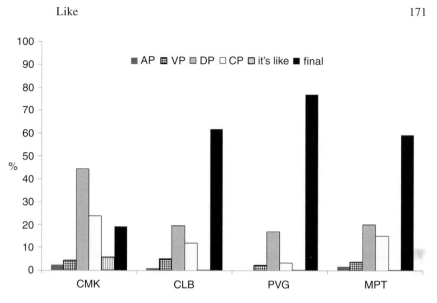

Figure 8.3 Frequency of discourse *like* contexts across communities

northern dialects of English, as in (18a-b). However, *like* may also occur before a CP, before a DP and elsewhere, as in (18c-f). Figure 8.3 shows the frequency of each of these contexts in each community.

(18)   Sentence final
       a. I divn't think anybody likes to be old *like*, do they? (MPT/h)
       b. Oh, I had a wee run in it last night *like*. But she had to go with me *like*.
          (PVG/f/M/57)

       Before CP
       c. But er – *like* I knew that it had its drawbacks of course. (PVG/c)
       d. *Like* well I still see lot of old lads in t'yard now. (MPT/a)

       Before DP
       e. And they had been er dressing her up *like* the day afore. (CMK/q/F/89)
       f. I'll just have a shower in t'morning I think and I'll warm it *like* on my bed.
          (MPT/e)

Figure 8.3 shows how the tokens of discourse *like* in the data are distributed according to these contexts in each community.[10]

With the exception of Cumnock, the vast majority of forms occur in clause-final position in every community (the black bars). In Cumnock, DP and CP position *like* tokens represent the most frequent positions. The overarching finding is that all communities exhibit a range of uses, but these three are the most frequent.

What does the study of 'like' tell us about dialects?

The findings for *like* are provocative in a number of ways. First, this data demonstrates that discourse *like* is *not* a North American phenomenon. Indeed, with the exception of quotative *like*, all the uses reported in North America are present in these elderly people. Second, these results suggest that discourse *like* had already made a grammatical shift towards discourse particle (rather than marker) well before its surge in frequency in North America. It is interesting that the clause-final use of *like* is not among the attested uses of discourse *like* in the current literature on North American varieties of English. It is curious why this use of *like* did not get transported whereas all the other uses did; or if it did get transported, it must have disappeared quickly. This is something that also warrants further investigation. Perhaps there are North American dialects in which sentence-final *like* still exists. The question of why all the other uses of *like* accelerated in North America is an independent question that can only be answered by finding spoken North American English from the relevant time periods.

Champing the blankets

[Interviewer] I suppose the blankets had just been once a year washed were they? [Charlie] Oh aye, just in the spring. It's a saying yet, it's the saying yet about here. 'This would be a good day for blankets.' [Local interviewer] Tell Jackie about when Aunty Bessie was champing the blankets. Afore she'd the twins. You telt me years ago, her waters broke when she was champing the blankets. [Charlie] Aye, that's right, aye. [Local interviewer] What did yous put them in? [Charlie] A tub. Wooden tubs, we had, aye. [Local interviewer] Oh I loved it. It was great. Oh, the lovely warm water was squelching through your toes. [Interviewer] Oh, you actually did it with your feet, did you? [Charlie] Aye. (Charlie Buchanan, 70, CMK)

General extenders

Pigs, hens, everything, ducks and anything that was getting fed, cows and everything was fed with prittas. (Rose Donovon, 89, CLB, 001)[11]

Another frequent expression in the Roots Archive is what is called a 'general extender' (GE), an expression that typically comprises a conjunction (i.e. *and*, *or*) and a generic or indefinite pronoun, as in (19).

(19) a. I'm an onion man or a scallion or leeks *or something like that*. I don't like turnip. (CMK/c)
      b. Your bed was pulled out onto the verandas, fresh air, sun *and everything*. (PVG/$)
      c. We couldn't get any books, particularly any books – er technical books, you know like chemistry *or anything like that*. (MPT/043)
      d. A Scotch accent is very pleasant to listen to, the rolling R's *and all*. (PVG/003)
      e. But she just did nae want to go to a college or university *or that*. She just felt she'd had enough stress *and all that*. (CLB/039)

A unifying characteristic of GEs is that they (1) occur in utterance final position and (2) often evoke a general category of similar objects that the speaker has in mind (Dubois, 1992: 198). For example, the use of *or something like that* in (19a) calls to mind a specific group of vegetables. The GE in (19b), *and everything*, refers first to another group of attributes relating to the outdoors. In (19c) the GE refers to a type of book and in (19d) to the different aspects of Scottish accent.

Yerkin

Paul he come up to ours there … And Paul was saying something till him you know about the way they used to fix their boots theirselves and sew the yerkins. He sat er listened awhile and then he sat and studied … He says, 'what was it you said er was in the boots?' (Laughs). He didn't know what the yerkin was, you see … I had to sew them whenever they ripped. He says, 'What was it you said there something was in the boots?' See I never heared word of a rip (laughs). (Molly Ellis, 89, CLB, 017)

Historical perspective

GEs have been in use for hundreds of years. They can be traced as far back as the fourteenth century in written documents (Poutsma, 1926: 914) and undoubtedly have always been in language. The earliest documented forms were fixed expressions such as *and such, and so forth, et cetera*. All of these older forms are found in the dialect data, albeit rarely, as in (20).

(20) a. We had … different factories over there from like buttons to mowing machines to electrical instruments for hospitals *etcetera*. (MPT/017)
  b. He was doing the lambing *and such*. (CMK/021)
  c. My boyfriend brought me back on his bike it – there was a siren, you know and bombs dropping *and so forth*. (YRK/007)
  d. He went down to the countryside selling groceries *and what have you*. (CMK/018)

Two basic types of GEs have been described in the literature, those with *and*, conjunctive, and those with *or*, disjunctive as in (21).

(21) a. I think we'll go and have a cup of tea and a biscuit or a cake *or something*. (CMK/021)
  b. And there were no cars *or anything*. (CLB/036)
  c. I says to her, 'What he means is, do we get anything with it, a drink *or something like that*?' (PVG/001)

There is a core set of generic pronouns that tend to occur in GEs, including *thing(s), stuff, anything, something, everything, nothing*; however, a few unique and idiosyncratic forms occur as well, as in (22). In some cases, dialectal variants of the generic pronouns occur, as in *ocht* in (22d).

(22) a. They supply shops with crisps *and all these fast food things*. (CLB/032)
  b. Youse are putting these men into expense for white coats and hats and boots *and all this old nonsense*. (PVG/007)

   c. Aye, well, I say she would tell you how many folk passes through *and all such as that.* (MPT/005)

   d. If you had put er anything in your hair you would nae get into the choir. You had no earrings, lipstick *or ocht like that.* (CLB/002)

In addition, a type that occurs in the Roots Archive that, as far as I am aware, is unattested elsewhere in the literature, are those with a generic but no conjunction, as in (23).

(23)   a. She teaches *kind of thing,* just in a wee part-time basis. (CMK/b)

      b. I think there's maybe about fourteen *something like that.* Aye. (CLB/a)

Examination of the historical record shows that GEs with *and* developed first and those with *or* arose somewhat later. The earliest GE with *or* is *or something,* which is attested in the early 1800s and *or whatever* in the early 1900s (Tagliamonte and Denis, 2010). This suggests that there is developmental historical layering in this system over time that may be visible in the dialect data.

Synchronic perspective

GEs have been widely studied in contemporary varieties of English in England, Ireland and Scotland, the United States, Canada and Australia (e.g. Britain and Sudbury, 2002; Norrby and Winter, 2001; O'Keeffe, 2004; Overstreet, 1999; Pichler and Levey, 2011, Cheshire 2007). A standard set of forms are commonly reported, including *or something, and everything, and things (like that), and stuff (like that)* (Biber et al., 1999: 116). Another common observation is that GEs are rising in frequency, with higher use typically associated with younger individuals, often females. Further, GEs are often associated with different levels of formality. This is likely in part due to their wide-ranging variety, from forms that are almost literary (e.g. *and so forth*) to those that are highly vernacular (e.g. *and that*). GE use in general is said to be typical of conversational language. GEs are also often associated with class and other socio-economic groupings. For example, certain GEs such as *and things* are associated with middle-class individuals, while others, e.g. *and that* (Cheshire, 2007: 165) or *and that lot* (Stenström and Andersen, 1996: 102), are associated with working-class individuals. At the same time, GEs are claimed to have interactional uses, apparently functioning to mark in-group affiliation and rapport, e.g. *and ting* 'and things' in Trinidad (Youssef, 1993).

Rooting around

Shaun was rooting through ... hashing about among stuff, you know, looking for stuff and always getting stuff. (Andrew Myers, 63, MPT 001)

   Researchers have also noticed that the generic words in GEs do not always match their referents. Grammatically, generics such as *thing(s)* should refer to count nouns and those with *stuff* should refer to mass nouns; however, that is not always the case. Nor do GEs always have a clear-cut set they can potentially refer to, as in (24) (e.g. Winter and Norrby, 2000: 4).

(24)   a. Aye, she could nae cope with the stairs. My mother's *had both her hips broken and that*. (CMK/007)
       b. Dan used to live in Belfast and where he *served his time and all*. (PVG/008)
       c. And we all got measured and got wir kilts and wir red tunics with the white piping on it, *sporrans and everything*. (CMK/028)

One wonders what should be inferred by the GE *and that* in (24a) and what else might be involved in 'serving one's time' in (24b). Note too the in-group, cultural knowledge required to interpret (24c). One needs to know what a 'sporran' is in order to interpret the GE.[12] This characteristic of GEs reveals that, although one of their functions is generalization to a set (Aijmer, 1985), there may be other functions.

This peculiar mismatch in form and function is attributed to grammatical changes in the function of GEs. As GEs develop, the constructions are thought to get shorter. For example, forms such as *and things like that* may evolve into *and things*. Part of the development of GEs is thought to be due to an extension in function. For example, while starting out as a generalization to a set, they come to be used for all kinds of generalizations. At a later stage, they apparently may not generalize to a set at all. Thus, the forms *and that* and *and all* in (24) could be the result of this type of development.

Methodology

In order to examine the nature of GEs in the Roots Archive, every expression with a conjunction and/or generic in a clause-final position was extracted. This provided a total of 1,687 GEs across the four communities. Each token was then coded for the form of the GE, the generic (e.g. *thing, stuff, something*, etc.), the length of the construction (e.g. *and things* vs *and things like that*), its co-occurrence with any other discourse marker or particle in the same clause (e.g. *ken, you know, I mean*, etc.), the community, and the individual.

Distributional analysis

Table 8.1 provides an inventory of the major GEs in the Roots Archive.[13] The table summarizes the nearly 88 different types in the data by grouping the GEs according to generic. The most frequent form of each category is displayed first followed by a combination of all the other variants of that generic type.[14] Table 8.2 provides a breakdown of the most frequent fixed expressions that are grouped together as 'other' in Table 8.1.

Table 8.1 *Distribution of GEs in the Roots Archive*

General Extender Type	%	N
and that	23.9	**318**
and all	19.7	**262**
and all that	4.0	53
Combined *and (all) (that)*	27.8	639
or something	18.8	**249**
or something + variants	6.3	84
and things	3.3	56
and things + variants	10.6	**179**
and everything	6.6	**112**
and everything + variants	0.7	12
or anything	4.7	63
or anything + variants	2.6	35
and stuff	1.8	24
and stuff like that + variants	0.8	10
Other	13.6	205
TOTAL GEs		1,687

Table 8.2 reveals that nearly a full third of all GEs in the data are some combination of *and (all) (that)*. Variants with the generic *something* or *thing* make up the bulk of the remainder, followed by *everything*, *anything* and *stuff*. The large catch-all category 'Other' comprises innumerable idiosyncratic forms along with a group of fixed expressions that include *and what not, and such, and all the rest*, etc., all well under 2% of the data.

In sum, the Roots Archive is consistent with previous research on GEs in that the GE system is rich in variation of forms. However, the particular GE inventory in these communities contrasts markedly with existing reports in the literature. The two conspicuous differences are (1) the rarity of variants with generic *stuff* and (2) the frequency of the forms *and that, and all, and all this*. Earlier research on this area of the grammar has suggested that variants with *stuff* as well as the form *and that* represent more recent layers in this system. While this data corroborates the claim that *and stuff* is an innovation, it demonstrates that the GE *and that* is old fashioned.

The next step is to consider whether the Roots Archive communities are differentiated with respect to this overall picture.

Figure 8.4 confirms that the communities have a parallel pattern with respect to their inventory of GEs. It is evident that *and (all) (that)* is the prevailing GE in every community; indeed, in Cumnock, Cullybackey and Maryport it dominates the system by a wide margin (the black columns). The GE type with *something* is most robust in Cumnock and Cullybackey, whereas in Portavogie and Maryport variants with *thing* are the most frequent. The rate of use of

Table 8.2 *Distribution of 'Other' GEs in the Roots Archive*

General Extender Type	%	N
and what have you	.02	36
or nothing	.02	34
or what	.01	28
and all the rest of it	.02	21
and so on	.009	16
and such	.008	14
and what not	.007	12
Remaining GEs	.026	44
TOTAL		205

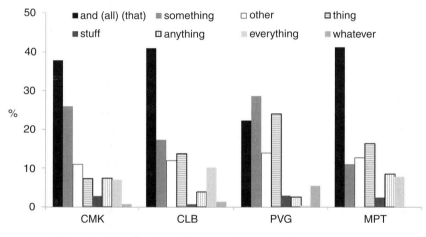

Figure 8.4 Distribution of GE types by community

forms in the 'other' category is relatively stable throughout. None of the communities show more than a few tokens of *stuff* or *whatever*, the two forms that are reported as frequent in contemporary varieties. These discrepancies between these conservative dialects and the contemporary dialects suggest that there has been considerable change in this system over time.

Constraints analysis

The status of GEs in terms of linguistic change varies greatly across the studies that have approached this system quantitatively: (1) in Montreal, Canada, in the 1990s GEs were found to be constrained by social factors and register differences (Dubois, 1992); (2) in Toronto, Canada, in the 2000s, only the favoured generic was changing (*thing(s)* → *stuff*), but patterns of use remained stable in apparent time (Tagliamonte and Denis, 2010); (3) in Reading, Milton Keynes and Hull in the 2000s GEs were found to be undergoing grammatical extension and change, and the state of grammatical development differed depending on the specific GE, i.e. *and that* and *and everything* were found to be the most grammaticalized; (4) in a study of the British National Corpus *or something* was the most grammaticalized (Erman, 1995: 146); (5) in Berwick-upon-Tweed, England, in the 2000s GEs were found to have important social conditioning (Pichler and Levey, 2011); (6) finally, in York (c. 1997) a development towards the generic *stuff* was found, much like what is reported for Toronto, Canada (Denis, 2011). These findings are mixed, and it is difficult to know how to interpret the discrepancies.

Our Tom

Now our Tom couldn't make a wheel. He packed it in trying 'cos he couldn't get it right. Them old cartwheels. And father just used to look at them – they're perfect when he finished. 'I don't know how he gets them like that', our Tom used to say, 'I don't know how he gets them that way.' (Bob Ellis, 78, MPT, 027)[15]

The Roots Archive offer critical insights to interpret and explain these disparate findings. They will give us some insight into an earlier stage in the history of the GE system. This will contribute to the broader question of grammaticalization as well as offering further insights into the nature of change at the discourse-pragmatic level of grammar.

Note that a central issue that emerges from the literature is whether or not GEs have been subject to grammatical change or lexical replacement. The two main indicators of grammaticalization are (1) a change from longer GEs to shorter ones and (2) a change from collocation of GEs with other discourse features to lack of collocation effects. The key evidence for lexical replacement is marked change in the use of the generic but no shifts in the contextual grammatical constraints.

Children

[007] Bairns. [008] In the east coast they talk about bairns, don't they? [007] It's a lovely word. [008] They use it all the time. [1] But you never say weans? [007] No, I think we got that from the Glasgow ... But bairns is a lovely word. [008] Bairns is actually nicer. [007] It's a beautiful word, bairns. [008] It's far nicer than weans. (Joan Dewar, 67, CMK, 007 and Morag Harris, 65, CMK, 008)[16]

Length of the GE   Research on three English towns in the 2000s found a high frequency of *and that* (Cheshire, 2007: 164, table 4). Following Aijmer (2002: 227), Erman (1995: 145) and others, Cheshire reasoned that this was the result of a gradual loss of the longer GE forms due to erosion, a mechanism

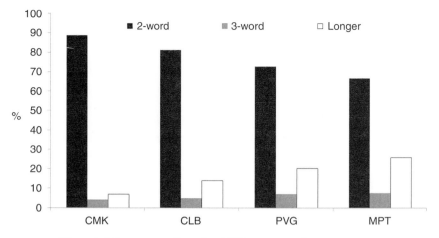

Figure 8.5 Frequency of length of GE by community

of grammaticalization (Cheshire, 2007: 167). In this hypothesis, longer GEs such as *and things like that* would have been present at earlier stages in the development of the GE system. Then, these would have gradually evolved into shorter GEs to arrive at a situation of frequent use of *and things*. If this trajectory is accurate, we would expect a greater number of longer GEs in the Roots Archive. Figure 8.5 tests this possibility by comparing the frequency of short and long GEs in each community. It provides a striking demonstration that the shortest GEs are predominant across all communities in the Roots Archive. Interestingly, the longer GEs show the highest frequency in Maryport. This is the locale that has previously exhibited the most advanced profile among the Roots Archive communities. If anything, this suggests that the *longer* GEs are developmentally advanced rather than the short ones!

Definition

Erosion in grammatical change refers to the loss of phonetic substance. As forms undergo grammatical development, they tend to shorten, lose stress and become dependent on surrounding words, e.g. *because* → *'cos*, *going to* → *gan*, etc.

However, Figure 8.5 groups all of the GEs together. Figures 8.6–8.9 now split the data so that the results for the forms with the highest frequency can be viewed across communities. In addition, I separate each generic so as to view the long and short forms in each type separately.

Figures 8.6–8.9 confirm that the long vs short phenomenon reported in the overall perspective in Figure 8.5 accurately reflects the situation for each GE

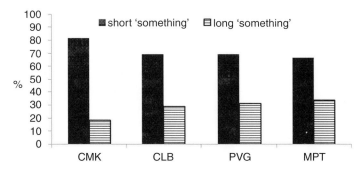

Figure 8.6 Proportion of long vs short variants with generic 'something'

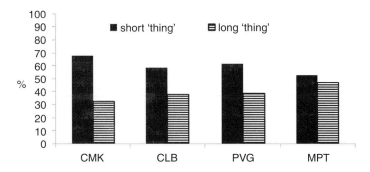

Figure 8.7 Proportion of long vs short variants with generic 'thing'

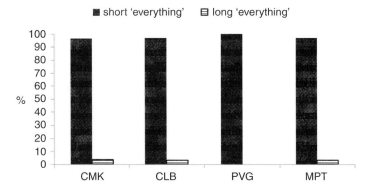

Figure 8.8 Proportion of long vs short variants with generic 'everything'

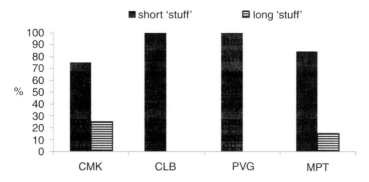

Figure 8.9 Proportion of long vs short variants with generic 'stuff'

type and for each community. There is no evidence for a trajectory of change from longer to shorter GEs in this data.

Collocation of GEs with discourse features Another proposed indicator of grammatical change in the GE system is collocation with other discourse-pragmatic expressions. Cheshire (2007: 185) argues that as the GEs develop new pragmatic functions, they no longer require the support of other discourse markers. In this hypothesis not only would longer GEs such as *and things like that* occur more often at earlier stages in the development of the GE system, but they would also co-occur with discourse markers to a greater extent than would shorter GEs. If this trajectory is accurate, we would expect a greater number of longer GEs in the Roots Archive to co-occur with discourse particles.

Table 8.3 tests this possibility in the Roots Archive by tabulating which discourse particles co-occur with each of the main GE types (compare Cheshire, 2007: 186, table 9).

The most frequent discourse features used with GEs in the Roots Archive are *you know* (N = 76), *aye* (N = 25) and *ken* (N = 25). Most of the GEs co-occur with these forms. However, the GE with *stuff* rarely occurs with any discourse feature. Moreover not a single one occurs with *or anything*. The 'Other' category is distinguished from the other GE types by the occurrence with *like* and *I don't know*. Importantly, *and (all) that* co-occurs with the most wide-ranging discourse features in these materials. This contrasts with the claim made for *and that* in English dialects.

It must be kept in mind that discourse features in general are infrequent with GEs in the Roots Archive. The most robust forms combined represent less than 10% of the GE data. In sum, here too there is no evidence for the proposed trajectory of change from reliance on discourse features to stand-alone GEs.

Table 8.3 *Co-occurrence patterns with general extenders and discourse features*

General Extender	Discourse Marker									
	you know	*aye*	*ken*	*I mean*	*eh*	*just*	*anyhow*	*like*	*kind of*	*I don't know*
and (all) (that)	✓	✓	✓	✓	✓			✓		
something	✓	✓	✓	✓			✓			
thing	✓	✓	✓		✓					
everything	✓	✓		✓		✓				
stuff			✓							
anything										
Other		✓			✓			✓		✓

There is simply a paucity of discourse features in these communities (in comparison with contemporary varieties), whereas GEs are abundant.

Ken

Aye, I used to say oh I'm no a great singer. Never mind I'm used to say I'm no a great singer but the folk love to hear the all songs ken that I was singing. And er, this man said to me this night about this song he kent when he was young and his mother sang it. And er, he started to sing it and I did ken it. (Joan Dewar, 67, CMK)[17]

What of 'and that'? Finally, let us consider how the major GE type *and (all) that* distributes across communities. Recall that the form *and that* is the pivotal form proffered as evidence that the GE system is changing over time. The argument is that it is the most advanced in terms of grammaticalization based on tests for frequency, length and co-occurrence with discourse features. Figure 8.10 plots the frequency of each of *and all*, *and that* and *and all that* in the Roots Archive. It reveals that the distribution of these forms is highly differentiated from one community to the next. Maryport favours the *and that* variant, Portavogie favours *and all that* and Cumnock and Cullybackey favour *and all*. Perhaps not surprisingly, these two also share the same pattern of frequency. Overall, however, we can now see that *and that* is relatively frequent across communities, but most especially in Maryport, in north-west England.

What does the study of general extenders tell us about dialects?

The study of GEs in the Roots Archive has offered a glimmer into an earlier stage in the general extender system, at least in northern varieties of English.

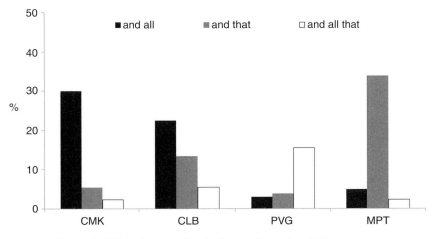

Figure 8.10 Distribution of *and all*, *and that* and *and all that* by community

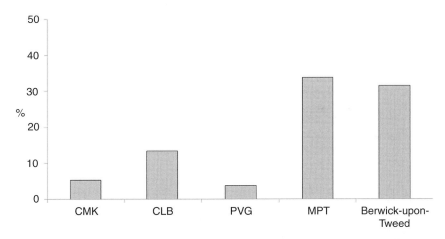

Figure 8.11 Proportion of *and that* in the Roots Archive compared to Pichler and Levey, 2011, Berwick-upon-Tweed, England

Given the competing hypotheses regarding the current status of the GE system in contemporary varieties in England (and elsewhere), this is an important addition to the current body of knowledge. As with many of the foregoing studies, both frequency and patterns of use combine to show the inner workings of the system across dialects. Further, the comparative evidence from the overall frequency of *and that* in the Roots Archive compared to contemporary varieties in Reading, Milton Keynes, Hull and Berwick-upon-Tweed suggests that *and that* was/is a conservative feature of northern English dialects. Consider the distributional data in Figure 8.11.

It is instructive to keep in mind that *and that* was also found to be 'firmly entrenched' in working-class speech in Reading, Milton Keynes and Hull (Cheshire, 2007: 165). Thus, it may be the case that the interpretation of *and that* is not an advancing GE in England, but rather the retention of a conservative northern feature generally and an extension of its use from working-class speech to more general usage.

Sheuch

[025] You ken how the sheuchs run through Lugar and the warm water coming fae the (inc)? Well Margaret White aye, said that Mrs. Donis learnt them to wash pots. They did them all out there, Aye,she says. [007] Can you imagine that? Can you imagine you'd take your pots outside to this sheuch? (CMK/ E\sther Hamilton, 88, 025)[18]

Dialect puzzle 8.1

The discerning reader will be able to answer the following questions by carefully reading the examples and dialect excerpts in Chapter 8.

Questions

a. Find a dialect word for 'story'.
b. Find a nonstandard intensifier.
c. Identify an expression for 'talking about'.
d. Spot evidence of erosion of an initial syllable.
e. Where is there a use of *like* for approximation?
f. Find verbal –*s* with 2nd person plural.
g. Spot an instance of definite article reduction.
h. Find a nonstandard 2nd person plural pronoun.
i. Identify an unusual variant of 'do not'.
j. Find an example that has three *like* tokens.

Answers

a. *Yarn.*
b. *She was right friendly.*
c. *One of her friends was on about this lad.*
d. *It was sort of 'tween.*
e. *I was only like forty.*
f. *We says.*
g. *Like well I still see lot of old lads in t'yard now.*
h. *Youse are putting these men into expense for white coats and hats and boots …*
i. *I divn't think anybody likes to be old, do they?*
j. *All builders is the same now, like. That Barnwood like he's the same. It's always over the time, five or six weeks like.*

---

9 Comparative sociolinguistics

> But I mean when you look at the time now and look at the times we had then, you could nae compare them.
>
> (Rob Paisley, 78, CLB, 008)

In this chapter, I take a step back from the individual linguistic analyses and consider the findings from an overarching perspective. All told, I have shown the results of twelve accountable variation analyses of linguistic features spanning morphology to discourse. Each of the linguistic features examined throughout the chapters has applied a specific set of methodological principles to the study of language variation and change. These include (1) accountability, (2) proportional analysis and (3) an analysis of constraints, i.e. patterns of use. Each study also offers a unique perspective – variable phenomena consistently studied across an array of related synchronic northern dialects. This type of analytic method fulfils the rigorous requirements held to be best practice in the comparative sociolinguistic enterprise, namely accountable analysis of distributions and constraint hierarchies across linguistically and socially related varieties. In addition, I have augmented the variation studies with a series of cursory comparisons of the most frequent words, expressions and verb forms in the data, all of which have peppered the excerpts, quips and stories interspersed throughout the text. Although comparative sociolinguistic interpretation can be complicated by numerous factors, social and otherwise, the broad perspective of mutually reinforcing data sets and consistently applied analysis go a long way towards offering a unified interpretation.

Rue the day!

Aye, she says I've a surprise for thou'. I says 'oh aye, what sort of a surprise?' She says, 'I don't know whether it's a surprise or a shock.' I says 'what?' she says, 'oh Jackie's changed car'. I says 'is he getting Morris thousand then?' she says 'no'. I says, 'what the hell's he getting?' she says 'an (inc)'. I says 'oh'. Talk about letting low down and that. I says, 'thou'll rue it'. And mind I said, 'don't come to me when thou do for changing a good car like for till that bloody thing'. Eh, it was a damn nuisance! (Phil Stephenson, 84, MPT, 022)[1]

Frequency and patterns in language use

Analysis of the *frequency* of individual linguistic forms provided an important first step in characterizing the nature of variation in the Roots Archive and the British Dialects Archive. In most cases the dialects differ in the rate of use of one variant over another (e.g. *for* instead of *because*, *that* instead of *who*, *will* instead of *going to*, etc.). Viewed in cross-variety perspective, these rates can be locally situated, but perhaps most importantly put into broad supra-local relationship with each other. The Northern Ireland communities consistently exhibit higher rates of older forms, e.g. *that*, *will/'ll*, *have to*, etc. Further, using frequency as a measure of development across communities we can determine how far linguistic change has progressed. This is most clearly visible in the comparisons showing a relatively greater infiltration of newer forms in Maryport than Cumnock, Cullybackey or Portavogie, e.g. fewer *–s*'s on 3rd person plural nouns, zero adverbs, conjunctive *for*, infinitive *for to*, etc.

In contrast to the dramatic differences in frequency of forms, the *patterns* that underlie these often expose intra-community parallels. For example, *who* is a rare relative pronoun in all of the dialects; however, in every case *who* is used more often for human referents than others. Another example is that each community uses different adverbs, but all of them use more abstract manner adverbs ending in *–ly* than concrete ones. This means that, while the communities are different with respect to rate of selection of form, they are the same in terms of the systems of grammar that produced them. These overarching similarities reveal, of course, that all the dialects are part of a broader whole.

Contrastive inter-community patterns provide evidence for the progression of linguistic change, i.e. how a change is taking place, or pinpoint the stage of development represented by the variety in question, hence rate of change. For example, with regard to relativizers, the development of the WH- forms was a change that came into English dialects encouraged by contact with French. When linguistic change comes from outside in this way, the change can be expected to begin in areas of contact and spread outwards. In the case of the WH- forms, the change had both an external origin (French) and a socially prestigious point of development (the court in London). Thus, linguistic change can be expected to proceed from the higher societal echelons to the lower ones and from London into the north. An externally oriented change such as this is expected to be different from linguistic change that arises from within the language itself. This difference contrasts *who* and *which*, external, as opposed to *that* and zero, which were present in the language from as far back as records go.

Stages of development and rates of change

When trends are compared across a large inventory of linguistic features and put in context as changes from outside or inside, the optimal explanation for dialect differences can be established. In some cases, differences in the details of individual constraints can be correlated with the relative degree of separation from mainstream varieties and/or the standard language. In this case, we may explain dialect asymmetries as differential participation in ongoing linguistic change. Varieties that have evolved in peripheral as well as culturally cohesive regions, such as Northern Ireland, are more likely to preserve obsolescent forms and patterns from earlier stages in the history of the change. Those that have evolved in situations with greater exposure to mainstream developments, such as York or Henfield, exhibit more extensive layering of forms (diversity) as well as patterns of use that can be interpreted as more fully advanced along the path of change. The conception of a variety as standard vs nonstandard undoubtedly plays into this as well. Further research is required in order to examine how and when individuals make a choice between a 'dialect' form and a standard one. In sum, there is a confluence of many possibilities that might explain why northern dialects are different: their peripherality, their non-standardness, their working-class quality, the simple fact that they are dialects (rather than standard varieties). While there is an inextricable association of regional dialects with lower social status, we must also keep in mind that other factors may play into this correlation as well. Moreover, these varieties may also be different because they arose from a distant history of language contact and assimilation from different languages entirely, i.e. Celtic, Gaelic, Norse.

Words from the wise

'The greatest dialect-related problem in the UK are the attitudes and prejudices many people hold towards non-standard dialects' (Trudgill, 1983: 199). At the same time, 'If we examine the aesthetic evaluations that are normally made in Britain of non-standard prestigious accents, it is clear that, by and large, rural accents are regarded as aesthetically much more pleasing than urban accents by the vast majority of British people' (Trudgill, 1983: 218).

In sum, the patterns underlying the use of linguistic features are crucial for understanding the relationship among dialects and for understanding linguistic variation and change generally. They provide the critical means to infer the deeper similarities and differences across dialects than is possible from a single dialect alone or a study of words or sounds alone or simply a study of forms divorced from their system.

Twiddle

I remember once up at depot I come across this engine driver stuck in t'middle at woods. His engine had conked out. And he had a starting handle. Though he usually started off a morning by electric starters. But er if they were out and the engine stopped had to use starting handle. And they were hard to turn. And I was walking down towards this fellow, saw him struggling, and I says till him 'does thou want a twiddle?' And he says 'Aye, if thou can.' So we gave it a turn, but that's what this other lad, although he was Cumberland born and bred, didn't know what twiddle was. (Jack Dobson, 66, MPT, 025)[2]

The socio-cultural context

In the next section, I will synthesize the results from the case studies presented in this book – twelve analyses of linguistic features from morphology to discourse. Dashes indicate that the data for that community was not analysed. Recall that a critical fact about the linguistic features in these case studies is that none of them are categorical phenomena. Each linguistic feature varies *across* all communities. It is not the case that the feature appears in one or another community but not the others. Table 9.1 provides an overview of the results from these studies. The ticks indicate the communities that patterned similarly with respect to the linguistic feature in question, while the crosses mark the varieties that stood apart.

Table 9.1 provides a striking demonstration that Cullybackey and Portavogie pattern together in contrast to the other communities. For example, in the case

Table 9.1 *Comparison of linguistic features across communities*

Dialect word or pronunciation	CMK	CLB	PVG	MPT
Word endings				
Verbal *–s*	✗	✓	✓	✗
[lexical verbs, present is; past was]				
Adverb *–ly*	✓	✓	–	✗
Aux contraction				
is	✓	✓	–	✗
are	✓	✓	✗	✗
will	✓	✓	✗	✗
Joining sentences				
Relative *that*	✓	✓	✓	✓
Complement zero	✓	✓	✓	✓
Conjunctive *for*	✗	✓	✓	✗
Causal *for to*	✗	✓	–	✓
Time, necessity and possession				
Future *go*	✓	✓	✓	✗
Necessity *have to*	✗	✓	✓	✗
Possession *have*	✗	✓	✓	✗
Expressions				
Discourse *like*	✓	✓	✓	✗
General extenders*	✓	✓	✓	✓

*But in some cases the communities go their own way

Table 9.2 *Comparison of select words and expressions across communities*

Word or expression	CMK	CLB	PVG	MPT
Aye discourse marker	✓	✓	✓	✓
Aie 'always'	✗	✓	✓	✗
Crack 'fun' expression	✗	✓	✓	✓
Haim 'home'	✗	✓	✓	✗
Ocht/och discourse marker	✓	✓	✓	✗
Till 'to'	✗	✓	✓	✓
Wheen 'a few'	✗	✓	✓	✗
Wir 'our'	✓	✓	✓	✗
Weans 'children'	✓	✓	✓	✗
Yan 'one'	✗	✓	✓	✓
Yin 'one'	✓	✓	✗	✗
Youse	✗	✓	✓	✗
Thee/thou	✗	✗	✗	✓
Eh discourse marker	✗	✗	✗	✓

of verbal *–s*, Cullybackey and Portavogie patterned similarly in having higher rates of verbal *–s* in 3rd person plural in contrast to Cumnock and Maryport, which had lower rates (see Figures 5.1–5.3). Nevertheless, there are three linguistic features that unify the three communities Cullybackey, Portavogie and Cumnock. These are adverb *–ly*, future *go* and discourse *like*. Further, there are three linguistic features that unite all communities: relative *that*, complement zero and general extenders. I will return to this observation below.

Cukoo

[Interviewer] Did you hear the cuckoo yet? Oh I have nae heard it this years. Neither the cuckoo nor the corncrake. (Jimmy Parnell, 90, CLB, 007)

Let us also consider some of the most frequent distinguishing words and expressions of these communities, which are notable in the examples and excerpts throughout the book. Table 9.2 shows a comparison of a number of the more prominent forms in the corpora. The ticks simply indicate that the word or expression in question exists in the community.[3]

Words from the wise

'[I]t is quite possible that from early times there existed doublets for many nouns, one of which might be selected by one dialect, another by another' (Lass, 1994: 133).

Supportive to Table 9.1, Table 9.2 reveals that Cullybackey and Portavogie once again pattern together in virtually every case. Many of these dialect words are found in both communities, e.g. *aie* 'always', in (1a) and *haim* 'home' in (1b). Here too, however, there are linguistic features that unite Cullybackey, Portavogie and Cumnock, as set apart from Maryport, e.g. use of *wir* and *weans*, as in (1c-d), *yin* as in (1e). Further, and also similar to Table 9.1, some features unify all the communities, in particular the discourse marker *aye*, which is the most prevalent discourse marker in each locale, as in (1f). It is worth mentioning here that *aye* has long been reported to be 'nearly universal and uniform' (Brockette, 1825) and one of the most characteristic northern English words.[4] These findings confirm this.

(1)   a. I was *aie* horrid careful with my two or three shilling, like. Dances, I'd have went to round about Marygate and Binverden and Ballywall and round that and there. They were grand crack! (CLB/019)[5]
      b. I'm gan *haim* on holiday. (PVG/008)
      c. The daughter gives us *wir* dinner every Sunday night. (CLB/007)
      d. And Lynne and the two *weans*. Young fellow come there sit down on the seat. And when you spoke till him – never seen as mannerly *weans* as them two *weans*. (CLB/017)
      e. You needed to make sure that everybody's all gone the *yin* road at the *yin* time. If they started waltzing and *yin* went *yin* road and another went another. (CLB/019)
      f. Eighteen was he? [006] *Aye*, he wasn't much more like. *Aye*, he drove too hard like. [008] You had a bike? [006] Oh *aye*, had three or four big bikes, Michael. (PVG/008,006)

Another salient characteristic of the Roots Archive that arises from observing the quips and stories is the morphology on certain high-frequency verbs. Table 9.3 shows a comparison of a number of these verbs. Once again the ticks simply indicate that the form exists in the community.

Table 9.3 shows that Cullybackey and Portavogie stand together on every count. They share all of the verb forms. In one case, all the communities are similar, namely in using the forms *telt/selt* as the past tense of 'tell' and 'sell' respectively, as in (2a).[6] Among the other forms, the by now familiar three-by-one pattern holds: Cumnock, Cullybackey and Portavogie have *taen*, as in (2b) and *kilt*, as in (2c) and the various forms of 'go', as in (2d), in contrast to Maryport, which has none of these. Nonstandard verb forms have been reported throughout the English-speaking world; however, to date there are no systematic studies, so areal distribution and system(s) underlying these uses are so far not known.

(2)   a. If the truth was *telt* he'd be glad to get away. (CMK/004)
      b. He's the yin that *taen* that photo of me. (CMK/028)
      c. And the smell would've *kilt* you; it was absolutely atrocious. (CMK/021)
      d. I mind the old woman she *gied* me sixpence. (CLB/009)

Table 9.3 *Comparison of dialect verb forms across communities*

Verb form	CMK	CLB	PVG	MPT
Taen past tense 'take'	✓	✓	✓	✗
Kilt past tense 'kill'	✓	✓	✓	✗
Telt past tense 'tell'	✓	✓	✓	✓
Selt past tense 'sell'	✓	✓	✓	✓
Telled past tense 'tell'	✗	✓	✓	✓
Selled past tense 'sell'	✗	✓	–	✓
Gies/gied/gieing/gien past/perfect/progressive 'give'	✓	✓	✓	✗

Table 9.4 *Comparison of dialect pronunciations across communities*

Dialect word or pronunciation	CMK	CLB	PVG	MPT
Wie 'with'	✓	✗	✗	✗
Tway 'two'	✓	✓	✗	✗
No 'not'	✓	✓	✓	✗
Fae 'from'	✓	✓	✓	✗
Nae 'not'	✓	✓	✓	✓
O 'of'	✗	✗	✓	✗
Divn't 'don't, didn't'	✗	✗	✗	✓
Lal 'little'	✗	✗	✗	✓
Nowt/owt 'nothing/anything'	✗	✗	✗	✓

The Roots Archive is also characterized by innumerable unique pronunciations of certain function words. Table 9.4 shows a comparison of some of the most frequent ones, with ticks again indicating that the word or expression in question exists in the community.[7]

In this case there is not a single item that is uniquely present in only Cullybackey and Portavogie. Instead, the dividing line appears to be Maryport vs the others. For example, Maryport has *laal* 'little', *nowt* 'nothing' and *owt* 'anything', as in (3a-b), and *divn't* 'didn't/don't', as in (3c), but the other communities do not, and Maryport does not have some of the words that the others have, e.g. *fae* 'for', *no* 'not', as in (3d). Cumnock is the only community that has *nae* 'not' and *wie* 'with', as in (3e). Portavogie is unique in having *o* 'of', as in (3f).

(3)   a. This poor body had never had *owt* to do with kids afore you know. (MPT/004)
      b. I'm not a Samaritan, I'm not *nowt*. I'm just an ordinary lad. (MPT/036)

    c. I *divn't* like to tell folk that bit. Because I *divn't* think anybody likes to be old like, do they? (MPT/008)

    d. He's away out this morning and he's *no* coming home the night. (CMK/039)

    e. And it's all done *wie* wee dobs of glue. (CMK/004)

    f. Every side *o'* that hill has a different name. (PVG/003)

In sum, when the communities are compared across these many different dimensions, we gain a comprehensive portrait of the complex patterns of similarity and difference across northern English. Unsurprisingly, the Northern Irish communities stand together. In many cases, there is a unity across Cumnock, Cullybackey and Portavogie reflecting the age old Ulster–Scots connection. Further, the Scotland–England national border is dramatically visible in the patterns that set Maryport off from the other locations. Finally, there is pan-variety parallelism. Recall from Table 9.1 that all the communities share the same (variable) system in each case and it is only in the subtle weights and constraints of variation that the differences emerge. Indeed, it is critical to reiterate that nearly all these linguistic features are variable, not categorical, across every community and every speaker. Thus, northern English may not be effectively defined by an overarching feature pool, but by a composite of systems that jockey between the local and the supra-local.

Nevertheless, perhaps the most arresting finding of this exploration of dialects is not the local idiosyncracies (since that is, of course, expected), but the overarching layers of history that are discovered when the underlying constraints are viewed in cross-variety perspective. The type of linguistic feature targeted for investigation plays a critical role in determining the similarities and differences amongst varieties. The dialect features that operate on one level of the grammar do not behave like those of another. This may prove to be fundamental to cross-variety comparisons more generally and to future analyses focusing on small differences between dialects (i.e. micro-parametric differences) in particular.

Lose the dialect

Sometimes I try to talk a little bit, you know I lose mi dialect. So I'm more better understood. But er it's all wrong. (Andrew Myers, 63, MPT, 003)

Further, the community differences and similarities discovered here, if they can be found in the localities to which the ancestors of our speakers migrated, may provide important evidence to track the origin and subsequent development of transplanted varieties around the world. Indeed, the complexity of this broader endeavour bears much further investigation. For example, locations elsewhere in the world, where emigrants from these areas represented a substantial proportion of the founding populations, should also exhibit features and patterns of language use akin to those found in these dialect areas. Interpreted comparatively alongside these findings, we may be able to understand developments in these locales more easily.

Dialect puzzle 9.1

Go back to the story entitled *The dram* in Chapter 1 and see how many linguistic features of interest you can spot in the story.

Answers

a. Use of *afore* for 'before'.
b. Several discourse markers, *you see, you know*.
c. Past tense form of 'learn' as *learnt*.
d. Quotatives *say, think*.
e. Contraction of an auxiliary on a noun, *man'll*.
f. Relative pronoun *that* for human animates, *he was an engineer that …*

Dialect puzzle 9.2

Consider the use of the word *old*, which is used in many of the examples and stories. What can you observe about its usage?

Answer

In some cases it is used with its original meaning 'having the characteristic or showing signs of age', e.g. in *the old pits*, but in other cases the meaning has extended to reflect the speaker's attitude, e.g. *it was a drizzly old morning.*

Dialect puzzle 9.3

Take a close look at the quotatives in *The birthday present*. What linguistic feature tends to distinguish the protagonist's quotatives from the other people in the story?

Answer

The protagonist's quotatives are nearly always introduced by past tense verbs; the others are in present tense, or have no quotative at all.

a. *I thought.*
b. Ø *'It's on for tomorrow.'*
c. *I thought.*
d. *He says.*
e. Ø *'No!'*
f. Ø *'You won't be frightened, now?'*
g. *They said* (post position).
h. *I said.*
i. *I said.*
j. *He says.*

Dialect puzzle 9.4

Re-examine the examples in Chapter 8. What form – not so far noted – occurs across many of the examples?

Answer

Use of *just* is surprisingly frequent.

10   The legacy of British and Irish dialects

I would nae want tae gie mi brogue away.

(Robin Mawhinney, 55, PVG, 002)[1]

In this chapter I ponder the legacy of these amazing dialects and consider what gifts they offer us for the future. Together the findings provide a synthetic perspective from many different subsystems of grammar as represented by the elders of twelve different communities in Scotland, England and Northern Ireland at the turn of the twenty-first century (2001–2003). The research programme as a whole complies with the standards for comparison laid out in earlier research, including the case for historical connection, 'the joint weight of several sets of data' (Schneider, 2004) and accountable comparative methodology. Let us now consider the conclusions that can be drawn from the results.

Overall, the dialects of the Roots Archive are highly conservative. Indeed, the variety spoken by the oldest generation of individuals in the outlying, off-the-beaten track locations lag far behind what is going on in the urban centres and mainstream populations of Britain. Features that are moribund or gone forever virtually everywhere in the world can be studied here. The peripherality of some of the communities is a critical part of the explanation for long-term maintenance of these features. For each linguistic feature I have examined, the communities exhibit a profile that is consistent with an earlier stage in the ongoing development of that system in English more generally. As historical linguistics has documented, relic areas preserve antiquated features. Yet it is astounding that the tracks of history endure so long. The unique socio-cultural milieu of the North has contributed a great deal to this extensive long-term, socially ingrained, maintenance. As Chesshyre (1987) enshrined in his evocative description of Scotch Corner, the 'north is another country'.

> **Words from the wise**
>
> '[I]t is … likely that certain regionalisms will resist outside influence. There may be structural reasons for a variety to resist a specific prestige feature, but cultural, social and economic differences may turn out to be an even more efficient wall against southern influence.' (Ihalainen, 1994: 263)

I will now review the findings from each of the linguistic features in turn, considering what we have learned from each of them.

Endings with –s and –ly

The –s endings of lexical verbs and present and past tense *be* can be traced back to the thirteenth century in Northumbria, and perhaps hark back further into the depths of time. To some people these –s's are a legacy of the Celtish language (e.g. Filppula, Klemola and Paulasto, 2008; Klemola, 2000; Viereck, 1999). Supportive to this research is the fact that the individuals in the Roots Archive continue to use the –s endings and maintain the foremost historically documented constraint on its use – the northern subject rule. The fact that –s endings are also found in other locations in Britain and southern Ireland (McCafferty, 2003, 2004) does not mitigate this fact. This is because there is a *qualitative* difference in the patterns of use from north to south: in the north –s occurs almost exclusively with 3rd person plural noun phrases, as exhibited by the Roots Archive.[2] In the south, the –s ending has spread to 3rd person plural pronouns, a context that only ever took the –s ending in the north if it was separated from the subject. This type of perturbation in the nature of the constraints that operate on linguistic variation is expected in the case of diffusion of features from one location to another or from one population to another (Labov, 2007). The constraints underlying the variation tend to generalize or change from their original patterning. This subtle but critical distinction provides a new angle for tracking the origins of transported dialects that employ the –s endings. The decisive contexts to watch out for are –s's with 3rd person pronouns and when the verb is not adjacent to its subject.

Atlantic crossing

Oh aye, them days it was desperate getting to America. You see, with that long in the boat, six-to-eight weeks in the boat, you know. Mind they suffered something them 'uns went away there too. And there's Irishmen and Irish people everywhere in America. (Rob Paisley, 78 CLB, 008)[3]

The –ly on adverbs exhibited robust variation between –ly and zero in all the Roots communities. The results reveal both local and universal patterns. From the overall distribution of zero adverbs (36%) and the fact that they exist everywhere, they might simply have been considered a generalized feature of nonstandard English grammar. However, once individual lexical items are distinguished, it becomes obvious that certain adverbs are popular in one place and some in others. Among manner adverbs only, we tested for a well-known historical constraint (concrete vs abstract). Every community has this contrast, exposing longitudinal systematic patterning in the development of this adverb (Nevalainen, 1994a, 1994b). The inter-community stability of this constraint, regardless of overall frequency and across six centuries, provides a dramatic confirmation of the idea that morphological variants change over time, their patterning remaining constant (Kroch, 1989). In contrast, intensifying adverbs present a highly differentiated array from one community to the next. First, the selection of the particular intensifier differs by community. Second, the propensity for zero or –ly on intensifiers differs as well. Thus, the use of intensifiers stands out as a salient marker of particular communities and thus of locality. This suggests that this feature may be a particularly useful diagnostic for cross-variety comparison. More broadly, the combination of constant and local feature within a single variable highlights the complexity of the linguistic system and how this plays out in contexts of change.

NEG/AUX contraction

The promising diagnostic of NEG/AUX contraction is one of those often-attested diagnostics of the relative northern location of a community, i.e. higher rates of AUX contraction in the north. However, I discovered that there is actually no absolute north–south regional pattern. Instead, two varieties stood out for their parallelism – Cumnock and Cullybackey. This is not surprising, of course, given the seventeenth-century population movements from the Lowlands of Scotland to Northern Ireland during the Ulster Plantations. Indeed, much of the quantitative linguistic evidence uncovered by the analyses reflects this age-old socio-historical link between these two localities. This provokes an interesting question: given this strong, regionally circumscribed features, could it be that the NEG/AUX patterns visible in these communities were transported elsewhere? This is especially compelling given the parallels that have already been established between Ulster Scots and Appalachian English in the United States (Montgomery, 1989, 1997; Montgomery and Chapman, 1992). If these patterns were not transported, it is equally interesting to wonder why they were not. Indeed, if the current literature on NEG/AUX contraction is any indication (e.g. Yaeger-Dror, 1997; Yaeger-Dror et al., 2002), it does not appear that AUX contraction is robust in any dialect in the United States. This may be due to the fact that, unlike the case of verbal –s, there was no uniform parallelism across all the northern dialects with this linguistic feature. The northern England community, Maryport, differs from Cullybackey and Cumnock. This means that competing variants must have been transported to North America.

Yet there does seem to be some evidence for distinct regional patterns in the United States, e.g. there is more AUX contraction with *be* in the southern United States (Yaeger-Dror et al., 2002). Thus, further research on this variable may be fruitful.

Conjunctive *for*

The obsolescing conjunction *for* is on the brink of extinction. There was simply too little data here for conclusive investigation. Unfortunately, for this feature we are too late to establish the basis for any cross-variety correspondences other than that this feature exists. This highlights the worst problem for tracking the history of dialects. Many of the older features we may be interested in are gone. But this is an empirical question. To my knowledge this feature has not been studied, or sought out, elsewhere in the English-speaking world.

Oh the women all hurried with their working, ken. And Aunty Mary and er yin or tway of the weans was just getting bathed, and she had to bath them 'cos old Tom would nae've done it. He would nae've put them to bed. [Local Interviewer] Men did nae do that then. [025] And she had a pail of cold water and all got a pot of cold water over them to make them sleep quick (laughs). So they did. Oh mother, nowadays they'd get the cruelty. [Local Interviewer] That's right, aye, you'd be jailed. Oh dear! [025] Aye, for old Tom was an old crab. (Esther Hamilton, 88, CMK, 025)

Relative *that*

Given the findings for the relative pronoun system, the conflicting claims in the literature regarding the WH- words can now be interpreted more fully. Indeed, this system is actually an ideal diagnostic for understanding the gulf between written and spoken varieties of English. The WH- words have not infiltrated the Roots Archive communities nor indeed have they made much headway in other British dialects. This confirms the idea that spoken varieties lag behind the standard (Romaine, 1980: 222) and that peripheral nonstandard varieties lag even further behind (not simply those with Scots heritage). Moreover, the cross-variety perspective reveals that Scots and English dialects are not diametrically distinct, nor qualitatively dissimilar. In fact, the differences are a matter of degree. Nowhere is this more obvious than in the comparison between Cumnock and Maryport. These two varieties consistently pattern together. Even more astonishing is the comparison between these two varieties and the southern communities, Wincanton and Tiverton. This juxtaposition reveals that it is not the case that the northern dialects are so different from the southern ones. They all share many patterns of relative pronoun use: *that* and zero are the dominant forms, and the ranking of the major constraints is parallel. The real difference is between York and everywhere else, whether north or south.

Instead of a Scots–English split, or a north–south split, these results suggest that it is the relative proximity of the dialects to mainstream norms that is definitive. Thus, the key comparative element for future research is to determine to what extent a variety has incorporated the WH- words, and if so the precise contexts where they are used and under what conditions. Further, given the strong prestige association of the WH- words, at least at the root, it will be informative to track how this plays out in different communities, under varying social conditions.

The zero complementizer

The zero complementizer is alive and well in the dialect data and shows no direcrepancy amongst the communities on any count. This result stands out as peculiar, simply because it is so different from all the other findings (where there are consistent differences of one kind or another). Nor is the presence or absence of complementizer *that* in these data entirely explained by processes of grammaticalization, the primary explanation in the literature. While forms such as *I think*, *you see* and *I mean* (i.e. discourse markers with complement-taking verbs) are frequent in the data, they do not explain *all* the contexts of zero. Outside of this small set of constructions that are clearly functioning as discourse markers, the remaining zeros are relatively mundane. Most are not epistemic, nor parenthetical. Yet zero prevails. Similarly, the complexity principle does not entirely explain the use of zero either. While it is evident that constructions that are more complex have a greater probability of an overt complementizer, this too does not explain the complex array of factors impinging on the variation. I can only conclude that all these influences are operating on the grammatical system together. Complexity functions as an overarching processing constraint – a universal we might expect in all levels of grammar, not simply on the complementizer system. The fact that all the communities pattern virtually identically in this regard provides strong corroboration of such an interpretation. Corroborating evidence from elsewhere in the grammar would consolidate this. It may be the case that other linguistic features involving markers of clause linking and hierarchical structure are also prone to complexity constraints. Grammaticalization is an independent process impacting on linguistic systems that targets particular, and likely the most frequent, collocations. For example, the 2nd person singular pronoun + verb 'know' (i.e. *you know*) evolves into a pragmatic marker for ratification. I suggest that these may be the entry points for further change as the pragmatic markers spread from one location to another in the phrase structure (e.g. *You know that I like you → I like you, you know*) and increase even more in frequency. In this way, the collocation pattern itself is like an arrowhead in the initial motivation of this development leaving the imprint of the original contextual pattern on the changing grammar. The findings from these dialect studies contribute to the increasing body of research arguing for a strong relationship between frequency and reanalysis in linguistic change.

Yet even these explanations end up puzzling. Put in context with the many studies of the complementizer system, both synchronic and diachronic, there is a paradox. There has been long-term, steady change from overt *that* to zero over several centuries. With this feature all the communities pattern exactly alike and are entirely parallel to contemporary varieties. Yet on all other counts the Roots dialects have been found to be conservative. Again we are forced to think about the nature of the data under investigation and the dichotomies of standard/nonstandard, written/spoken, etc. In this case, the dialect data strongly advocates a far greater distance between written and spoken language than previously thought, which means that extrapolating linguistic change from comparisons across diachronic written datasets and synchronic spoken data sets requires more considered argumentation. In terms of broader comparison, the prediction would be that other dialects elsewhere, whether peripheral or mainstream, would pattern similarly with respect to their complementizer systems. If they do not, it will be critical to assess the local conditions that could have perturbed this solidly entrenched patterning.

You know

Mary Turner come with a twenty-pound note. And er I says, 'Hang on, Mary 'til I get some change and I'll change it for you.' Well um, Molly Hamilton come 'I'll change it, I'll give you two tens for it' you know. Well, they were putting this money down and I said 'Now hang on, hang on.' So I got Mary's change till her and I says 'Now clear off' (laughs). I says, 'clear off' I said 'showing off with your twenty-pound note' you know. Well, she was just laughing but you couldn't have said that till some folk you know. (Lucy Fisher, 73, MPT, 029)[4]

Infinitive *for to*

The *for to* infinitive, like conjunctive *for*, is a feature that is fading away. The fact that it lingers in the north is another straightforward reminder (especially in conjunction with the other findings) that these dialects preserve an older era in the history of dialects. The fact that two causal connectors with *for* are moribund may be an indication that there is a broader evolution going on in the grammar of English. It could be the case that English has lost other causal connectors as well. It could also be the case that the demise of the connector *for* is due to the fact that the form has grammaticalized into other areas of the grammar. Consider the fact that *for* occurs 18,318 times in the combined Roots Archive and British Dialects Archive. Thus, it is clearly vigorous in other systems of the grammar. It is worthwhile to question how different linguistic systems are organized and how a form that functions in one domain may evolve across the boundaries of the grammar into another function. These are questions that could be answered by a larger study in which the forms and functions of one domain are studied across domains, in essence a cross-system comparison within the same grammar.

Future *going to*

Although future *going to* is making strong inroads in English in the mainstream, and particularly in North America, the results from the Roots Archive enable us to peek into the early days of its development. Because the future uses of *going to* are only beginning to develop in these varieties, the results provide a window into the early stages of this linguistic change. A developing theme in the findings presented in this book is that constraints are not uniformly constant in the evolution of change. In the case of future *going to*, we find, as with other systems of grammar (e.g. stative possessive), that some constraints stay stable over time, supporting the Constant Rate Effect (Kroch, 1989), yet other constraints evolve, in this case temporal reference and grammatical person. This means that the Constant Rate Effect may not be operational in all changes or it may only be reflected in certain types of constraints. When a grammaticalizing form undergoes extension or specialization, the visible consequence is levelling across categories rather than maintenance of contrasts (e.g. Tagliamonte, 2003). Contemporary research on the future temporal reference system will do well to track the development of *going to* not only in these northern varieties, but also across dialects of English elsewhere. It may be the case that *going to* is continuing to evolve in the future temporal reference system. But it could as easily be the case that the division of labour has become specialized between *will* and *going to*. Both possibilities are measurable and can be discerned in the nature of the constraints underlying usage. The fact that some of the same collocation patterns reported in North America (e.g. *going to* favoured for questions) exist in these peripheral localities where *going to* rarely occurs suggests again that patterns in language use are a pervasive part of the grammar. Whether they remain constant over time in all types of change and in all circumstances is an empirical question.

Deontic *have to*

The study of deontic modality exposed a previously unknown tendency towards increasing use of *have to* (rather than *have got to*). Here too, the question of what type of data is under investigation becomes critical. While *have got to* may have taken over in the standard written language, the spoken language is going its own way. Indeed, the trajectory of change in the northern English situation suggests that there has been a reversal in this change. Where once British varieties were evolving towards *have got*, it appears that *have to* may be resurging. This may be due to the fact that *have to* is becoming more and more auxiliary-like as time goes on. Alternatively, it may be the result of ongoing grammatical developments that are not necessarily related to its auxiliary status, i.e. grammaticalization. Broader study of the system of deontic modality across other major varieties of English will present a unique opportunity to track the development of this sub-system of grammar at a time when contemporary British dialects expose an unusual twist in the course of its history. The reversal itself is provocative, especially given its timing and location – mid-twentieth century, northern England. The answer can only lie in expanding the comparative enterprise or by extending the research programme to consider questions about actuation. This means being able to identify the force that shifts the direction of change. In this case, the chances are it was a change from above, from outside the community and perhaps even from outside the British Isles. What remains is to determine from where and by whom.

Possessive *have*

The study of possessive *have* offered consolidating evidence for the developing picture presented by the convergence of results across linguistic features, namely, the idea that constraints reflect different processes. Some are extraordinarily persistent across time and space (*have got* is favoured with concrete complements). This is true regardless of whether *have got* is just beginning to penetrate the community grammar (as in Northern Ireland), whether the variability between *have got* and *have* is robust (Wheatley Hill), or whether *have got* has nearly taken over the whole system (younger generation in York). Other constraints, however, have differential weightings depending on location (*have got* is undifferentiated by subject type in Scotland), and grammatical person is not significant at later stages of development (southern England).

This demonstrates that morpho-syntactic change is influenced by multi-dimensional factors that do not necessarily operate in the same way or take the same developmental path. I suggest that patterns that remain constant across communities reveal the underlying mechanism of a change, in this case the reanalysis of *got* as a marker of stative possession. Effects that differ across communities point to dialect-specific differences (Scots) or highlight a particular stage in a protracted process (i.e. non-significance at a later stage of development as in southern England). In other words, a comparison of different competing constraints operating on the same linguistic change offers insight into their independent contributions to the same change. How this differs across varieties of English may uncover further nuances to the mechanisms of change. In terms of broader comparison, the complexity of the stative possession system, combining linguistic and social patterns, offers a rich diagnostic for future study.

Discourse *like*

One of the mysteries of contemporary English is how and why discourse *like* has surged to supremacy in North American varieties of English. The Roots Archive shows us that this feature was present in the ambient language of earlier centuries. While the analysis I have conducted here was cursory, further study of *like* across generations in these communities would undoubtedly expose the later stages of this change and perhaps the missing link between the Old World and New World grammar of this feature.

General extenders

In the early years of the twenty-first century, the study of discourse pragmatic features using systematic methods has come to the fore. General extenders, the parts of language that enable individuals to add a convenient catch-all term to the ends of their sentences, e.g. *and things like that*, are one of the most highly studied of these. Yet even with accountable analyses, the interpretation of features and their explanation requires more than simply a linguistic perspective. In the case of general extenders, conflicting hypotheses abound. The question is to determine whether they are still grammaticalizing (i.e. changing) or whether their use is more akin to stable variation. Information from the Roots Archive and the British Dialects Archive offers key evidence to piece this puzzle together. As with some of the other features I have considered, general extenders in contemporary English in large part mirror what is found in the dialect data. Yet the proportions of certain items vary, and in some cases particular forms are found more often in one locality than another. For example, all the varieties share the use of variants with *thing* and *stuff* (the generics that make the extender possible). Yet there is a distinct development with regard to which generic is more prominent. At the same time, some varieties prefer certain forms, e.g. *and that* is dominant in northern England while *and all* is preferred in Northern Ireland. As with the intensifying adverbs, there are parts of the general extender system that remain constant across communities and others that are regionally circumscribed. In conducting broader comparisons, the different aspects of this area of grammar offer new means to tease apart cross-variety parallels and distinctions.

Northern power
Well, I used to make miself understood till a certain extent, but yan of them – she was a laal bit, you know, thought she was a bit better than the rest of us in a way, I suppose.

She turned round to me ya day and she looked, 'Can I ask you a question?' I says, 'What's that?' 'Why don't you speak right?' She right into it like 'Why can't you speak right?' I says 'Oh, oh, just – just a minute, mi lass' … I thought I'll just put it on. I'll let thou know I can talk. I said 'just a minute, lass, just a minute. Has thou understood us?' 'Aye' Right, I says 'frae now, when I do mi talking, thou won't understand us'. But I says 'where's thou frae?' Down York or summat. I said how many miles away is it frae here?' Oh, I didn't know. So she said how many miles it was. I said I'm twenty-nine mile away frae yam. I said you don't tell me to talk right. I said, when you're up here, you talk like me. I said, 'Well I don't want to talk like thee. It's as simple as that!' No, why should you? Well, they've – they've nae answer. No, to hell with it. I won't change my way of talking! (Andrew Myers, 63, MPT, 001)[5]

A cross-variety perspective

These studies from morphology to pragmatics show us a range of different scenarios. When variation in different systems of grammar is subject to rigorous investigation, and different dialects and regions are compared and the results can be triangulated, it becomes evident where the parallels and differences lie. Certain areas of the grammar are flush with variation and allow regions, communities and groups to set themselves off from others. Other systems of grammar are more narrowly circumscribed and are remarkably solid across the board. In order to conduct broader comparative studies, it will be important for analysts to know which facets are which.

The findings presented in this book suggest that variables cannot be viewed a priori as part of only one level of grammar, but must be examined in terms of the multiple constraints that operate upon them (see also Poplack and Tagliamonte, 1989, 2001; Tagliamonte, 2002a). This means that the questions become even more interesting. We need to know what types of feature or constraint may be co-opted for regional, social and other cultural nuances and which cannot. We need to clarify the relationship between linguistic change and the spread of features in a community and across communities. Similarly, at broader levels the nature of internal change and external diffusion across regions, countries and oceans remains to be discovered. In the twenty-first century, as global networks become more entrenched, these questions will become even more provocative.

Implications for transported dialects

A key point to sum up the contributions of this book is the foundation it offers for research on dialects elsewhere, wherever English is spoken. To go back to the original motivation for this project, my question was: can we find the roots of English by studying relic dialects back at the source? I hypothesized that dialects from the regions of the largest migrations into North America during the early colonization period should shed light on the origins and development of English where the ancestors of those migrants settled. In the antipodes, where population mixes from Great Britain and Ireland were in different proportions, the results may be quite different. Indeed, the findings presented here could as easily be extended to any variety of English that can trace its roots to these locales.

We do not, of course, know why colonial varieties of English around the world have the characteristics that they do – although we can look … at British English dialects and attempt to make sensible explanations. (Trudgill, 1986: 161)

Building directly on Mufwene's theories of ecological setting and feature pool (1996, 2001), theories about the formation of new dialects (Trudgill et al., 2000) and dialects in contact (Trudgill, 1986), the findings from the twelve linguistic features that were investigated permit me to make a number of speculations. I suggest that if the source varieties all share the same linguistic feature, a preponderance of *will* for future temporal reference, for example, as well as the constraints on its use, the feature will stand an excellent chance of being transported intact, as well as being selected into offspring dialects. The showcase variable, verbal *–s* in 3rd person plural, is precisely this type. No wonder it has engendered so much research in the study of transatlantic dialect connections. Not only does it endure in the contemporary peripheral dialects back at the source, it is also found in many transported dialects as well. In contrast, where the source dialects are differentiated, e.g. use of *and that* in northern England vs *and all* in Northern Ireland, the features that are transported are mixed from the outset, both in form and patterning. This type of cross-dialectal variation will have consequences for the selection process. Features that are marginal or marked when viewed against the total cohort of linguistic features will be less likely to find their way into the developing dialects. Variable NEG/ AUX contraction is a feature of this type. Two out of the three source dialects use the form *'ll not*, the other uses *won't*. This means that *'ll not* might be expected to have selective advantage. Yet it is the form *won't* that was actually selected into North American varieties (Yaeger-Dror et al., 2002). It is interesting to speculate why this would be the case. Here, we may appeal to the rest of the structured set in the language. Most of the other forms in the input dialects are NEG contraction, e.g. *wouldn't, haven't, hasn't, hadn't*. Therefore, in this case, it appears that what gets selected is the form that matches the rest of the system, pushing out the marked variant *'ll not*. The evidence from adverbs permits further elaboration of these general processes. Given the high frequency of zero adverbs in this data, we might predict that it too would have had selective advantage in North American dialects. Indeed, research suggests that the zero adverb is far more frequent in North America than Britain (Opdahl, 2000). The reason for this is now apparent. The transported dialects likely had more instances of zero than mainstream British dialects do today, predisposing the emergent dialects to use it (see also Tagliamonte and Ito, 2002). Given the findings for intensifiers, however, we might expect that peripheral dialects in North America and other locales relevant to these founding dialect areas might retain their ancestor's intensifiers as well – *terrible* and/or *awful* with varying rates of *real* vs *really* and *near* vs *nearly*. However, we do not know what intensifiers, general extenders, verb forms, discourse markers and many other of the linguistic features noted in this book may be used in relic areas in North America or elsewhere, at least not yet. Research on intensifiers (Ito and Tagliamonte, 2003; Labov, 1985) and general extenders (Cheshire, 2007; Denis, 2011; Pichler and Levey, 2011; Tagliamonte and Denis, 2010) has flourished into a wide-ranging set of new accountable and comparable studies. Further study of layering and conditioning of these and other linguistic systems will offer interesting new insights for cross-dialectal comparison.

Form vs constraints

Cross-variety comparisons are only as good as their comparability. The type of study presented in this book offers evidence that can test similarities and differences in the comparison of Old and New World varieties of English on a comprehensive scale. The results demonstrate that the frequency of a given feature in one community cannot unambiguously establish if that form or its frequency is unique to that community or how it can be situated amongst others. Moreover, unless underlying linguistic factors and lexical distributions are taken into account, conclusions may be questionable.

In the United States, regional circumscription of source dialects in Britain, Northern Ireland and Ireland are often impossible to pin down precisely. Montgomery laments that 'existing sources may never permit exact estimation of the British and Irish component in American English', despite the fact that 'that component substantially and unmistakably indicates the general origin of American English in the British Isles'(Montgomery, 2001: 151). He concludes that:

Descriptions of … input varieties are far from adequate and much historical work is needed on earlier, nonstandard varieties from all parts of the British Isles. (Montgomery, 2001: 152)

Given the results I have reported here, in conjunction with earlier findings, it may be the case that linguistic features that have previously been relegated to the area of 'generalized vernacular features' may actually provide ideal evidence for disentangling the origins of different dialects. As we have seen, the progress of linguistic variables that have been changing gradually over several hundred years is reflected across dialects. Their progress along the cline of grammaticization can be viewed in geographically simulated linguistic change (e.g. Poplack and Tagliamonte, 1999). Although communities may share the same linguistic forms, the varying frequency of incoming forms and conditioning of factors that operate on those forms offer important insights into the relative degree of separation of the communities from mainstream varieties. In this way, the imprint of dialect origins and development may be subtly etched in the contrasting patterns of alliance or variance in linguistic weights and constraints (Labov, 1982: 76).

Despite widely divergent frequencies of features across dialects – which might lead one to think that the dialects are quite different among themselves – there are typically parallel constraints. These constraints provide a measure of the underlying grammar and attest to a coherent evolving system at a broader level. At the same time, the relative strength of the constraints can be quite different across dialects. Indeed, the evidence from the frequency of forms along with the constraints on its use, viewed comparatively, show us that the dialects are at varying points in the general trajectory of change. This suggests that the development of the system under investigation must be taken into account. It shows how related dialects are similar, how they may be differentiated, and how they fit in with the rest.

While the ranking of constraints may sometimes be universal (Wolfram, 2000), linguistic features such as deontic modality, possessive *have* and future *going to* are complex enough to have embedded within them the tracks of dialect-specific tendencies as well. Only attention to the multiplex of factors and the details of their operation can disentangle which ones are which. I suggest, therefore, that Poplack and Tagliamonte's (1989) 'strong hypothesis' about comparative sociolinguistic methods is not too strong at all. In fact, the combined results from the studies presented here permits me to re-emphasize the importance of rigorous standards for cross-variety comparison (Poplack and Tagliamonte, 2001: chapter 5; Tagliamonte, 2002a). Harris (1986: 193) once asked why a saliently nonstandard British feature (he was referring to periphrastic *do*) became so widely established in Atlantic contact vernaculars, yet no other such identifying features have. However, as we have seen, in many cases the dialects of the Roots Archive and the British Dialects Archive share innumerable features. In fact, it is quite remarkable how many shared features there are once you start looking. The evidence building from this groundswell of shared retentions establishes a strong basis for an explanation of common ancestry (e.g. Poplack and Tagliamonte, 2001). Only where substantive linguistic data exists can appropriate linguistic analysis be performed that can determine the character of the 'diagnostic' forms and functions. The sociohistorical record is often fraught with ambiguous interpretations, making it near impossible to disentangle population mixes, proportions of different dialect speakers, and the myriad of social influences that may have been operating at the time of the founders and subsequently. This is why the linguistic evidence is imperative.

Indeed, the linguistic lines of evidence converge in demonstrating both the steadfast retention and systemic nature of linguistic features across the communities. Even linguistic features on the verge of extinction, and especially relic forms, can retain diachronic patterns in systematic linguistic conditioning. Indeed, many of the dialect features have remained intact (see also Campbell and Muntzel, 1989). This contradicts suggestions that variables at the end point of change in language may display unusual or 'unnatural' patterning. In fact, this study offers an alternative to the claim that during the process of obsolescence there may be upheaval in the 'natural ordering of constraint effects' (Wolfram and Schilling-Estes, 1995: 711). In the Roots Archive and the British Dialects Archive obsolescing features continue to maintain a complex set of constraints and patterns of constraints that can be traced in the history of English. Of course, it is incumbent upon future research to determine the conditions under which constraints endure and those that lead to their perturbation and demise.

Hidings

Well, we'd owt to do. Aye, aye. Same as policeman. If policeman catched you in the orchard or doing owt wrong, you know and he didn't – he never took you up. An old fellow called Dick Thornbury. He was spot on, he were. And eh, he used to gie you a hiding with stick. And if you come yam and said I'd a hiding off – you daren't say you'd had a hiding off Dick Thornbury. And you couldn't say you'd yan off school teacher, 'cos you got another when you got yam. That's what they used to say, if thou'd had a hiding off, you were doing summat wrong. It was as simple as that. (Andrew Myers, 63, MPT, 001)[6]

Grammatical change

The comparative and contrastive cross-dialectal patterns are particularly relevant for understanding underlying mechanisms of change, namely grammaticalization. Grammaticalization is conceived of as a series of transitions, forming a path or trajectory over time (Hopper 1991: 22–31). As the number of choices gradually gets smaller, the survivors assume more general grammatical meanings or specialize for particular semantic functions (Hopper and Traugott 1993: 22–28). Indeed, underlying the overall frequency of forms in each of the studies are revealed remarkable patterns of linguistic change, not only across generations within a single community (where there is generational data to examine this), but also across (multiple) communities. These changes appear to be proceeding through systematic processes (e.g. extension, specialization) deriving from earlier patterns of use and/or ongoing grammaticalization. In such situations the fallout of grammaticalization involves shifts and re-weighting of constraints as grammaticalizing morphemes take on revised functions in the grammar (Hopper, 1991: 23).

Layering of functionally equivalent forms specialized for different lexical items, constructions or meanings is typical of grammaticalization. The variability in the dialect data (essentially layering) records the longitudinal process of centuries. By providing a vivid snapshot of the different degrees of grammaticalization attained by different forms, dialect data offers a unique insight into this process (Hopper and Traugott, 1993: 23). At the same time, traces of the original lexical meaning of the forms continue, which can be explained by the principle of persistence (Hopper, 1991: 23). Indeed, for some features, such as the abstract vs concrete effect for stative possessive *have got* or the abstract vs concrete distinction for dual form adverbs, the constancy of constraints across generations and the extent to which these parallel historically attested variation is remarkable. Such findings strongly support Kroch's Constant Rate Effect in demonstrating how the mix of two opposed settings of a single grammatical parameter may change drastically over time, but maintain the same constraints. It may be the case that the linguistic changes I have demonstrated here reflect bona fide grammatical change. However, they may be the result of some other process such as lexical replacement, dialect shift or structural reanalysis, These types of questions have implications not only for grammaticalization theory, but also for bridging the gap between different sub-domains of linguistics.

Each of these aspects of grammatical change is put in perspective by comparing and contrasting the details of linguistic conditioning on linguistic variables in a single community as well as across communities. In this regard, the consistent findings of these studies show that grammatical change can be profitably viewed from a synchronic cross-variety perspective. Variable inter-variety distributions across generations as well as cross-dialectal differences suggest that linguistic change is not progressing at the same rate in all speech communities. However, these different rates of change make the incremental stages of linguistic development visible and, as such, reveal the underlying mechanism guiding the change itself. These patterns tell the story of shifting norms and practices at the community level, while at the same time preserving the pathways of language change.

The complexity of this situation bears much further investigation. Indeed, as more community-based data is collected it will become increasingly possible to track grammatical change in synchronic data. Where early dialectological reports showed that sound change could be viewed across dialects of a language, this is true also of morpho-syntactic change and discourse-pragmatic change. In the last couple of decades, corpus linguists have effectively demonstrated that language change is proceeding at quite different rates across the major varieties of English. Here I can confirm that language change is also proceeding at different rates in dialects of the same variety of English. Where traditionally the contrast between mainstream (urban) dialects and those in rural locales was vital, here I can also add that the contrast between northern

Englishes and any other is critical as well. Of course, language change has probably always proceeded at different rates across communities as well as according to key components of the social and cultural situation. These findings confirm that this is still very much true. How the spoken vs written contrast elucidates change more generally is a new frontier.

The rationale for a quantitative perspective

It is important to point out that the findings that arise from quantitative study are often not always intuitively obvious. The type of large-scale comparison conducted here permits a unique perspective by offering a graphic demonstration of the complexity of the northern English and Northern Ireland dialect situation, while at the same time exposing the broad regional similarities amongst some varieties. In the morphological component, we have been able to establish patterns of similarity and difference amongst the same northern varieties (see also Tagliamonte and Smith, 2000, 2001). Thus, perhaps the most important conclusion for the broader concerns of the comparative endeavour is that the type of linguistic feature targeted for investigation plays a critical role in determining the similarities and differences amongst varieties. Those that operate on one level of the grammar may not behave like those of another, either with respect to patterns of use and development or with respect to obsolescence or diffusion. Compare the robust use of *aye* vs verbal *–s*. These understandings may prove to be fundamental to cross-variety comparisons in the ongoing search for cross-variety, and even global, connections.

Is it just an Uster-Scots thing?

The cumulative evidence unfolding from these chapters reveals that there is a dramatic divide between the Northern Ireland communities and their neighbours across the Irish Sea in Cumnock and Maryport. However, a simple interpretation of dialect differentiation may mask the fact that Northern Ireland retains older forms due to the social, cultural and geographic separation. The cross-variety perspective points to the latter interpretation. This is because the difference across communities is not absolute, but relative. Moreover, and perhaps most telling, the underlying patterns of use are for the most part parallel. Thus, we can argue that Northern Ireland retains older features to a far greater extent. In comparison, the same features are receding in Lowland Scotland and northern England. Yet many of the features reported to be likely candidates for northern English are extremely infrequent (Montgomery, 1997, 2001). I found very few double modals, virtually no stative progressives, no positive *anymore*, no a-prefixing on verbs, no affirmative *does*, no finite *be*, etc., even though many of these persist in isolated North American dialects (e.g. Montgomery, 1989). On the other hand, there are plenty of other features elsewhere in the grammar, as is well exemplified in the examples, quotes and quips. If we were to turn our sights onto transported dialects in the light of this cornucopia of features, we may end up discovering many 'new' phenomena for analysis.

Where the dichotomies lie

It is critical too to confront what these accumulating findings offer for elucidating the contrast between peripheral and mainstream, between dialectal, regional and supra-local and between standard and nonstandard. Evidently, language change does not proceed in these vernacular dialects as it does in the standard language. Nor does it proceed in the same way in peripheral dialects as it does in those most closely associated with mainstream developments. Indeed, if these results are any indication, there are dramatic differences between vernacular and mainstream norms. Such differences may become particularly pronounced in the case of linguistic innovations that involve change from above, as with the WH- relative markers or the modal *must*. Further exploration of the dichotomy between change from above vs change from below across different synchronic dialect situations will provide much further insight into the social mechanisms of language change and their interaction with the layering and specialization of linguistic forms. Moreover, there is still much more work to be done in deciphering how standard and nonstandard forms co-exist in the same speaker, in the same conversation, and even in the same sentence. The relationship between how individuals use these features in discourse interaction remains an important research question. Similarly, the dialectic between individual behaviour and community behaviour, especially under conditions of obsolescence, needs deeper cross-variety scrutiny.

Blackberry jam

Sometimes you hardly got a wee bit of butter on your bread in them times. And yet we used to go out and gather blackberries and make blackberry jam. (Laughs) I can mind that. Aye, surely to goodness they're lovely. [3] Yes they're lovely. [005] They're – oh, blackberry jam's lovely. I never got any of this year's. [3] Have you not? [005] No. [3] Oh, I like the blackberry jam. [005] Aye, so do I, it's lovely, surely it's lovely. (Kate McBride, 88, CLB, 005)[7]

Language structure?

One of the provocative questions that is also raised by this research is whether cross-variety differences impinge on language structure. They may be the result of grammatical change alone, or they may be interpreted as parametric variation (e.g. Cornips and Corrigan, 2005; Henry, 1995). For some researchers there are two sources of variation: variation in the design of the feature structure of the categories and variation in the range of spellout options (Adger, 2006, 2007; Adger and Smith, 2010). The analyst must determine which features are which and what impact this difference has on variation, constraints and change. Further exploration of these types of questions is critical not only for informing linguistic theory, but also for bridging the gap between formal theories of grammar, historical linguistics and sociolinguistics. The Roots Archive alone comprises four different communities from at least three dialect areas, while the British Dialects Archive offers a clear north to south perspective. This gives us the unique capacity to test recent developments in the areas of parametric dialect differences (Cornips and Corrigan, 2002; Henry, 1995; Wilson and Henry, 1998), morphosyntactic variation (Kroch, 1994), dialect typology (Kortmann, 2002) and parametric change (Roberts and Roussou, 2003).

The younger generation

The data this book is based on is heavily biased towards the oldest generation (c. 1997–2003). Because the 'Back to the Roots' research program focused on the oldest and most insular speakers only, there is no information on the pathways of change in apparent time in the same communities. Yet the evidence from York reveals astonishing change across generations, particularly among the individuals born after the Second World War. Future fieldwork must address these gaps in our knowledge. Further data from different generations of individuals in the peripheral communities is sorely needed. More information on change across generations in non-peripheral, more standard varieties is also required. Research programmes from London to Glasgow offer new insights for comparison (e.g. Cheshire et al., 1989; Cheshire, Fox, Kerswill, Khan and Torgersen, 2007–2010; Kerswill, 1995, 2003; Kerswill and Cheshire, 2004–2007; Stuart-Smith, 1999, 2002–2005). For the time being, however, this study fills in part of the picture of the current state of variation and change in numerous systems of grammar.

Twang

She come in … had coffee and I says er 'are you Scotch? Where about in Scotland do you live?' She says, 'how do you know I'm Scotch? I've been here a long time.' I says, 'I divn't care how long you've been here.' I says 'the Scotch never ever loses their twang'. (Elsie Williams, 86, MPT)[8]

Northern English

Northern English is a singular resource in the controversial showground of linguists who track the origins and development of English. Lucky for us, it has endured across centuries and may not fade away entirely any time soon. Although there are reports that the dialects are dying, it is interesting that the predictions of their demise have been going on for at least three decades (e.g. Tidholm, 1979). More relevant is that this dire prophecy may not even be fulfilled into the twenty-first century:

[O]f all the varieties of English remaining within England at the beginning of this new Millennium it is Northern English especially its distinctive accents, that will survive the longest. (Wales, 2006: 211)

Dialects are a tremendous resource for understanding the grammatical mechanisms of linguistic change. Dialects are also the storehouse of the heart and soul of culture, history and identity. Delving deep into the nuts and bolts of language, deeper than words and phrases and expressions, down into the grammar, we discover a treasure trove. Beneath the anecdotes and nonce tales are hidden patterns and constraints that are a system unto themselves, reflecting the legacy of regional factions, social groups and human relationships. As language evolves through history, its inner mechanisms are evolving, but not in the same way in every place nor at the same rate in all circumstances – it will always mirror its own ecology. The step-by-step methodology I have employed here has given us the means to crack this hidden orderliness. At the same time, the cross-variety perspective has given us a critical bird's-eye view of the steps in the evolving processes, at least in the dialects studied here. The findings from the combined research on the Roots Archive and the British Dialects Archive lay out the promising new research potential for tracking global changes into the twenty-first century. The next step is to extend the broad accountable comparisons begun here beyond the British Isles and out into the global arena of dialects in other locations, contexts and countries. As I write these lines, there is already another north country in my dreaming.

Notes

ACKNOWLEDGEMENTS

1 The names of all the individuals cited in the examples are pseudonyms; however, the ages are real. The communities they live in are rendered as short forms as follows: BCK = Buckie; CLB = Cullybackey; CMK = Cumnock; MPT = Maryport; PVG = Portavogie; SAM = Samaná; TIV = Tiverton; WIN = Wincanton; WHL = Wheatley Hill; YRK = York. The format of each reference is pseudonym, age, community acronym and speaker identification number or letter. In this excerpt, note the use of the definite article reduction, a phenomenon that is often referred to by the acronym 'DAR' in the literature and orthographically rendered as *t'*. Also notice the discourse marker *you know*, which tends to occur at the end of a sentence in these dialects. The sequence *yan, tan, thethera* is a sheep-counting rhyme used by shepherds in northern England. These notes on linguistic features in the data are not meant to be exhaustive.

1   INTRODUCTION

1 Note the particle *nae* for 'not', the use of *just* as 'simply'.
2 Note the use of discourse features *aye* and *ken*; *somebody* rather than *someone* followed by use of *a body* in the generic; *yin* for 'one'; inverted, *says*; the expression *it's a good job*; the syntactic structure *it's no weans you've got* 'you've got no children'; use of *can nae, would nae* for 'wouldn't', 'couldn't'.
3 In addition to the features being commented upon, notice the use of *our* as a kinship term for identifying family members, *our Robert, frae* for 'from', *divn't* for 'didn't', the sentence tag *eh*, and discourse marker *well*.
4 The term 'turf' refers to peat, which was used as a household fuel in lieu of firewood. Peat bogs were more plentiful than trees in many areas of the north. Considerable time was spent cutting turves of peat, drying them and stacking them.
5 Note the use of demonstrative *that*, preterit *done*, *'tis* for 'it is', discourse features *you know what I mean* and *like, till* as a preposition, zero subjects, e.g. Ø *makes like a track*, discourse particle *you know*.
6 I cannot begin to list the vast number of books, articles, dialect repositories, dictionaries and other materials that are currently available on northern dialects in the British Isles. Any of the references in the bibliography can be used as a jumping off point for further exploration. Two recent corpora compilation projects are worthy of mention: the Newcastle Electronic Corpus of Tyneside English http://research.ncl.ac.uk/necte/ Accessed 2 February 2012 and the Freiburg English Dialect Corpus www2.anglistik. uni-freiburg.de/institut/lskortmann/FRED/ Accessed 2 February 2012.

7 Note the use of 2nd person plural *youse* and *ain* for 'own'.

8 Note the use of discourse features *you know* and *I mean* as well as comparative *as* and the general extender *all this sort of stuff.*

2   DIALECTS AS A WINDOW ON THE PAST

1 Note the use of discourse markers *aye*, *mind* and discourse particles *you see*, *you know*; the term *them'uns*; non-standard agreement with *is*, e.g. *there's Irishmen*; demonstrative *them*; and the cultural word *oatcake.*

2 Appalachian English is a variety spoken in the Appalachian Mountains in the United States.

3 Despite this Canadian's contention, *muck*, as in 'to muck out a room or closet' meaning to give it a good cleaning is used all over Britain, not simply in Scotland.

4 Note the use of *muck out* to mean 'give something a good cleaning'; the expression *on a morning* for 'every morning'.

5 Note the use of *muck in* to mean 'to join in and help out'; use of *ot* for 'of'; non-standard agreement with *–s*; discourse marker *aye* in sentence final position.

6 Note the dramatic use of quotative *say* to introduce and to end the constructed dialogue, e.g. *'No, I do not' he says 'I thought he was being obscene!' he says, Says to Joe, says*; use of *wi* for 'with'; *wee* for 'small'; and of course the dialect word *pinkie.*

7 The excerpts in (10a) and (10b) illustrate the standard use of *whenever* which has a habitual reading; whereas (10c) from Northern Ireland illustrates the quintessentially Irish use of *whenever* with a punctual reading (see Trudgill and Hannah, 1985).

8 Note the use of *sie* for 'say'; *this* for 'one'; absence of *do* support in questions.

9 Note the use of discourse marker *aye*; preterit *seen*; demonstrative *them*; *mi* instead of 'my'; double negatives, *there never was nothing*; the placement of 'ever', *ever I seen*. The term *zip fastener* for what would be 'zipper' today.

10 This is not to say that the North has not influenced the development of other dialects of British English. In mediaeval and early modern times many innovations in the south had diffused from the north, for example verbal *–s*. In many cases, it was the south of England, and in particular the south-east, that was conservative.

11 Note the use of *o* for 'of'; the zero plural on *mile;* the general extender *or something*; discourse features *you know, aye.*

12 Note the use of discourse marker *aye*; zero subjects; the intensifier *very*; non-standard agreement with *there*; contraction on a noun; the expression *that's right* and *like you know what I mean.*

13 *English dialect dictionary* (Wright, 1900).

14 *Survey of English dialects* (Orton and Halliday, 1963).

15 This construction does not occur in the Buckie or Cumnock data.

16 Note the use of discourse *like* in sentence final position and *you know what I mean*; *till* for 'to'; *nae* for 'no'. Dated and/or uncommon lexical items, *petticoats*, *clogs.*

17 In New Zealand the input dialects are recoverable from the archives of the Origins of New Zealand [ONZE] project http://www.canterbury.ac.nz/ucresearchprofile/ group.aspx?groupid=1. For further information, see Gordon, Campbell, Maclagan, Sudbury and Trudgill, 2004; Gordon and Hay, 2008; Trudgill, 2004.

18 In these discussions of typical foods in the north, it is clear that leeks, onions and cabbage were a staple. Note the different words for 'potatoes', e.g. *tatties* in Maryport and *spuds* in Cullybackey. You will notice that there are at least three other words for 'potato' in the Roots Archive. Look for them!

19 Note the non-agreement in *there wasn't any fancy puddings*; demonstrative *them*; sentence final *like*; general extender *and that*; discourse marker *you know*; *of* absence in *out the garden*.

20 Scotch Corner is a well-known northern reference point at the junction of two trunk roads in England, i.e. the point where the A1 meets the A66, which goes further north-west across the Pennines.

21 Beowulf is an epic poem from Old English. The hero of the epic is Beowulf and the 'monster' is Grendel, who Beowulf defeats in battle. The poem is considered one of the most important works in Anglo-Saxon literature.

22 Note the zero relative; the use of *till* for 'to'; non-agreement with the plural existential *there*.

23 The relative conservatism of forms is an interesting consideration. For example, the form *teached* is historically innovative, attested from the fourteenth century. *Taught* is older, going back to Old English. The forms *taen* and *haen* are variants of the verb *take* and *have* respectively. For further discussion of these forms, see Smith, 2004.

3   THE ROOTS ARCHIVE

1 Note the use of punctual *whenever*; *mi* for 'my'; *went* as a past participle; preterit *come*; *fae* for 'from'; discourse marker *you see*.

2 In some cases false starts, repetitions and hesitations were removed from these excerpts to facilitate comprehension.

3 Note the use of *would nae* for 'wouldn't'; *have to* as a deontic modal; reduplication of the subject, e.g. *The Cumbrian, he*; indefinite *you*.

4 Note sentence final use of *you know* and *right*.

5 Note non-standard agreement with existential *there*.

6 This is a transcription convention that means that there was a section of the audio recording that was 'incomprehensible' to the transcriber.

7 Note the use of narrative *I says*; discourse marker *you know*; the expression *gan off*.

8 Note the Northern Subject Rule in operation with *my fish is fresh*; negative *does nae*; nonstandard *does*; use of *o'* for 'of'; quotative *I says*; use of future *going to* in negative context; demonstrative *them*; dialect word *stane*; negation without *do* support.

9 Note the use of *I seen*; discourse marker *you see*; *miself* for 'myself'.

10 Note the use of the Northern Subject Rule with *if the prittas was good*; *when prittas was*; *them was*; note too that the 3rd person pronoun *them* takes the *–s* ending; the form *wee'uns*; the past tense *boilt*; the general extender *or whatever you were feeding*; the use of *mind* for 'remember'; demonstrative *them*; *for to* as 'in order to'; and of course the dialect word 'pritta' which means 'potato'.

11 The 1851, 1901 and 1951 census reports list residents having a birthplace in Yorkshire at 83%, 82% and 72% respectively. The 1851 census reports that 51% of the household heads had been born in Durham and Northumberland (Armstrong, 1974).

12 Note the reduplication of the subject in *this guy, he* ...; use of a nonstandard verbal *–s* with *we was*; the expression *we were sat* for 'we were sitting'; the expression *to be on*; the lack of the definite article in *he's only one*; and the combination of relative pronouns *that* and *who* in the last sentence.

13 Note the use of *really* as 'truly', an older layer in the grammaticalization chain from lexical word to intensifier in more contemporary varieties.

14 Among the many studies on features in York, a number of results highlight the conservative nature of York English. For example, the relatively high rates of non-standard *was* in 2nd person singular (13%) may be a holdover from earlier stages in the history of English where this context was singled out as being propitious for this form in northern Britain. The frequency of *was* in 1st person plural (i.e. *we was*) is likely a remnant as well since the SED reports its use in York as an anomaly for the north. Finally 3rd person plural pronoun *they was* is absent. This pattern too is consistent with the historical record. This corroborates the hypothesis that these patterns are holdovers from an earlier stage in the history of English when such differential rates of nonstandard *was* were typical. The uses in York, although limited in frequency, show that these earlier patterns have not yet fully fallen out of the grammar. In contrast, existential *was* could be seen as increasing over time. Past-reference *come* occurs more frequently with first and third person singular subjects in historical English dialects (Long, 1944; Morris, 1911). In fact, Morris (1911: 40) specifically attributes the tendency toward use of past-reference *come* in contexts such as *he come yesterday* to analogy with the preterit singular of the verb *come* in Old Norse, which was also *kom*, thereby reinforcing preterit *come* in the eastern parts of Britain (Brunner, 1963: 76; Tidholm, 1979: 140). Yorkshire, in north-east England, had extensive contact with Norwegian and Danish at earlier times. The tendencies still visible among the older individuals in the York English Corpus may well be due to the lingering effects of an older regional dialect with some Scandinavian influence.

15 Note the general extenders *and all that sort of thing*; the discourse features *you know* and *I mean*; *like* for 'as' and 'as if'; zero subjects.

16 Note the cleft in *by the old Blundell's Garage, it was*; the general extender *and that*; the preposition *out* in 'out Hay Park'; zero subjects as in *went up there and worked for so long*; the discourse marker *you know*; *like* for 'as if' in sentence initial position; and non-agreement with existential, *there was newts*.

17 Note the intensifiers in this excerpt, *awful* and *very*; the string of relative pronouns *that I know that has come ... that's been built ...*; also striking is the plethora of adjectives *delightful*, *proud*, *nice* and even a superlative *friendliest village*. It is interesting to speculate whether these features correlate with other of the findings presented in this book regarding Henfield.

18 Note the use of verbal *–s* in this excerpt. Only one present indicative verb has no *–s*! Note the use of *'tis* for 'it is'; relative pronoun *who*; general extender *and that*; zero subjects.

19 Note the unusual use of *who* for an inanimate, *places*. We might wonder whether this is hypercorrection, especially given the use of *who* in one of the following sentences. This man might be over-using the prestige form. Further examination would determine this.

4   METHODS OF ANALYSIS

1 There is a striking example of inherent variability in this excerpt, what I would call a 'supertoken'. Can you spot it? Note the use of demonstrative *them*; verbal *–s* in 3rd person plural, *them women was* but 3rd person plural pronoun with no *–s*, *they were*; reduplicated subject, *there was a woman, she*; the 2nd person plural *yous*; the expression *manys a time*; the word *daft*.

2 Note the use of the cleft in *A small pony ... he was*; *thee* for 'you'; discourse marker *you see*; zero subjects *went to Bampton Fair, had fed and grassed it, and kept him for*.

3 Note the use of *dinna* for 'don't'; *thisel'* for 'yourself' (or 'oneself'). The translation of this quip would be something like: 'Don't use "thou" with anyone older than yourself.' What does this suggest about the 'rules of usage' for *thee/thou*?

4 Further analysis using logistic regression can assess the direction of effect of these patterns, their significance and relative importance when all factors are considered simultaneously (e.g. Tagliamonte, 2006, 2007, 2012).

5 Note the use of preterit *come*; discourse markers *you see, you know*; use of *mi* for 'my'; demonstrative *that there*; general extender *or whatever*; discourse *like*; use of *our*, as in 'our Grace' to refer to family members; definite article reduction *t'buckets*; the expression *I tell you*.

6 For further discussion of comparative sociolinguistics, see Poplack and Tagliamonte, 2001; Tagliamonte, 2006, 2012.

5   WORD ENDINGS

1 Note the alternation between *somebody* and *someone*; the use of the zero adverb *quick*; the negative particle *no*; the all purpose quotative verb *says* (regardless of grammatical person); and the use of the velar fricative in *nicht*, 'night'. This form/ pronunciation only occurred in Portavogie.

2 Note the use of *fae* for 'from'; *afore* for 'before'; *naebody* for 'nobody'; the general extender *and everything*.

3 They are also rare in written documents; N = 22 in Giner and Montgomery's research on Yorkshire English (Giner and Montgomery, 1997: 178).

4 In the cross-variety comparisons of the Roots Archive and the British Dialects Archive the communities will be presented in geographic order from (more or less) north to south – Buckie, Cumnock, Cullybackey, Portavogie, Maryport, Wheatley Hill, York, Tiverton, Wincanton, Henfield. Note that the communities investigated differ from one study to the next.

5 The Helsinki Corpus is a 1.5-million-word collection of English texts spanning 850– 1710, a time period that encompasses Old to Early Modern British English (Kytö, 1993a: 2). The corpus is particularly useful for the study of diachronic change in the English language in that it provides a controlled sample for different periods, genres, and registers.

6 Note the use of sentence final *there, now* and discourse marker *you know*; the non-standard verb *knowed*; zero relative pronoun, *there were a boy in Ballycare told me that*; *till* for 'to'; alternation between *right* and *rightly*; verbal *–s*, *the lambs was*; *were* regularization; *be* as a habitual marker, *maybe somebody else be looking for a foster mother*.

7 Note the use of intensifier *awful*; *fae* for 'from'; preterit *come*; quotatives alternate between *saying* and *said*.

8 Note the use of the zero subject relative; the nonstandard preterit *sung*; the intensifier *very*; the use of a quotative at either side of the constructed dialogue, *well, says I, 'it's very strange,' says I.*

9 The majority of *nearly* tokens are found in CLB – 85 tokens for a proportion of 40.7% of all *nearly* tokens in the Roots Archive. As Table 5.2 shows, this does not skew the overall distributional results because *nearly* is ranked one of the three most frequent items in all communities.

10 In the OED, however, there is no mention of the use of *near* in adverbial function, e.g. *Well it was nearly a fortnight's wages* (PVG/018).

11 In contexts of *had*, NEG contraction occurs nearly exclusively; the contracted form *'d not* is not used (Hiller, 1987: 535; Kjellmer, 1998: 181; Quirk et al., 1985: 122). The reason that AUX contraction does not occur in this context is explained in two ways: (1) it is avoided due to the ambiguity of *I'd*. It could represent *I would* or *I had* (Quirk et al., 1985: 122); (2) it is avoided due to the phonological clash between [t] and [d] in *it'd* and *that'd* (Kjellmer, 1998: 181).

12 Note the use of *no* for 'not'; preterit *come*. Did you catch the zero subject at the beginning?

13 Although the use of *ain't* is pervasive in some dialects (e.g. Cheshire, 1982), there were only twelve instances in the data (TIV = 10; WHL =2). The use of *amn't* is attested for Scots dialects; however, none occurred in these materials and there were only seven tokens of *aren't*.

14 Note the use of the associative plural *and them*; the discourse feature *here*; the intensifier *very*; the *–body* variant of the indefinite pronoun; the negative particle *nae*; the use of *feller* for male person; *wi* for 'with'.

15 Note preterit *run*; the causal connector *for to*; the expression *don the door*.

6   JOINING SENTENCES

1 While researchers tend to refer to the WH- forms as standard, this skims over the fact that there is a nonstandard WH- form, *what*, which is a relatively normal relative pronoun in much of the south of England (Poussa, 1988; Trudgill, 2003).

2 The British National Corpus (BNC) was collected between 1991 and 1994, http://www.hcu.ox.ac.uk/BNC/index.html. From these materials Tottie (1997) selected eight conversations. The overall frequency of *who* was only 9% and *which*, 8% N = 575.

3 Note the use of *nae*; dialect term 'bool' and the use of 'wee' for small.

4 In the early stages, some researchers argue that þæt/*that* continued to predominate. Later however, there arose a tendency to confine þæt to restrictive clauses (Romaine, 1980: 222).

5 Note the use of 'wee' for small; *mind you* as a discourse marker; *did nae* for negative; *gaad* for past tense 'go'; the *–body* variant for the indefinite pronouns; the conjunction *whiles*. Imagine 'kicking the peats out of the fire'!

6 For additional information on methodological considerations, see Tagliamonte, Smith and Lawrence, 2005.

7 Note the use of *feller* for a young male; use of *there's* in the context of 'folk'; *wee* for 'small'; discourse marker *well*; *terrible* as in intensifier; *ma* for 'mother'; *folk* for 'people' and of course the different pronunciations of 'dog'.

8 Note the use of demonstrative *them*; the existential *it*; preterit *come*; discourse features *of course* and *you know*.

9 The two entries for Ayr come from the same study by Macaulay (1991).

10 Note the use of the directive 'get yourself'; the past tense negative *hadn't*; *yam* for 'home'; absence of definite articles and/or preposition, e.g. *I got up pit*; the non-canonical sentence structure in *'Twas young Doctor Rafferty, I seen*; 'poorly' for *sick*; preterit *seen*; definite article reduction; reduced *cos* for 'because'; discourse marker *eh* and the negative tag *weren't they*; the expressions *get yourself away*.

11 Note the use of 'wee' for *small*; the consistent use of *–s* with a plural referents; and demonstrative *them* in subject position.

12 This corpus comprises 116 eight-minute recorded conversations between university students at the University of California. The data totals 240,000 words (Thompson and Mulac, 1991a: 240).

13 This variety of Canadian English is spoken in Québec City, the capital of Québec, which is predominantly French speaking.

14 Elsness' data come from the Capital Syntax Data Corpus, which consists of 64 of the 500 texts making up the Brown University Corpus of American English, 128,000 words (Elsness, 1984: 520).

15 Note sentence final *like* and *like you know; till* as 'to'; zero subject with *seemed*.

16 Note the use of discourse marker *aye*; *tha* for 'you'; *div* for 'do'; *summat* for 'something'.

17 Note the position of the adverb in the first sentence; the use of sentence final *you know*; the demonstrative *thon*; the plural *sheafs*.

18 Note the past tense of ride = *rid*; conjunctive *whiles; for* for 'to'; use of present tense for conditional; the use of *–er, you're oftener* rather than 'more often'. Only in Cullybackey did the lexical item 'slippy' turn up. Where it turned up elsewhere (Somerset and York), the pronunciation was 'slippery'.

19 It does not occur at all in the London-Lund Corpus (Altenberg, 1984) and is less frequent than *because* in the Lancaster-Oslo-Bergen Corpus. The overall ratio is 15 to 85 in the British National Corpus (Rissanen, 1998a:398–399).

20 Note the use of *them* instead of 'those'; dialect words *spud, farls, fadge; mi* for 'my'; *them* for 'those'; discourse marker *you know; whiles* for 'during that time'; *wee* for 'small'.

21 Note the use of *nae* for 'not'; the discourse features *ken, aye*; the *a–* prefix on *afore* 'before'; the use of preposition *in*; the dialect word *kye* for 'cows'.

22 Note the use of preterit *done*; pronoun *thee; 'cos* for 'because'; *yam* for 'home'; non-standard agreement with 1st person singular, *I's; gas* for 'goes'; discourse marker *you know*.

23 In addition to the words mentioned in the metalinguistic commentary, note the expression *as they say* and discourse marker *you know*.

7   TIME, NECESSITY AND POSSESSION

1 Note the supertoken!

2 In one spontaneous spoken sentence note use of the *–body* variant in *everybody*; the use of stative *has; o'* for 'of'; *ain* for 'own'; *haen* for 'have'; the dialect word *brogue*, which refers to a person's accent.

3   *Blether* is a word that means to talk longwindedly without making very much sense. A related word is *blather*.

4   There were 278 future-in-the-past contexts, representing 5% of the total number of tokens. Despite the fact that only those contexts that were interchangeable with *would* were included, they were rendered as *going to* 98% of the time.

5   Tag questions, which were categorically *will*, and rare instances of *about to* were excluded (Tagliamonte and Poplack, 1986).

6   The Archer Corpus is a multi-genre corpus of British and American English covering the period 1650–1999 http://www.llc.manchester.ac.uk/research/projects/archer/ accessed 1 November 2011.

7   Note the use of *o* for 'of'; *wee* for 'small'; discourse marker *now*; negative contraction with *isn't* in question.

8   Note the use of discourse marker *like* in sentence-final position; *were* in 1st person singular; use of *summat* for 'something'; preterit *come*; *till* for 'to'; *her* for 'she'; *thou* for 'you'; quotative *I says*; the expression *on about*; *lass* for 'female'.

9   Use of *must* for deontic modality; shortened form of 'because' with *cos*.

10 Note the use of *yin* for 'child'; *till* for 'to'; preterit *come*; quotative *I says* and *says I*; discourse marker *aye, you see*; *whiles* for 'during that time'; the indefinite pronoun *somebody*; cleft *it was him*; preterit *knowed*; zero relative pronouns.

11 Note the contraction after noun phrases.

12 Most of Krug's data come from written sources: the Brown Corpus consists of American English texts from 1961; the LOB corpus, which is the Lancaster/Oslo-Bergen Corpus, a similarly constituted corpus of British English; the 'Frown' and 'FLOB' corpora, short forms for the Freiburg versions of Brown and LOB, which match their predecessors but are texts from 1991–2. Krug also considers the relatively smaller spoken section of the British National Corpus (for further discussion, see Krug, 2000: 31–6).

13 Note the use of *mi* for 'my'; discourse features *you see, mind, anyway*; contracted 'had to', *I'd to be ready*; a zero definite article, *Mary went out on front with Ø old mac on*; zero subjects; definite article reduction *t'airfield, on t'wing*; *t'pilot*; the expression *by gum*; sentence tag *do you*.

14 The negated forms were divided between *mustn't* (N = 6) and *don't have to* (N = 7), *haven't to* (N = 3) and *haven't got to* (N = 3). The questions were *have to* (N = 7) and *have got to* (N = 5).

15 The earlier form of 'must', *mon/maun*, once found in these northern areas, was not present in these data. For further discussion, see Corrigan, 2000.

16 Note discourse marker *aye*; the form *onyway* for 'anyway'; *wi* for 'with'; *mi* for 'my'.

17 Buckie and Wheatley Hill have been removed from consideration in this analysis because they each had fewer than five tokens of subjective obligation.

18 The verb 'have' can also be used with dynamic meaning, e.g. *I have coffee with breakfast.* This is apparently a North American innovation. For a detailed analysis of the change from stative to dynamic *have*, see Trudgill, Nevalainen and Wischer, 2002.

19 Note the Yorkshire cleft, *it worries me, does that*; the so-called 'dangling preposition', *she really belongs to*; the discourse features, *mind you, I suppose* and possibly the first instance of *really*. Do the two instances mean the same thing?

20 Note the use of discourse features *aye, och, you know*; nonstandard agreement with *were*; use of *–body* variant of the indefinite pronoun, *everybody*; zero relative

pronoun; *no* for 'not'; *whiles* for 'at that time' or 'during the time that'; *at* for 'with'; nonstandard preterit *throwed, done*; *nae* for 'no'.
21 Note use of *o* for 'of'; a zero complementizer.
22 Note the use of intensifier *right*; *wee* for 'small'; the discourse marker *ken*; the *–body* variant of the indefinite pronoun 'somebody'; use of *fae* for 'since'.

8   EXPRESSIONS

1 Note the use of *shall* and the main verb *have* in the questions! The lexical item *conundrum* is striking.
2 Nouns are modified by adjectives and determiners.
3 Note the juxtaposition between the formal forms *thou* and *shalt* and the fact that the sentence exhibits negative concord.
4 Note the use of *you know* as a discourse marker; *'ve got* for deontic modality.
5 Note the use of *yin* for 'one'; *fae* for 'from'; *off* for 'past'; the discourse marker *ken, aye; aback* for 'behind'; preterit *seen;* 3rd person plural *–s; no* for 'not'.
6 Note the use of discourse marker *you know*; *wheen* for 'a few'; the expression *bit of crack*; *to you, to me*, to refer to people's place of residence; the use of *the day; the morra* to refer to 'the day'; not also the word *morra* to refer to 'tomorrow'.
7 Note the use of *like* at the ends of sentences; demonstrative *them*; nonstandard verb form *hae* for 'have'.
8 Note the use of demonstrative *them;* the indefinite pronoun *nobody*; elision of 'would'; 3rd person noun phrase with *–s*; discourse *like*; relative *that*; use of *feared* for 'afraid'; intensifier *terribly*. What is *sure* doing in this excerpt?
9 In comparison, an interview with two young women in Toronto, Canada in 2002 contained 1,226 instances of *like* (in all functions) in a single hour of conversation that contained 12,778 words.
10 Due to the infrequency of discourse *like* in these materials, the analysis did not go beyond a simple count of the tokens where *like* appeared and a rudimentary account of their frequency out of the total number of words in each corpus.
11 Note that *pritta* is a dialect word for 'potato'.
12 A *sporran* is part of a man's Scottish Highland dress. It is a small pouch worn around the waist in front of the kilt.
13 There were 88 different forms in all. As with many linguistic variables several main forms dominate the system, while most occur only once or twice.
14 Each of the categories comprises a large number of variants. For example, included in the category 'thing' are the following forms: *and this kind of thing, and that sort of thing, and that kind of thing, this sort of thing, or this sort of thing, and all these things, and all that sort of thing, and all sorts of things, and things, kind of thing, that kind of thing, this sort of thing, type of thing, sort of thing, that sort of thing, and all little things like that, or that sort of thing, and all these kinds of things, or things like that, and all the things, and all these sort of things, and all this sort of thing, things like that, all this sort of thing, all that sort of thing* and *all things like that*. A similar multi-faceted group is found for 'stuff'.
15 Note the expression *pack it in*; the shortened form of 'because' as *'cos*; the demonstrative *them*.
16 Note the sentence structure in *it's a beautiful word, bairns*; the use of *–s* with a plural noun.

17 Note the use of *no* for 'not'; the discourse marker *aye*; and dialect form *kent*, past tense of 'to know'.

18 Note the use of *ken* for 'know'; *fae* for 'from'; discourse marker *aye*; the past tense form *learnt*.

9   COMPARATIVE SOCIOLINGUISTICS

1 Note the use of general extender *and that*; quotative *says* in 1st person singular; discourse markers *aye, eh, mind, then*; *thou* for 'you'; discourse *like*; *till* for 'for'; some expletive words *hell, damn*.

2 Note the use of preterit *come*; definite article reduction, *t'middle*; zero definite article, had to use Ø *starting handle*; *fellow* for indefinite male; quotative *says*; *till* for 'to'; *thou* for 'you'; discourse marker *aye*.

3 The discerning reader will recognize the wealth of variation that could potentially be studied. Many such studies are planned or are in the works.

4 There are a total of 15,797 instances of *aye* across the four communities; N = 7,236 in Cumnock (total characters 1,875,374), N = 3,027 in Cullybackey (total characters 1,172,536), N = 1,333 in Portavogie (total characters 491,974) and N = 4,201 in Maryport (total characters 2,122,633).

5 Note the intensifier 'horrid', in *horrid careful* and the use of the expression *grand crack*.

6 Indeed, a quick search of the British Dialects Archive for all potential verbs ending in *–lt* revealed that *built, felt, spoilt* and *smelt* occur across all the dialects. However, *telt* is confined to the Roots Archive communities plus Buckie and Wheatley Hill. It never occurs in York, Wincanton or Henfield. Other verbs in *–lt* occur in the Roots Archive, including *swelt, pult* and *selt*, but also not in York, Wincanton or Henfield. Of course, it could also be that these relatively rare verbs simply never turned up in the interviews in these locations. Nevertheless, the consistency of the patterns suggests an underlying commonality – verbs in *–lt* are northern and vernacular.

7 In a few cases, rare instances of a form in a community were ignored, such as a single token of *nowt* in Portavogie, etc.

10   THE LEGACY OF BRITISH AND IRISH DIALECTS

1 Note the use of *nae* as negative particle; *tae* as 'to'; *gie* as 'go'; *mi* for 'my'; the cultural word *brogue* for 'dialect' or 'accent'.

2 Of course another location for nonstandard use of *–s* is in 1st person singular quotatives, e.g. *I says*. A study of the distribution and patterning of this feature is warranted.

3 Note the use of discourse features *aye, you see, you know, mind*; *'uns* for 'ones'. Can you spot the zero relative pronoun?

4 Note the use of preterit *come*; quotative *I says*; note the use of *I'll*; *till* for 'to'; discourse marker *you know*; a couple of interesting expressions, e.g. *hang on, clear off*.

5 Note the use of *miself* and *mi* for 'myself' and 'my'; *yan* for 'one'; *laal* for 'little'; discourse features *you know, aye, right*; parenthetical expression *I suppose*; *ya* for 'one'; quotative *I says*; *thou* and *thee* for 'you'; *summat* for 'something'; *frae* for

'for'; *yam* for 'home'; general extender *or summat*; *nae* for 'no'; aux contraction in *they've nae answer* and *I won't change*.

6 Note the use of *owt* and *summat* for 'nothing' and 'something'; nonstandard preterit *catched*; *yam* for 'home'; *thou* for 'you'; *yan* for 'one'; expression *hiding off* for a 'beating'; *gie* for 'give'; and the cleft in *He was spot on, he were*.

7 Note the use of *wee* for 'small'; demonstrative *them*. Have you noticed that this form tends to occur as a collocation, i.e. *Them times*; discourse marker *aye*; the dialect word *mind* for 'remember'; the expression *surely to goodness*; the local interviewer's use of *have* for questions, *have you not?*; the adverb *surely*; and the adjective *lovely*.

8 Note the alternation between present and past morphology, e.g. *I says; I said;* the use of *divn't* for 'don't'.

References

Abbott, Edwin Abbott (1879). *A Shakespearian grammar.* London: Macmillan.

Adger, David (2006). Combinatorial variability. *Journal of Linguistics* 42(3): 503–30.

(2007). Variability and modularity: A response to Hudson. *Journal of Linguistics* 43(3): 695–700.

Adger, David and Smith, Jennifer (2010). Variation in agreement: A lexical feature-based approach. *Lingua* 120: 1109–34.

Aijmer, Karin (1985). What happens at the end of our utterances? – The use of utterance final tags introduced by 'and' and 'or'. In O. Togeby (ed.), *Papers from the eighth Scandinavian Conference of Linguistics.* Copenhagen: Institut for Philologie. 366–89.

(2002). *English discourse particles: Evidence from a corpus.* Amsterdam and Philadelphia: John Benjamins.

Aitken, A. J. (1984). Scottish accents and dialects. In P. Trudgill (ed.), *Language in the British Isles.* Cambridge: Cambridge University Press. 94–114.

Alford, Henry (1864). *A plea for the Queen's English: Stray notes on speaking and spelling.* London: Strahan.

Altenberg, Bengst (1984). Causal linking in spoken and written English. *Studia Linguistica* 38(1): 20–69.

Andersen, Henning (1973). Abductive and deductive change. *Language* 49(4): 765–93.

(1988). Center and periphery: Adoption, diffusion, and spread. In J. Fisiak (ed.), *Historical dialectology: Regional and social.* Berlin: Mouton de Gruyter. 39–83.

Anderwald, Lieselotte (2002). *Negation in non-standard British English.* London and New York: Routledge.

Anttila, Raimo (1989). *Historical and comparative linguistics.* Amsterdam and New York: John Benjamins.

Arends, Jacques (1995). The socio-historical background of creoles. In J. Arends, P. Muysken and N. Smith (eds.), *Pidgins and creoles: An introduction.* Amsterdam and Philadelphia: John Benjamins. 15–24.

Armstrong, Alan (1974). *Stability and change in an English county town: A social study of York, 1801–51.* Cambridge: Cambridge University Press.

Ashcroft, Elise (1997). *A study of the copula in Sussex.* Undergraduate dissertation, University of York.

Bailey, Guy (2002). Real and apparent time. In J. K. Chambers, P. Trudgill and N. Schilling-Estes (eds.), *The handbook of language variation and change.* Malden: Blackwell Publishers.

Bailey, Guy, Wikle, Tom, Tillery, Jan and Sand, Lori (1991). The apparent time construct. *Language Variation and Change* 3(3): 241–64.

Bailyn, Bernard and DeWolfe, Barbara (1986). *Voyagers to the west: A passage in the peopling of America on the eve of the revolution.* New York: Knopf; distributed by Random House.

Baldi, Philip (1990). Introduction: The comparative method. In P. Baldi (ed.), *Linguistic change and reconstruction methodology.* Berlin: Mouton de Gruyter. 1–13.

Ball, Catherine (1996). A diachronic study of relative markers in spoken and written English. *Language Variation and Change* 8(2): 227–58.

Barber, Charles Laurence (1976). *Early modern English.* London: André Deutsch.

Barry, Michael V. (1981). The southern boundaries of northern Hiberno-English speech. In M. V. Barry (ed.), *Aspects of English dialects in Ireland.* Belfast: Queen's University. 52–95.

Bauer, Laurie (1994). *Watching English change: An introduction to the study of linguistic change in standard Englishes in the twentieth century.* London and New York: Longman.

Baugh, Albert C. (1935). *A history of the English language.* New York: D. Appleton-Century Company.

Beal, Joan (1993). The grammar of Tyneside and Northumbrian English. In J. Milroy and L. Milroy (eds.), *Real English: The grammar of English dialects in the British Isles.* New York: Longman. 187–213.

(1997). Syntax and morphology. In C. Jones (ed.), *The Edinburgh history of the Scots language.* Edinburgh: Edinburgh University Press. 355–77.

Beal, Joan C. and Corrigan, Karen P. (2002). Relatives in Tyneside and Northumbrian English. In P. Poussa (ed.), *Relativization on the North Sea littoral.* Munich: Lincom Europa. 125–34.

Belcher, William (1813). *Observations on the use of the words shall and will, chiefly designed for foreigners and persons educated at a distance from the metropolis, and also for the use of schools, containing XXXV rules.* Canterbury: William Belcher.

Berglund, Ylva (1997). Future in present-day English: Corpus-based evidence on the rivalry of expressions. *ICAME Journal* 21: 7–19.

Biber, Douglas, Johansson, Stig, Leech, Geoffrey, Conrad, Susan and Finegan, Edward (1999). *Longman grammar of spoken and written English.* Harlow: Longman.

Bickerton, Derek (1975). *Dynamics of a creole system.* New York: Cambridge University Press.

Bolinger, Dwight (1980). *Language: The loaded weapon.* London: Longman.

Brainerd, Barron (1989). The contractions of *not*: A historical note. *Journal of English Linguistics* 22(2): 176–96.

Brinton, Laurel J. (1996). *Pragmatic markers in English.* Berlin: Mouton de Gruyter.

Britain, David (2007). *Language in the British Isles.* Cambridge: Cambridge University Press.

Britain, David and Sudbury, Andrea (1999). There's tapestries, there's photos and there's penguins: Variation in the verb BE in existential clauses in conversational New Zealand and Falkland Island English. In M. C. Jones and E. Esch (eds.), *Language change: The interplay of internal, external and extra-linguistic factors.* Berlin: Mouton de Gruyter. 211–40.

(2002). There's sheep and there's penguins; Convergence, 'drift' and 'slant' in New Zealand and Falkland Island English. In M. C. Jones and E. Esch (eds.), *Language change: The interplay of internal, external and extra-linguistic factors.* Berlin: Mouton de Gruyter. 211–40.

Brockette, John Trotter (1825). *A glossary of North Country words.* Newcastle: T. and J. Hodgson (for E. Charnley).

Brunner, Karl (1963). *An outline of Middle English grammar.* Oxford: Blackwell Publishers.

Bybee, Joan L. and Pagliuca, William (1987). The evolution of future meaning. In A. G. Ramat, O. Carruba and G. Bernini (eds.), *Papers from the 7th international conference on historical linguistics.* Amsterdam and Philadelphia: John Benjamins. 107–22.

Bybee, Joan L., Perkins, Revere D. and Pagliuca, William (1994). *The evolution of grammar: Tense, aspect, and modality in the languages of the world.* Chicago: University of Chicago Press.

Bynon, Theodora (1977). *Historical linguistics.* Cambridge: Cambridge University Press.

Campbell, John C. (1921). *The southern highlander and his home land.* New York: Russell Sage foundation.

Campbell, Lyle and Muntzel, Martha C. (1989). The structural consequences of language death. In N. C. Dorian (ed.), *Investigating obsolescence: Studies in language contraction and death.* Cambridge: Cambridge University Press. 181–96.

Chambers, J. K. (2000). Universal sources of the vernacular. In U. Ammon, P. H. Nelde and K. J. Mattheier (eds.), *Special issue of Sociolinguistica: International yearbook of European sociolinguistics.* Tübingen: Max Niemeyer Verlag. 11–15.

(2001). Vernacular universals. In J. M. Fontana, L. McNally, T. M. Turell and V. Enric (eds.), *Proceedings of ICLaVE !: The First International Conference on Language Variation in Europe.* Barcelona: Universitate Pompeu Fabra. 52–60.

(2004). Dynamic typology and vernacular universals. In B. Kortmann (ed.), *Dialectology meets typology: Dialect grammar from a cross-linguistic perspective.* Berlin and New York: Mouton de Gruyter. 127–45.

Chambers, J. K. and Trudgill, P. (1980). *Dialectology.* Cambridge: Cambridge University Press.

Chaudenson, Robert (1992). *Des îles, des hommes, des langues: Essais sur la créolisation linguistique et culturelle.* Paris: L'Harmattan.

Cheshire, Jenny (1982). *Variation in an English dialect: A sociolinguistic study.* Cambridge: Cambridge University Press.

(1994). Standardization and the English irregular verb. In Stein, D. and Tieken-Boon von Ostade, I. (eds.), *Towards a standard English 1600–1800.* Berlin and New York: Mouton de Gruyter. 115–33.

(2007). Discourse variation, grammaticalisation and stuff like that. *Journal of Sociolinguistics* 11(2): 155–93.

Cheshire, Jenny, Fox, Sue, Kerswill, Paul, Khan, Arfaan and Torgersen, Eivind (2007–2010). Multicultural London English: The emergence, acquisition and diffusion of a new variety. Research project funded by Economic and Social Science Research Council (ESRC) Grant.

Cheshire, Jenny, Edwards, Viv and Whittle, Pamela (1989). Urban British dialect grammar: The question of dialect levelling. *English World-Wide* 10(2): 185–225.

Cheshire, Jenny and Milroy, James (1993). Syntactic variation in non-standard dialects: Background issues. In J. Milroy and L. Milroy (eds.), *Real English: The grammar of English dialects in the British Isles.* New York: Longman. 3–33.

Chesshyre, Robert (1987). *The return of a native reporter.* London: Viking.

Christian, Donna, Wolfram, Walt and Dube, Nanjo (1988). *Variation and change in geographically isolated communities: Appalachian English and Ozark English.* Tuscaloosa, AL: American Dialect Society.

Christy, Craig (1983). *Uniformitarianism in linguistics.* Amsterdam and Philadelphia: John Benjamins.

Clarke, Sandra (1997a). On establishing historical relationships between New World and Old World varieties: Habitual aspect and Newfoundland Vernacular English. In E. W. Schneider (ed.), *Englishes around the world.* Amsterdam and Philadelphia: John Benjamins. 277–93.

(1997b). The search for origins: Habitual aspect and Newfoundland vernacular English. *Journal of English Linguistics* 27(4): 328–40.

Close, R. A. (1977). Some observations on the meaning and function of verb phrases having future reference. In W.-D. Bald and R. Ilson (eds.), *Studies in English usage: The resources of a present-day English corpus of linguistic analysis.* Frankfurt am Main and Berne: Peter Lang. 125–56.

Coates, Jennifer (1983). *The semantics of the modal auxiliaries.* London: Croom Helm.

Cobbett, William (1818/1983). *A grammar of the English language, in a series of letters.* Amsterdam: Rodopi.

Conradie, C. J. (1987). Semantic change in modal auxiliaries as a result of speech act embedding. In M. Harris and P. Ramat (eds.), *Historical development of auxiliaries.* Berlin: Mouton de Gruyter. 171–80.

Cornips, Leonie and Corrigan, Karen (2002). Convergence and divergence in grammar. In P. Auer, F. Hinskens and P. Kerswill (eds.), *The convergence and divergence of dialects in contemporary societies.* Cambridge: Cambridge University Press.

Cornips, Leonie and Corrigan, Karen (eds.) (2005). *Syntax and variation: Reconciling the biological and the social.* Amsterdam and Philadelphia: John Benjamins.

Corrigan, Karen (1997). The acquisition and properties of a contact vernacular grammar. In A. Ahlqvist, and V. Capková (eds.), *Dán Do Oide: Essays in Memory of Conn R. Ó Cleirigh.* Dublin: The Linguistics Institute of Ireland. 75–93.

(2010). *Irish English, Volume 1: Northern Ireland.* Edinburgh: Edinburgh University Press.

Corrigan, Karen P. (2000). 'What bees to be maun be': Aspects of deontic and epistemic modality in a northern dialect of Irish English. *English World-Wide* 21(2): 25–62.

Crowell, Thomas L. (1955). Predating 'have to', 'must'? *American Speech* 30(1): 68–9.

(1959). 'Have got', a pattern preserver. *American Speech* 34(2): 280–6.

Crozier, A. (1984). The Scots-Irish Influence on American English. *American Speech* 59: 310–31.

Crystal, David (1986). I shall and I will. *English Today* 5 (Jan.–Mar.): 42–4.

(1995). *The Cambridge encyclopedia of the English language.* Cambridge: Cambridge University Press.

Cukor-Avila, Patricia (1997). Change and stability in the use of verbal *-s* over time in AAVE. In E. W. Schneider (ed.), *Englishes around the world.* Amsterdam and Philadelphia: John Benjamins. 295–306.

Curme, George O. (1947). *English grammar.* New York: Barnes and Noble.

(1977). *A grammar of the English language.* Essex, CT: Verbatim.

D'Arcy, Alexandra (2005a). *Like: Syntax and development.* PhD Dissertation, University of Toronto.

(2005b). Tracking the development of discourse 'like' in contemporary (Canadian) English. *Doctoral Thesis Proposal.* Toronto, Canada, 16 March.

(2006). Lexical replacement and the like(s). *American Speech* 81(4): 339–57.

(2007). *Like* and language ideology: Disentangling fact from fiction. *American Speech* 82(4): 386–419.

(2008). Canadian English as a window to the rise of *like* in discourse. In M. Meyer (ed.), *Focus on Canadian English. Special issue of Anglistik. International Journal of English Studies.* Heidelberg: Winter. 125–40.

Dailey-O'Cain, Jennifer (2000). The distribution of and attitudes towards focuser *like* and quotative *like. Journal of Sociolinguistics* 4(1): 60–80.

Danchev, Andrei and Kytö, Merja (1994). The construction *be going to* + infinitive in Early Modern English. In D. Kastovsky (ed.), *Studies in Early Modern English.* Berlin: Mouton de Gruyter. 59–77.

Dekeyser, Xavier (1984). Relativi[z]ers in Early Modern English: A dynamic quantitative study. In J. Fisiak (ed.), *Historical syntax.* Berlin: Mouton de Gruyter. 61–87.

Denis, Derek (2011). Innovators and innovation: Tracking the innovators of *and stuff* in York English. *University of Pennsylvania Working Papers in Linguistics* 17(2). http://repository.upenn.edu/pwpl/vol17/iss2/8/ accessed 29 March 2012.

Denison, David (1998). Syntax. In S. Romaine (ed.), *The Cambridge history of the English language, 1776–present day.* Cambridge: Cambridge University Press. 92–329.

Dieth, Eugen (1932). *A grammar of the Buchan dialect.* Cambridge: Heffer.

Donner, Morton (1991). Adverb form in Middle English. *English Studies* 72: 1–11.

Dubois, Sylvie (1992). Extension particles, etc. *Language Variation and Change* 4(2): 163–203.

Durham, Mercedes (2011). Right dislocation in Northern England: Frequency and use – perception meets reality. *English World-Wide* 32(3): 257–79.

Dyer, S. (1891). *Dialect of the West Riding of Yorkshire.* Brighton: Yorkshie.

Edwards, Viv and Weltens, Bert (1985). Research on non-standard dialects of British English: Progress and prospects. In W. Viereck (ed.), *Focus on: England and Wales.* Amsterdam and Philadelphia: John Benjamins. 97–139.

Elsness, Johan (1984). *That* or zero? A look at the choice of object clause connective in a corpus of American English. *English Studies* 65: 519–33.

Emma, Ronald David (1964). *Milton's grammar.* The Hague: Mouton and Co.

Erman, Britt (1995). Grammaticalization in progress: The case of *or something.* In I. Moen, H. Gram Simonsen and H. Lødrup (eds.), *Papers from the XVth Scandinavian Conference of Linguistics, Oslo, January 13–15, 1995.* Oslo: Department of Linguistics, University of Oslo. 136–47.

Evans Wagner, and Suzanne Sankoff, Gillian (2006). Age grading in the Montréal French inflected future. *Language Variation and Change* 23(2): 2011.

F. (1838). *The grammarian: or the English writer and speaker's assistant, comprising shall and will made easy to foreigners, with instances of their misuse on the part of the natives of England.* Dublin?: np.

Facchinetti, Roberta, Krug, Manfred and Palmer, Frank (eds.) (2003). *Modality in contemporary English.* Berlin and New York: Mouton de Gruyter.

Feagin, Crawford (1979). *Variation and change in Alabama English: A sociolinguistic study of the white community.* Washington, DC: Georgetown University Press.

Filppula, Markku (1999). *The grammar of Irish-English.* London: Routledge.

Filppula, Markku, Klemola, Juhani and Paulasto, Heli (2008). *English and Celtic in contact.* New York: Routledge.

Finlay, C. (1988). *Syntactic variation in the speech of Belfast schoolchildren.* PhD Dissertation, University of Ulster at Jordanstown.

Fischer, David Hackett (1989). *Albion's seed: Four British folkways in America.* New York and Oxford: Oxford University Press.

Fischer, Olga (1992). Syntax. In N. Blake (ed.), *The Cambridge history of the English language*, Volume II: *1066–1476.* Cambridge: Cambridge University Press. 207–408.

(2007). *Morphosyntactic change: Functional and formal perspectives.* Oxford: Oxford University Press.

Fleischman, Suzanne (1982). *The future in thought and language: Diachronic evidence from Romance.* Cambridge: Cambridge University Press.

Forsström, Gösta (1948). *The verb 'to be' in Middle English: A survey of the forms.* Lund: C.W. K. Gleerup.

Fowler, H. W. and Fowler, F. G. (1931). *The King's English.* Oxford: The Clarendon Press.

Fries, Charles Carpenter (1925). The periphrastic future with 'shall' and 'will' in modern English. *Publications of the Modern Linguistic Association of America* 40: 963–1024.

(1927). The expression of the future. *Language* 3(2): 87–95.

Gauchat, Louis (1905). L'unité phonétique dans le patois d'une commune. In *Aus romanischen Sprachen und Literaturen: Festschrift Heinrich Morf.* 175–232.

Geisler, Christer (2002). Relativization in Ulster English. In P. Poussa (ed.), *Relativization on the North Sea littoral.* Munich: Lincom Europa. 135–46.

Giner, Maria F. Garcia-Bermejo and Montgomery, Michael (1997). Regional British English from the nineteenth century: Evidence from emigrant letters. In A. S. Thomas (ed.), *Current methods in dialectology.* Bangor: University of Wales. 167–83.

(2001). Yorkshire English two hundred years ago. *Journal of English Linguistics* 29(4): 356–62.

Godfrey, Elisabeth (1997). *An analysis of verbal -s marking in Devon English.* MA thesis, University of York.

Godfrey, Elisabeth and Tagliamonte, Sali A. (1999). Another piece for the verbal -s story: Evidence from Devon in Southwest England. *Language Variation and Change* 11(1): 87–121.

Gordon, Elizabeth, Campbell, Lycle, Maclagan, Margaret, Sudbury, Andrea and Trudgill, Peter (2004). *New Zealand English: Its origins and evolution.* Cambridge: Cambridge University Press.

Gordon, Elizabeth and Hay, Jennifer (2008). *New Zealand English.* Edinburgh: Edinburgh University Press.

Grant, W. and Main Dixon, J. (1921). *Manual of modern Scots.* Cambridge: Cambridge University Press.

Grant, W. and Murison, D. D. (eds.) (1931–1976). *The Scottish national dictionary.* Aberdeen: Aberdeen University Press.

Greenbaum, Sidney (1977). Judgement of syntactic acceptability and frequency. *Studia Linguistica* 31(2): 83–105.

Gregg, Robert J. (1985). *The Scotch–Irish dialect boundary in the province of Ulster.* Ottawa: Canadian Federation for the Humanities.

Gwynne, Parry (1855). *A word to the wise, or: Hints on the current improprieties of expression in writing and speaking.* London: Griffith and Farran.

Haegeman, Lilliane (1981). *The use of will and the expression of futurity in present-day British English.* Part 1: *Future time expression in a corpus of Standard British English.* DPhil Dissertation, University College, London.

Harris, J. (1993). The grammar of Irish English. In J. Milroy, and L. Milroy (eds.), *Real English: The grammar of English dialects in the British Isles.* New York: Longman. 139–86.

Harris, John (1986). Expanding the superstrate: Habitual aspect markers in Atlantic Englishes. *English World-Wide* 7(2): 171–99.

Hedevind, Bertil (1967). *The dialect of Dentdale in the West Riding of Yorkshire.* Stockholm: Almqvist and Wiksell.

Heine, Bernd, Claudi, Ulrike and Hünnemeyer, Friederike (1991). *Grammaticalization: A conceptual framework.* Chicago: The University of Chicago Press.

Henry, Alison (1995). *Belfast English and standard English: Dialect variation and parameter setting.* New York and Oxford: Oxford University Press.

(1998). Parameter setting within a socially realistic linguistics. *Language in Society* 27(1): 1–21.

Hermann, M. E. (1929). Lautveränderungen in der Individualsprache einer Mundart. *Nachrichten der Gesellschaft der Wissenschaften zu Göttingen, philosophisch-historische Klasse* 11: 195–214.

Heslop, Rev. Richard Oliver (1892). *Northumberland words: A glossary of words used in the county of Northumberland and on the Tyneside,* Volume 1. London: English Dialect Society/Kegan Paul, Trench, Trübner and Co.

Hickey, Raymond (ed.) (2004). *Legacies of colonial English: Studies in transported dialects.* Cambridge: Cambridge University Press.

Hickey, Raymond (2006). *Irish English: History and present day forms.* Cambridge: Cambridge University Press.

Hiller, Ulrich (1987). She isn't studying vs. She's not studying: An investigation into the choice between the two contracted variants of negated English auxiliaries. *Die Neueren Sprachen* 86(6): 531–53.

Hock, Hans Heinreich (1986). *Principles of historical linguistics.* Amsterdam: Mouton de Gruyter.

Hock, Hans Henrich and Joseph, Brian D. (1996). *Language history, language change, language relationship: An introduction to historical and comparative linguistics.* Berlin and New York: Mouton de Gruyter.

Hoenigswald, Henry M. (1960). *Language change and linguistic reconstruction.* Chicago: University of Chicago Press.

Holmqvist, E. (1922). *On the history of the English present inflections particularly -th and -s.* Heidelberg: Carl Winter.

Hope, Jonathon (1994). *The authorship of Shakespeare's plays: A sociolinguistic study.* Cambridge: Cambridge University Press.

Hopper, Paul J. (1991). On some principles of grammaticization. In E. C. Traugott and B. Heine (eds.), *Approaches to grammaticalization,* Volume 1: *Focus on theoretical and methodological issues.* Amsterdam and Philadelphia: John Benjamins. 17–35.

Hopper, Paul J. and Traugott, Elizabeth Closs (1993). *Grammaticalization.* Cambridge: Cambridge University Press.

Huddleston, Rodney and Pullum, Geoffrey, K. (2002). *The Cambridge grammar of the English language.* Cambridge: Cambridge University Press.

Hughes, Arthur and Trudgill, Peter (1979). *English accents and dialects: An introduction to social and regional varieties of British English.* London: Edward Arnold.
  (1987). *English accents and dialects.* London: Edward Arnold.

Hulbert, J. R. (1947). On the origin of the grammarian's rules for the use of 'shall' and 'will'. *Publications of the Modern Language Association of America* 62(4): 1178–82.

Ihalainen, Ossi (1994). The dialects of England since 1776. In R. Burtchfield (ed.), *The Cambridge history of the English language,* Volume 5: *English in Britain and overseas: Origin and development.* Cambridge: Cambridge University Press. 197–270.

Ito, Rika and Tagliamonte, Sali A. (2003). *Well weird, right dodgy, very strange, really cool:* Layering and recycling in English intensifiers. *Language in Society* 32(2): 257–79.

Jankowski, Bridget L. (2005). *'We've got our own little ways of doing things here':* Cross-variety variation, change and divergence in the English stative possessive. PhD Generals Paper, University of Toronto.

Jespersen, Otto H. (1909/1949). *A modern English grammar on historical principles,* Part VI: *Morphology.* London: George Allen and Unwin.
  (1940). *A modern English grammar on historical principles,* Part V: *Syntax.* London: George Allen and Unwin.
  (1961a). *A modern English grammar on historical principles*, Part VI: *Morphology.* London: Bradford and Dickens. 14–23.
  (1961b). *A Modern English Grammar on Historical Principles*, Part IV: *Present tense.* London: Bradford and Dickens. 46–59.

Jones, Megan (2000). *'They had these things what did go up across the sky'* – Nonstandard periphrastic do in the dialect of south-east Somerset. MA dissertation, University of York.

Jones, Megan and Tagliamonte, Sali A. (2004). From Somerset to Samaná: Pre-verbal *did* in the voyage of English. *Language Variation and Change* 16(2): 93–126.

José, Brian (2007). Appalachian English in southern Indiana: The evidence from verbal -s. *Language Variation and Change* 19: 249–80.

Kerswill, Paul (1995). Children, adolescents and language change. In P. Kerswill, R. Ingham, Y. Huang and L. Shockey (eds.), *Reading working paper in linguistics*. Reading: Department of Linguistic Science, University of Reading. 68–90.

(1996). Children, adolescents, and language change. *Language Variation and Change* 8(2): 177–202.

(2003). Dialect levelling and geographical diffusion in British English. In D. Britain and J. Cheshire (eds.), *Social dialectology: In honour of Peter Trudgill*. Amsterdam and Philadelphia: John Benjamins.

(2009a). Community type, dialect contact and change. Paper presented at *LSA Summer Institute 2009*. Berkeley, California, USA.

(2009b). Endogeny, exogeny, ideology and community typology: Modelling linguistic innovation, levelling and conservatism in a monolingual Old World society. Paper presented at the 7th UK Language Variation and Change Conference (UK-LVC7), Newcastle, England, 1–3 September.

Kerswill, Paul and Cheshire, Jenny (2004–2007). Linguistic innovators: The English of adolescents in London. Research project funded by ESRC Research Grant (RES-000–23–0680).

Kjellmer, Goran (1998). On contraction in Modern English. *Studia Neophilologica* 69(2): 155–86.

Klemola, Juhani (2000). The origins of the Northern Subject Rule: A case of early contact. In H. L. C. Tristram (ed.), *The Celtic languages*. Heidelberg: C. Winter. 329–46.

Klemola, Kaarlo Juhani (1996). *Non-standard periphrastic do: A study of variation and change*. PhD dissertation, University of Essex.

Kortmann, Bernd (2002). New prospects for the study of English dialect syntax: Impetus from syntactic theory and language typology. In S. Barbiers, L. Cornips and S. van der Kleij (eds.), *Syntactic Microvariation*. Amsterdam: SAND. www.meertens. knaw.nl/books/synmic accessed 8 May 2008.

Kortmann, Bernd, Burridge, Kate, Mesthrie, Rajend and Schneider, Edgar W. (eds.) (2004). *A handbook of varieties of English*. The Hague: Mouton de Gruyter.

Kroch, Anthony (1994). Morphosyntactic variation. In K. Beals, J. Denton, R. Knippen, L. Melnar, H. Suzuki and E. Zeinfeld (eds.), *Papers from the 30th regional meeting of the Chicago Linguistics Society*, Volume 2: *The parasession on variation and linguistic theory*. Chicago: Chicago Linguistics Society.

Kroch, Anthony S. (1989). Reflexes of grammar in patterns of language change. *Language Variation and Change* 1(3): 199–244.

Krug, Manfred (1998). *Gotta* – the tenth central modal in English? Social, stylistic and regional variation in the British National Corpus as evidence of ongoing grammaticalization. In H. Lindquist, S. Klintborg, M. Levin and M. Estling (eds.), *The major varieties of English*. Växjö: Växjö University. 177–91.

(2000). *Emerging English modals: A corpus-based study of grammaticalization*. Berlin and New York: Mouton de Gruyter.

Krug, Manfred Gunter (1994). *Contractions in spoken and written English*. MA Thesis, University of Exeter.

Kurath, Hans (1949). *A word geography of the Eastern United States.* Ann Arbor: University of Michigan Press.

   (1964). British sources of selected features of American pronunciation: Problems and methods. In D. Abercrombie, D. B. Fry, P. A. D. MacCarthy, N. C. Scott and J. L. M. Trim (eds.), *In honour of Daniel Jones: Papers contributed on the occasion of his eightieth birthday 12 September 1961.* London: Longmans. 146–55.

Kytö, Merja (1993a). *Manual to the diachronic part of the Helsinki Corpus of English Texts: Coding conventions and lists of source texts.* Helsinki: University of Helsinki, Department of English.

   (1993b). Third-person present singular verb inflection in early British and American English. *Language Variation and Change* 5(2): 113–39.

Labov, William (1963). The social motivation of a sound change. *Word* 19: 273–309.

   (1966). *The social stratification of English in New York City.* Washington, DC: Center for Applied Linguistics.

   (1972a). *Language in the inner city.* Philadelphia: University of Pennsylvania Press.

   (1972b). *Sociolinguistic patterns.* Philadelphia: University of Pennsylvania Press.

   (1982). Building on empirical foundations. In W. P. Lehmann and Y. Malkiel (eds.), *Perspectives on historical linguistics.* Amsterdam and Philadelphia: John Benjamins. 17–92.

   (1985). Intensity. In D. Schiffrin (ed.), *Meaning, form and use in context: Linguistic applications.* Washington, DC: Georgetown University Press. 43–70.

   (1989). The child as linguistic historian. *Language Variation and Change* 1(1): 85–97.

   (1994a). *Principles of linguistic change,* Volume 1: *Internal factors.* Cambridge and Oxford: Blackwell Publishers.

   (1994b). The use of the present to explain the past. In Labov, W. (ed.), *Principles of linguistic change.* Cambridge: Cambridge University Press. 9–27.

   (1998). Coexistent systems in African-American English. In S. Mufwene (ed.), *African-American English: Structure, history and use.* London: Routledge. 110–53.

   (2001). *Principles of linguistic change,* Volume 2: *Social factors.* Malden and Oxford: Blackwell Publishers.

   (2007). Transmission and diffusion. *Language* 83(2): 344–87.

Labov, William, Cohen, Paul, Robins, Clarence and Lewis, John (1968). *A study of the non-standard English of Negro and Puerto Rican speakers in New York City.* Philadelphia: US Regional Survey.

Landsman, Ned C. (1985). *Scotland and its first American colony 1683–1765.* Princeton, NJ: Princeton University Press.

Lass, Roger (1994). *Old English: A historical linguistic companion.* Cambridge: Cambridge University Press.

Le Page, Robert B. and Tabouret-Keller, Andrée (1985). *Acts of identity: Creole-based approaches to language and ethnicity.* Cambridge: Cambridge University Press.

Leech, Geoffrey (2003). Modality on the move: The English modal auxiliaries 1961–1992. In R. Facchinette, M. Krug, and F. Palmer (eds.), *Modality in Contemporary English.* Berlin and New York: Mouton de Gruyter. 223–40.

Leech, Geoffrey N. (1971). *Meaning and the English verb.* London: Longman.

Leech, Geoffrey N. and Svartvik, Jan (1975). *A communicative grammar of English.* London: Longman.

Lehmann, W. (1973). *Historical linguistics.* New York: Holt, Rinehart and Winston.

Lehmann, Winfred P. (1992). *Historical linguistics,* 3rd edition. London: Routledge.

Leiby, Austin N. (1985). Federal Writers' project. In J. S. Olson (ed.), *Historical dictionary of the New Deal: From inauguration to preparation for war.* Westport, CT: Greenwood Press. 191–92.

LeSourd, Philip (1976). 'Got' insertion. *Linguistic Inquiry* 7: 509–16.

Leyburn, James (1962). *The Scotch-Irish: A social history.* Chapel Hill: University of North Carolina Press.

Long, M. M. (1944). *The English strong verb from Chaucer to Caxton.* Menasha, WI: George Banta Publishing Co.

Lowth, Robert (1762/1775). *A short introduction to English grammar.* London: Printed by J. Hughs for A. Millar and J. Dodsley.

Macafee, Caroline (1983). *Varieties of English around the world: Glasgow.* Amsterdam: Benjamins.

(1992a). Characteristics of non-standard grammar in Scotland. www.abdn.ac.uk/~enl038/grammar.htm, accessed 15 December 2005.

(1992b). A short grammar of Older Scots. *Scottish Language* 11–12: 10–36.

Macaulay, Ronald K. S. (1991). *Locating dialect in discourse: The language of honest men and bonnie lassies in Ayr.* Oxford: Oxford University Press.

(1995). The adverbs of authority. *English World-Wide* 16(1): 37–60.

Mair, Christian (1997a). Parallel corpora: A real-time approach to the study of language change in progress. In M. Ljung (ed.), *Corpus-based studies in English: Papers from the seventeenth international conference on English language research on comptuerized corpora (ICAME 17).* Amsterdam: Rodopi. 195–209.

(1997b). The spread of the *going-to*-future in written English: A corpus-based investigation into language change in progress. In R. Hickey and S. Puppel (eds.), *Language history and linguistic modelling.* Berlin: Mouton de Gruyter. 1537–43.

(2006). *Twentieth-century English.* Cambridge: Cambridge University Press.

Mair, Christian and Hundt, Marianne (1997). 'Agile' and 'uptight' genres: The corpus-based approach to language change in progress. *International Journal of Corpus Linguistics* (4): 221–42.

Martin, Danielle (1999). *Copula variability in a northern British dialect: Contraction, deletion and inherent variability.* Unfinished MA thesis, University of York.

Martin, Danielle and Tagliamonte, Sali A. (1999). 'Oh, it beautiful'. Copula variability in Britain. Paper presented at New Ways of Analyzing Variation (NWAV) Conference, Toronto, Canada.

Masam, S. (1948). *A grammar of the dialect of West Riding: Historical and descriptive.* Tokyo: Azuma Shobo.

McCafferty, Kevin (2003). The northern subject rule in Ulster: How Scots, how English? *Language Variation and Change* 15(1): 105–39.

(2004). '[T]under storms is verry dangese in this countrey they come in less than a minnits notice …': The Northern Subject Rule in Southern Irish English. *English World-Wide* 25(1): 51–79.

McDavid, Raven I. (1985). Dialect areas of the Atlantic seaboard. In P. Benes (ed.), *American speech: 1600 to the present.* Boston: Boston University. 15–26.

McMahon, April M. S. (1994). *Understanding language change.* Cambridge: Cambridge University Press.

Meehan, Teresa (1991). It's like, 'What's happening in the evolution of like?': A theory of grammaticalization. *Kansas Working Papers in Linguistics* 16: 37–51.

Meillet, Antoine (1967). *The comparative method in historical linguistics.* Paris: Librairie Honoré Champion.

Melchers, Gunnel (1997). *This, than, yon:* On 'three-dimensional' deictic systems. In J. Cheshire and D. Stein (eds.), *Taming the vernacular: From dialect to written standard English.* London: Longman. 83–92.

Mencken, Henry Louis (1961). *The American language: Supplement II.* New York: Alfred A. Knopf.

    (1963). *The American language.* London: Routledge and Kegan Paul.

Miller, James (1993). The grammar of Scottish English. In J. Milroy and L. Milroy (eds.), *Real English: The grammar of English dialects in the British Isles.* New York: Longman. 99–138.

Miller, Jim and Weinert, Regina (1995). The function of *like* in dialogue. *Journal of Pragmatics* 23: 365–393.

Milroy, James (1992). *Linguistic variation and change.* Oxford: Blackwell.

Milroy, James and Milroy, Lesley (eds.) (1993). *Real English: The grammar of English dialects in the British Isles.* New York: Longman.

Milroy, Lesley (1980). *Language and social networks.* Baltimore, MD: University Park Press.

    (1987). *Observing and analysing natural language.* Oxford: Blackwell.

Mitchell, Bruce (1985). *Old English syntax,* Volumes 1, 2. Oxford: Clarendon Press.

Molloy, Gerald (1897). *The Irish difficulty: Shall and will.* London, Glasgow and Dublin: Blackie and Son.

Montgomery, Michael B. (1989). Exploring the roots of Appalachian English. *English World-Wide* 10(2): 227–78.

    (1997). Making transatlantic connections between varieties of English. *Journal of English Linguistics* 25(2): 122–41.

    (2001). British and Irish antecedents. In Algeo, J. (ed.), *The Cambridge history of the English language*, Volume 6: *English in North America.* Cambridge: Cambridge University Press. 86–151.

Montgomery, Michael B. and Chapman, Curtis (1992). The pace of change in Appalachian English. In M. Rissanen, O. Ihalainen, T. Nevalainen and I. Taavitsainen (eds.), *History of Englishes: New methods and interpretations in historical linguistics.* Berlin: Mouton de Gruyter. 624–39.

Morris, Marmaduke Charles Frederick (1911). *Yorkshire folk-talk: With characteristics of those who speak it in the North and East Ridings.* London: Brown.

Mufwene, Salikoko S. (1996). The founder principle in creole genesis. *Diachronica* 13(1): 83–134.

    (1997). The legitimate and illegitimate offspring of English. In M. L. Forman and L. E. Smith (eds.), *World Englishes 2000.* Honolulu: The University of Hawaii Press. 182–203.

    (1999a). Accountability in descriptions of creoles. In J. R. Rickford and S. Romaine (eds.), *Creole genesis, attitudes, and discourse: Studies celebrating Charlene J. Sato.* Amsterdam and Philadelphia: John Benjamins. 157–85.

(1999b). North American varieties of English as by-products of population contacts. In R. Wheeler (ed.), *The workings of language: From prescriptions to perspectives.* Westport, CT: Greenwood Publishing Group. 15–37.

(2000). Population contacts and the evolution of English. *The European English Messenger* 9: 9–15.

(2001). *The ecology of language evolution.* Cambridge: Cambridge University Press.

Murray, James A. H. (1873). *The dialect of the Southern Counties of Scotland: Its pronunciation, grammar and historical relations.* London: Philological Society.

Murray, Lindley (1795/1968). *English grammar.* English Linguistics 1500–1800 – A Collection of Facsimile Reprints, No.106. Menston: Scolar Press.

Mustanoja, Tauno F. (1960). *A Middle English syntax.* Helsinki: Société Néophilologique.

Nelson, Gerald (2004). The negation of lexical *have* in conversational English. *World Englishes* 23: 299–308.

Nesselhauf, Nadia (2006). The decline of 'be to' and the rise of 'be going to' in Late Modern English: Connection or coincidence? In C. Houswitschka, G. Knappe and A. Müller (eds.), *Anglistentag 2005 Bamberg.* Trier: WVT. 515–29.

(2007). Diachronic analysis with the internet? Will and shall in ARCHER and in a corpus of e-texts from the web. In M. H. Hundt, N. Nesselhauf and C. Biewer (eds.), *Corpus linguistics and the we.* Amsterdam and New York: Rodopi. 287–305.

(2010). The development of future time expressions in Late Modern English: Redistribution of forms or change in discourse? *English Language and Linguistics* 14(2): 163–86.

Nevalainen, Terttu (1994a). Aspects of adverbial change in Early Modern English. In D. Kastovisky (ed.), *Studies in Early Modern English.* Berlin and New York: Mouton de Gruyter. 243–59.

(1994b). Diachronic issues in English adverb derivation. In U. Fries, G. Tottie and P. Schneider (eds.), *Creating and using English language corpora: Papers from the Fourteenth International Conference on English Language on Computerized Corpora, Zürich 1993.* Amsterdam and Atlanta: Rodopi. 139–47.

(1997). The processes of adverb derivation in Late Middle and Early Modern English. In M. Rissanen, M. Kytö and K. Heikkonen (eds.), *Grammaticalization at work: Studies of long-term developments in English.* Berlin and New York: Mouton de Gruyter. 145–89.

Nevalainen, Terttu and Raumolin-Brunberg, Helena (2002). The rise of relative *who* in early Modern English. In P. Poussa (ed.), *Relativisation on the North Sea littoral.* Munich: Lincom Europa. 109–21.

Nicolle, Steve (1997). A relevance-theoretic account of *be going to. Journal of Linguistics* 33(2): 355–77.

Noble, Shawn (1985). To have and have got. Presented at New Ways of Analyzing Variation (NWAV) 14. Georgetown University, Washington, DC, USA.

Norrby, Catrin and Winter, Joanne (2001). Affiliation in adolescents' use of discourse extenders. *Proceedings of the Australian Linguistic Society.*

O'Keeffe, Ann (2004). 'Like the wise virgins and all that jazz': Using a corpus to examine vague categorization and shared knowledge. *Language and Computers* 52(1): 1–26.

Opdahl, Lise (2000). *LY or zero suffix?: A study in variation of dual-form adverbs in present-day English.* Frankfurt am Main: Peter Lang.

Orton, Harold and Halliday, Wilfrid J. (1963). *Survey of English dialects.* Leeds: E. J. Arnold.

Overstreet, Maryann (1999). *Whales, candlelight, and stuff like that: General extenders in English discourse.* New York: Oxford University Press.

Palander-Collin, Minna (1997). A medieval case of grammaticalization, *methinks.* In M. Rissanen, M. Kyto and K. Heikkonen (eds.), *Grammaticalization at work: Studies of long-term developments in English.* Berlin and New York: Mouton de Gruyter. 371–403.

Palmer, Frank R. (1974). *The English verb.* London: Longman.

(1979). *Modality and the English modals.* New York: Longman.

(1987). *The English verb.* Singapore: Longman.

Peitsara, Kirsti (2002). Relativizers in the Suffolk dialect. In P. Poussa (ed.), *Relativization on the North Sea littoral.* Munich: Lincom Europa. 167–80.

Peters, Hans (1994). Degree adverbs in early modern English. In D. Kastovsky (ed.), *Studies in Early Modern English.* Berlin and New York: Mouton de Gruyter. 269–88.

Pichler, Heike (2009). The functional and social reality of discourse variants in a northern English dialect: *I don't know* and *I don't think* compared. *Intercultural Pragmatics* 6(4): 561–96.

Pichler, Heike and Levey, Stephen (2011). In search of grammaticalization in synchronic dialect data: General extenders in north-east England. *English Language and Linguistics* 15(3): 441–71.

Pietsch, Lukas (2005). *Variable grammars: Verbal agreement in northern dialects of English.* Tübingen: Niemeyer.

Pitts, Walter (1981). Beyond hypercorrection: The use of emphatic *-z* in BEV. *Chicago Linguistic Society* 17: 303–10.

Pooley, Robert C. (1933). *Real* and *sure* as adverbs. *American Speech* 8(1): 60–2.

Poplack, Shana (ed.) (2000). *The English history of African American English.* Malden: Blackwell Publishers.

Poplack, Shana (2011). A variationist perspective on grammaticalization. In B. Heine and H. Narrog (eds.), *Handbook of grammaticalization.* Oxford.

Poplack, Shana and Sankoff, David (1987). The Philadelphia story in the Spanish Caribbean. *American Speech* 62(4): 291–314.

Poplack, Shana and Tagliamonte, Sali A. (1989). There's no tense like the present: Verbal *–s* inflection in Early Black English. *Language Variation and Change* 1(1): 47–84.

(1991). African American English in the diaspora: Evidence from old-line Nova Scotians. *Language Variation and Change* 3(3), 301–39.

(1999). The grammaticalization of *going to* in (African American) English. *Language Variation and Change* 11(3): 315–42.

(2001). *African American English in the diaspora: Tense and aspect.* Malden: Blackwell Publishers.

(2004). Back to the present: Verbal *-s* in the (African American) English diaspora. In R. Hickey (ed.), *Legacies of colonial English.* Cambridge: Cambridge University Press. 203–23.

Poplack, Shana and Walker, James (2002). A majority language in minority guise: The *future* of Quebec English. Paper presented at Canadian Linguistics Association (CLA). Dalhousie University, Halifax, Nova Scotia, Canada.

   (2003). An English 'like no other'? Language contact and change in Quebec. Paper presented at New Ways of Analyzing English (NWAV) 31. Stanford University, Palo Alto, California.

Poussa, Patricia (1988). The relative *what:* Two kinds of evidence. In J. Fisiak (ed.), *Historical dialectology: Regional and social:* Berlin: Walter de Gruyter. 443–74.

Poutsma, Hendrik (1926). *A grammar of Late Modern English.* Groningen: P. Noordhoff.

Pulgram, Ernst (1968). A socio-linguistic view of innovation: *-ly* and *-wise. Word* 24: 380–91.

Pyles, Thomas (1964). *The origins and development of the English language.* New York: Harcourt, Brace and World.

Pyles, Thomas and Algeo, John (1993). *The origins and development of the English language.* Orlando: Harcourt Brace and Company.

Quinn, Heidi (2004). Possessive have and have got in New Zealand English. Paper presented at New Ways of Analyzing English (NWAV) 33, University of Michigan.

   (2009). Downward reanalysis and the rise of stative HAVE got. In P. Crisma and G. Longobardi (eds.), *Historical syntax and linguistic theory.* Oxford: Oxford University Press. 212–30.

Quirk, Randolph (1957). Relative clauses in educated spoken English. *English Studies* 38: 97–109.

Quirk, Randolph and Greenbaum, Sidney (1973). *A university grammar of English.* Harlow: Longman.

Quirk, Randolph, Greenbaum, Sidney, Leech, Geoffrey and Svartvik, Jan (1985). *A comprehensive grammar of the English language.* New York: Longman.

Ramisch, Heinrich (1989). *The variation of English in Guernsey/Channel Islands.* Frankfurt am Main: Verlag Peter Lang.

Rice, Wallace (1932). Get and got. *American Speech* 7(2): 280–96.

Rickford, John (1986). Some principles for the study of Black and White speech in the south. In M. B. Montgomery and G. Bailey (eds.), *Language Variety in the South.* Alabama: University of Alabama Press. 38–62.

Rickford, John R. (1997). Prior creolization of African-American Vernacular English? Sociohistorical and textual evidence from the 17th and 18th centuries. *Journal of Sociolingusitics* 1(3): 315–36.

   (1998). The creole origins of African-American Vernacular English: Evidence from copula absence. In S. Mufwene, J. R. Rickford, G. Bailey and J. Baugh (eds.), *African-American English: Structure, history, and use.* London: Routledge. 154–200.

   (2006). 'Down for the Count'? The creole origins hypothesis of AAVE at the hands of the Ottawa Circle, and their supporters. Review article on *The English history of African American English*, ed. Shana Poplack. *Journal of Pidgin and Creole Languages* 21(1): 97–154.

Rissanen, Matti (1983). The Conjunction *for* in Early Modern English. *North-Western European Language Evolution* 14: 3–18.

(1984). The choice of relative pronouns in 17th century American English. In J. Fisiak (ed.), *Historical syntax*. Berlin: Mouton de Gruyter. 417–35.

(1991). On the history of *that*/zero as object clause links in English. In K. Aijmer and B. Altenberg (eds.), *English corpus linguistics: Studies in honour of Jan Svartvik*. London and New York: Longman. 272–89.

(1994). 'Candy no witch, Barbadoes': Salem witchcraft trials as evidence of Early American English. In H. Ramisch and K. Wynne (eds.), *Language in time and space: Studies in honor of Wolfgang Viereck on the occasion of his 60th birthday*. Stuttgart: F. Steiner. 183–93.

(1998a). Isn't it? or Is it not? On the order of postverbal subject and negative particle in the history of English. In I. Tieken-Boon van Ostade, G. Tottie and W. van der Wurff (eds.), *Negation in the History of English*: Berlin: Mouton de Gruyter. 189–205.

(1998b). Towards an integrated view of the development of English: Notes on causal linking. In J. Fisiak and M. Krygier (eds.), *Advances in English historical linguistics (1996)*. Berlin and New York: Mouton de Gruyter. 389–406.

Roberts, Ian and Roussou, Anna (2003). *Syntactic change: A minimalist approach to grammaticalization*. Cambridge: Cambridge University Press.

Robertson, Stuart (1954). *The development of Modern English,* rev. Frederic G. Cassidy. Englewood Cliffs, NJ: Prentice-Hall.

Rohdenburg, Gunter (1998). Clausal complementation and cognitive complexity in English. In F.-W. Neumann and S. Schülting (eds.), *Anglistentag Erfurt*. Trier: Wissenschaftlicher Verlag. 101–12.

Romaine, Suzanne (1980). The relative clause marker in Scots English: Diffusion, complexity and style as dimensions of syntactic change. *Language in Society* 9(2): 221–47.

(1982). *Socio-historical linguistics: Its status and methodology*. Cambridge: Cambridge University Press.

Romaine, Suzanne and Lange, Deborah (1991). The use of *like* as a marker of reported speech and thought: A case of grammaticalization in progress. *American Speech* 66(3): 227–79.

Ross, Claudia N. (1984). Adverbial change: Implications for a theory of lexical change. In D. Testen, V. Mishra and J. Drogo (eds.), *Papers from the parasession on lexical semantics*. Chicago: Chicago Linguistic Society. 243–9.

Royster, Jane F. and Steadman, John M. (1923/1968). The 'going-to' future. *Manly Anniversary Studies in Languages and Literature*. Freeport, NY: Books for Libraries Press. 394–403.

Rydén, Mats (1983). The emergence of *who* as a relativizer. *Studia Linguistica* 37: 126–34.

Sanders, Deborah (2002). *Family dynamics: The behaviour of relatives in contemporary spoken standard English*. Unpublished MA dissertation, University of York.

Sankoff, David (1988a). Sociolinguistics and syntactic variation. In F. J. Newmeyer (ed.), *Linguistics: The Cambridge survey*. Cambridge: Cambridge University Press. 140–61.

(1988b). Variable rules. In U. Ammon, N. Dittmar and K. J. Mattheier (eds.), *Sociolinguistics: An international handbook of the science of language and society,* Volume 2. Berlin: Walter de Gruyter. 984–97.

(1974). A quantitative paradigm for the study of communicative competence. In R. Bauman and J. Sherzer (eds.), *Explorations in the ethnography of speaking.* Cambridge: Cambridge University Press. 18–49.

Sapir, E. (1921). *Language: An introduction to the study of speech.* New York: Harcourt, Brace.

Schibsbye, Knud. (1965). *A modern English grammar.* London: Oxford University Press.

Schiffrin, Deborah (1987). *Discourse markers.* Cambridge: University of Cambridge Press.

Schilling-Estes, Natalie (1998). Investigating 'self-conscious' speech: The performance register in Ocracoke English. *Language in Society* 27: 53–83.

Schneider, E. W. (1981). *Morphologische und syntaktische Variablen im amerikanischen Early Black English.* Frankfurt am Main, Bern: Peter Lang.

Schneider, Edgar W. (1989). *American earlier Black English.* Tuscaloosa: The University of Alabama Press.

(1995). Verbal –*s* inflection in 'early' American Black English. In J. Fisiak (ed.), *Linguistic change under contact conditions.* Berlin: Mouton de Gruyter. 315–26.

(2004). The English dialect heritage of the southern United States. In R. Hickey (ed.), *Transported dialects: The legacy of non-standard colonial English.* Cambridge: Cambridge University Press.

Schourup, L. C. (1985). *Common discourse particles in English conversation.* New York: Garland Publishing.

Schourup, Lawrence (1999). Discourse markers. *Lingua* 107: 227–65.

Selkirk, E. O. (1981). *The phrase phonology of English and French.* Bloomington: Indiana University Linguistics Club.

Shorrocks, Graham (1997). Field methods and non-standard grammar. In H. Ramisch and K. Wynne (eds.), *Language in time and space.* Stuttgart: Franz Steiner. 212–22.

(1998a). *A grammar of the dialect of the Bolton area.* Part 2: *Morphology and Syntax.* Bamberg: Peter Lang.

(1998b). *A grammar of the dialect of the Bolton area.* Part 1: *Introduction, Phonology.* Bamberg: Peter Lang.

Siegel, Muffy E. A. (2002). Like: The discourse particle and semantics. *Journal of Semantics* 19: 35–71.

Singler, John Victor (1991). Copula variation in Liberian settler English and American Black English. In W. F. Edwards and D. Winford (eds.), *Verb phrase patterns in Black English and creole.* Detroit: Wayne State University Press. 129–64.

(1993). An African-American linguistic enclave: Tense and aspect in Liberian settler English. In H. Aertsen, and R. Jeffers (eds.), *Historical linguistics 1989: Papers from the 9th International Conference on Historical Linguistics.* Amsterdam and Philadelphia: J. Benjamins. 457–65.

Smith, Jen, Tagliamonte, Sali A. and Lawrence, Helen (2001). Disentangling the roots: The legacy of British dialects in cross-variety perspective. Paper presented at Methods in Dialectology (Methods XI) Conference, Joensuu, Finland.

Smith, Jennifer (1999). Negative concord in a Scottish dialect. Paper presented at New Ways of Analyzing Variation (NWAVE) 28. Toronto, Canada.

(2000). *Synchrony and diachrony in the evolution of English: Evidence from Scotland.* DPhil dissertation, University of York.

(2001a). Negative concord in the old and new world: Evidence from Scotland. *Language Variation and Change* 13(2): 109–34.

(2001b). *Ye ø na hear that kind o' things*: Negative *do* in Buckie. *English World-Wide* 21(2): 231–59.

(2004). Accounting for vernacular features in a Scottish dialect: Relic, innovation, analogy and drift. In C. Kay, S. Horobin, and J. Smith (eds.), *Perspectives on English historical linguistics.* Amsterdam: John Benjamins.

Smith, Jennifer and Tagliamonte, Sali A. (1998). '*We* were *all thegither … I think we was all thegither*': *was* regularization in Buckie English. *World Englishes* 17(2): 105–26.

Stenström, Anna-Brita and Andersen, Gisle (1996). More trends in teenage talk: A corpus-based investigation of the discourse items *cos* and *innit.* In C. E. Percy, C. F. Meyer and I. Lancashire (eds.), *Synchronic corpus linguistics: Papers from the sixteenth International Conference on English Language Research on Computerized Corpora, Toronto 1995.* Amsterdam: Rodopi. 189–203.

Strang, Barbara M. H. (1970). *A history of English.* London: Methuen and Co.

Stuart-Smith, Jane (1999). Glottals past and present: A study of T-glottaling in Glaswegian. *Leeds Studies in English* 30: 181–204.

(2002–2005). Contributory factors in accent change in adolescents. Research project funded by Economic and Social Science Research Council of the United Kingdom. Grant #R000239757.

Swan, Michael (1995). *Practical English usage.* Oxford: Oxford University Press.

Sweet, Henry (1898). *A new English grammar: Logical and historical.* Part 2: *Syntax.* Oxford: Clarendon Press.

(1900). *The history of language.* London: J. M. Dent and Co.

Sweetster, Eve E. (1988). Grammaticalization and semantic bleaching. In S. Axmaker, A. Jaisser and H. Singmaster (eds.), *Berkeley Linguistics Society: General session and parasesson on grammaticalization* (Berkeley Linguistics Society 14). Berkeley: University of California, Berkeley.

Szmrecsanyi, Benedikt (2003). 'Be going to' versus 'will/shall'. Does syntax matter? *Journal of English Linguistics* 31: 295–323.

Tagliamonte, Sali A. (1991). *A matter of time: Past temporal reference verbal structures in Samaná English and the ex-slave recordings.* PhD dissertation, University of Ottawa.

(1998). *Was/were* variation across the generations: View from the city of York. *Language Variation and Change* 10(2): 153–91.

(2001). *Come/came* variation in English dialects. *American Speech* 76(1): 42–61.

(2002a). Comparative sociolinguistics. In J. K. Chambers, P. Trudgill and N. Schilling-Estes (eds.), *Handbook of language variation and change.* Malden and Oxford: Blackwell Publishers. 729–63.

(2002b). Variation and change in the British relative marker system. In P. Poussa (ed.), *Relativisation on the North Sea littoral.* Munich: Lincom Europa. 147–65.

(2003). 'Every place has a different toll': Determinants of grammatical variation in cross-variety perspective. In G. Rhodenberg and B. Mondorf (eds.), *Determinants of grammatical variation in English.* Berlin and New York: Mouton de Gruyter. 531–54.

(2004). *Have to, gotta, must*: Grammaticalization, variation and specialization in English deontic modality. In H. Lindquist and C. Mair (eds.), *Corpus research on grammaticalization in English.* Amsterdam: John Benjamins. 37–55.

(2005). *So* who? *Like* how? *Just* what? Discourse markers in the conversations of young Canadians. *Journal of Pragmatics,* special issue (guest editors, Anna-Brita Stenström and Karin Aijmer) 37(11): 1896–915.

(2006). *Analysing sociolinguistic variation.* Cambridge: Cambridge University Press.

(2007). Quantitative analysis. In R. Bayley and L. Ceil (eds.), *Sociolinguistic variation: Theory, methods, and applications, dedicated to Walt Wolfram.* Cambridge: Cambridge University Press.

(2008). *So* different and *pretty* cool! Recycling intensifiers in Canadian English. Special issue of *English Language and Linguistics, Intensifiers (*guest editor Belén Mendez-Naya) 12(2): 361–94.

(2009). There *was* universals; then there weren't: A comparative sociolinguistic perspective on 'default singulars'. In M. Fillpula, J. Klemola and H. Paulasto (eds.), *Vernacular universals versus contact induced change.* Oxford: Routledge. 103–29.

(2011). Variation as a window on universals. In P. Siemund (ed.), *Linguistic universals and language variation.* Berlin and New York: Mouton de Gruyter. 128–70.

(2012). *Variationist sociolinguistics: Change, observation, interpretation.* Malden and Oxford: Wiley-Blackwell.

(in press). The verb phrase in contemporary Canadian English. In B. Aarts, J. Close, G. Leech and S. A. Wallis (eds.), *The English verb phrase: Corpus methodology and current change.* Cambridge: Cambridge University Press.

Tagliamonte, Sali A. and D'Arcy, Alexandra (2007). Frequency and variation in the community grammar: Tracking a new change through the generations. *Language Variation and Change* 19(2): 1–19.

Tagliamonte, Sali A, D'Arcy, Alexandra J. and Jankowski, Bridget (2010). Social work and linguistic systems: Marking possession in Canadian English. *Language Variation and Change* 22(1): 1–25.

Tagliamonte, Sali A. and Denis, Derek (2010). The *stuff* of change: General extenders in Toronto, Canada. *Journal of English Linguistics* 38(4): 335–68.

Tagliamonte, Sali A., Durham, Mercedes and Smith, Jen (2011). Grammaticalization at an early stage: Future 'be going to' in conservative British dialects. Paper presented at Linguistic Society of America, Portland, Oregon, January.

Tagliamonte, Sali A. and Hudson, Rachel (1999). Be like et al. beyond America: The quotative system in British and Canadian youth. *Journal of Sociolinguistics* 3(2): 147–72.

Tagliamonte, Sali A. and Ito, Rika (2002). Think *really* different: Continuity and specialization in the English adverbs. *Journal of Sociolinguistics* 6(2): 236–66.

Tagliamonte, Sali A. and Lawrence, Helen (2000). 'I used to dance, but I don't dance now': The habitual past in contemporary English. *Journal of English Linguistics* 28(4): 324–53.

Tagliamonte, Sali A. and Poplack, Shana (1986). Tense and aspect in Samaná English. Paper presented at New Ways of Analyzing English (NWAVE) 15. Stanford University.

Tagliamonte, Sali A. and Roeder, Rebecca Virginia (2009). Variation in the English definite article: Socio-historical linguistics in t'speech community. *Journal of Sociolinguistics* 13(4): 435–71.

Tagliamonte, Sali A. and Smith, Jennifer (2000). Old *was*; new ecology: Viewing English through the sociolinguistic filter. In S. Poplack (ed.), *The English history of African American English.* Oxford and Malden: Blackwell Publishers. 141–71.

(2001). Back to the roots: The legacy of British dialects. Paper presented at New Ways of Analyzing Variation Conference (NWAV) 30. Raleigh, North Carolina.

(2002). Either it *isn't* or it'*s not*: NEG/AUX contraction in British dialects. *English Word Wide* 23(2): 251–81.

Tagliamonte, Sali A., Smith, Jennifer and Lawrence, Helen (2005). No taming the vernacular! Insights from the relatives in northern Britain. *Language Variation and Change* 17(2): 75–112.

Thomason, Sarah Grey and Kaufman, Terrence (1988). *Language contact, creolization and genetic linguistics.* Berkeley and Los Angeles: University of California Press.

Thompson, Sandra and Mulac, Anthony (1991a). The discourse conditions for the use of the complementizer *that* in conversational English. *Journal of Pragmatics* 15: 237–51.

(1991b). A quantitative perspective on the grammaticization of epistemic parentheticals in English. In E. C. Traugott and B. Heine (eds.), *Approaches to grammaticalization.* Amsterdam and Philadelphia: John Benjamins. 313–29.

Tidholm, Hans (1979). *The dialect of Egton in North Yorkshire.* Gothenburg: Bokmaskine.

Torres-Cacoullos, Rena and Walker, James A. (2009a). The present of the English future: Grammatical variation and collocations in discourse. *Language* 85(2): 321–54.

(2009b). On the persistence of grammar in discourse formulas: A variationist study of *that*. *Linguistics* 47(1): 1–43.

Tottie, Gunnel (1997). Relatively speaking: Relative marker usage in the British National Corpus. In T. Nevalainen and L. Kahlas-Tarkka (eds.), *To explain the present: Studies in the changing English Language in honour of Matti Rissanen.* Helsinki: Société Néophilologique. 465–81.

Tottie, Gunnel and Harvie, Dawn (2000). It's all relative: Relativization strategies in early African American English. In S. Poplack (ed.), *The English history of African American English.* Oxford and Malden: Blackwell Publishers. 198–230.

Traugott, Elizabeth Closs (1972). *A history of English syntax: A transformational approach to the history of English sentence structures.* New York: Holt, Rinehart and Winston.

(1997 [1995]). The role of the development of discourse markers in theory of grammaticalization. Paper presented at the Twelfth International Conference on Historical Linguistics, University of Manchester, 1997. Manchester, England. Available online at: www.standford.edu/~traugott/ect.papersonline.html.

Traugott, Elizabeth Closs and Heine, Bernd (1991a). *Approaches to grammaticalization,* Volume 1. Amsterdam and Philadelphia: John Benjamins.

(1991b). *Approaches to grammaticalization*, Volume 2: Amsterdam and Philadelphia: John Benjamins.

Trudgill, Peter (1974). *The social differentiation of English in Norwich.* Cambridge: University of Cambridge Press.

(ed.) (1978). *Sociolinguistic patterns in British English.* London: Edward Arnold.

(1983). *On dialect: Social and geographical perspectives.* Oxford: Basil Blackwell.

(1984). *Language in the British Isles.* Cambridge: Cambridge University Press.

(1986). *Dialects in contact.* Oxford: Blackwell Publishers.

(1990). *The dialects of England.* Oxford: Blackwell Publishers.

(1996). Dialect typology: Isolation, social network and phonological structure. In G. Guy, C. Feagin, D. Schiffrin and J. Baugh (eds.), *Dialect typology: Isolation, social network and phonological structure.* Amsterdam and Philadelphia: John Benjamins. 3–22.

(1997). British vernacular dialects in the formation of American English: The case of East Anglian *do.* In R. Hickey (ed.), *Language history and linguistic modelling.* Berlin: Mouton de Gruyter. 749–58.

(1999). New-dialect formation and dedialectalisation: Embryonic and vestigal variants. *Journal of English Linguistics* 27(4): 319–27.

(2003). *The Norfolk dialect.* Cromer: Poppyland Publishing.

(2004). *New-dialect formation: The invevitability of colonial Englishes.* Oxford: Oxford University Press.

(2010). *Investigations in sociohistorical linguistics: Stories of colonization and contact.* Cambridge: Cambridge University Press.

Trudgill, Peter J. and Chambers, Jack (eds.) (1991). *Dialects of English: Studies in grammatical variation.* London and New York: Longman.

Trudgill, Peter J., Gordon, Elizabeth, Lewis, Gillian and Maclagan, Margaret (2000). Determinism in new-dialect formation and the genesis of New Zealand English. *Journal of Linguistics* 36: 299–318.

Trudgill, Peter J. and Hannah, Jean (1985). *International English: A guide to varieties of standard English.* London: Edward Arnold.

Trudgill, Peter, Nevalainen, Terttu and Wischer, Ilse (2002). Dynamic *have* in North American and British Isles English. *English Language and Linguistics* 6(1): 1–15.

Underhill, Robert (1988). Like is like, focus. *American Speech* 63(3): 234–46.

van den Eynden, Nadine (1993). *Syntactic variation and unconscious linguistic change: A study of adjectival relative clauses in the dialect of Dorset.* Frankfurt am Main: Peter Lang.

van den Eynden Morpeth, Nadine and Hogeschool, Lessius (2002). Relativisers in the Southwest of England. In P. Poussa (ed.), *Relativization on the North Sea littoral.* Munich: Lincom Europa. 181–94.

Van Draat, P. Fijn. (1910). *Rhythm in English prose.* Heidelberg: Carl Winter's Universitätsbuchhandlung.

Vet, Co (1984). Is there any hope for the 'futur'? In H. Bennis, and W. U. S. van Lessen Kloeke (eds.), *Linguistics in the Netherlands 1984.* Dordrecht: Foris. 189–96.

Viereck, Wolfgang (1999). Dialectal English verb morphology: Some observations. In G. A. Tops, B. Devriendt and S. Geukens (eds.), *Thinking about grammar: To honour Xavier Dekeyser.* Leuven: Peeters. 129–41.

Visser, Fredericus T. (1963–73). *An historical syntax of the English language.* Leiden: E. J. Brill.

Wagner, Susanne (2004). English dialects in the southwest: Morphology and syntax. In B. Kortmann, K. Burridge, R. Mesthrie, and E. W. Schneider (eds.), *A handbook of varieties of English.* The Hague: Mouton de Gruyter. 154–74.

Wakelin, Martyn F. (1977). *English dialects: An introduction.* London: Athlone Press. (1988). *The archaeology of English.* London: Batsford.

Wales, Katie (2000). North and South: An English linguistic divide. *English Today* 16(1): 4–15.

(2006). *Northern English: A social and cultural history.* Cambridge: Cambridge University Press.

Walker, James (2001). The 'ain't' constraint in Early African American English. Paper presented at the 3rd UK Language Variation and Change Conference (UK-LVC3). York, UK.

(2007). 'There's bears back there': Plural existentials and vernacular universals in (Quebec) English. *English World-Wide* 28(2): 147–66.

Walker, James and Cacoullos, Rena (2003). Taking a complement … variably. Paper presented at New Ways of Analyzing Variation (NWAV) 32, Philadelphia, 11 October.

Wardale, Edith Elizabeth (1937). *An introduction to Middle English.* London: Routledge and Kegan Paul.

Warner, Anthony (1982). *Complementation in Middle English and the methodology of historical syntax.* London and Canberra: Croom Helm.

(1993). *English auxiliaries: Structure and history.* Cambridge: Cambridge University Press.

Waters, Cathleen (2011). *Social and linguistic correlates of adverb variability in English.* PhD Dissertation, Department of Linguistics, University of Toronto.

Weinreich, Uriel (1954). Is a structural dialectology possible? *Word* 10: 388–400.

Weinreich, Uriel, Labov, William and Herzog, Marvin (1968). Empirical foundations for a theory of language change. In W. P. Lehmann and Y. Malkiel (eds.), *Directions for historical linguistics.* Austin: University of Texas Press. 95–188.

Wekker, H. C. (1976). *The expression of future time in contemporary British English.* Amsterdam: North Holland.

Wells, John C. (1982). *Accents of English.* Cambridge: Cambridge University Press.

White, Richard Grant (1927). *Words and their uses, past and present: A study of the English language.* Revised Edition. Boston: Houghton.

Whitney, William Dwight (1867). *Language and the study of language.* New York: Charles Scribner and Company.

Wilson, John and Henry, Alison (1998). Parameter setting within a socially realistic linguistics. *Language in society* 27(1): 1–21.

Winford, Donald (1992). Back to the past: The BEV/Creole connection revisited. *Language Variation and Change* 4: 311–57.

Winter, Joanne and Norrby, Catrin (2000). 'Set marking tags' and stuff. In J. Henderson, (ed.), *Proceedings of the 1999 Conference of the Australian Linguistic Society.* www.docstoc.com/docs/29168304/Set-Marking-Tags-%E2%80%93-and-stuff accessed 29 March 2012.

Wolfram, Walt (1993). Identifying and interpreting variables. In D. Preston (ed.), *American dialect research.* Amsterdam and Philadelphia: John Benjamins. 193–221.

(2000). Issues in reconstructing earlier African-American English. *World Englishes* 19(1): 39–58.

Wolfram, Walt and Schilling-Estes, Natalie (1995). Moribund dialects and the endangerment canon: The case of the Ocracoke Brogue. *Language* 71(4): 696–721.

(2006). *American English,* Second edition. Malden and Oxford: Blackwell.

Wood, Peter H. (1974). *Black majority: Negroes in colonial South Carolina from 1670 through the Stono Rebellion.* New York: Alfred Knopf.

(1989). The changing population of the Colonial South: An overview by race and region, 1685–1790. In P. H. Wood, G. A. Waselkov and T. M. Hatley (eds.), *Powhatan's mantle: Indians of the colonial southeast.* Lincoln and London: University of Nebraska Press. 25–103.

Wooley, Edwin C. (1907). *Handbook of composition.* Boston: D. C. Heath and Co.

Wright, Joseph (1892). *A grammar of the dialect of Windhill.* London: English Dialect Society.

(1898–1905). *The English dialect grammar.* Oxford: Clarendon Press.

(1900). *English dialect dictionary.* London: Henry Frowde.

Wright, Laura (2004). The language of transported Londoners: Third-person-singular present-tense markers in depositions from Virginia and the Bermudas, 1607–1625. In R. Hickey (ed.), *Legacies of colonial English: Studies in transported dialects.* Cambridge: Cambridge University Press. 158–71.

Wyld, H. C. (1927). *A short history of English.* London: John Murray.

Yaeger-Dror, Malcah (1997). Contraction of negatives as evidence of variance in register-specific interactive rules. *Language Variation and Change* 9: 1–36.

Yaeger-Dror, Malcah, Lauren Hall-Lew and Sharon Deckert (2002). It's not or isn't it? Using large corpora to determine the influences on contraction strategies. *Language Varation and Change* 14(1): 79–118.

(in press). *Be* contraction in American English: Evidence from different registers. In R. Reppen, D. Biber and S. Fitzmaurice (eds.), *Using corpora to explore linguistic variation.* Philadelphia: Benjamins.

Youssef, Valerie (1993). Marking solidarity across the Trinidad speech community: The use of *an ting* in medical counselling to break down power differentials. *Discourse and Society* 4(3): 291–306.

Zettersten, Arne (1969). *The English of Tristan da Cunha.* Lund: Gleerup.

Index